As Good as It Gets

As Good as It Gets

Love, Life, and Relationships

Fifty Days in the Song of Songs

STEPHEN M. CLARK

WIPF & STOCK · Eugene, Oregon

AS GOOD AS IT GETS
Love, Life, and Relationships
Fifty Days in the Song of Songs

Copyright © 2011 Stephen M. Clark. All rights reserved. Except for brief quotations in critical publications or reviews, no part of this book may be reproduced in any manner without prior written permission from the publisher. Write: Permissions, Wipf and Stock Publishers, 199 W. 8th Ave., Suite 3, Eugene, OR 97401.

Wipf & Stock
An Imprint of Wipf and Stock Publishers
199 W. 8th Ave., Suite 3
Eugene, OR 97401

www.wipfandstock.com

ISBN 13: 978-1-60899-623-0

Scripture taken from the Holy Bible, New International Version®, NIV®
Copyright© 1973, 1978, 1984 by Biblica, Inc.™
Used by permission of Zondervan. All rights reserved worldwide. WWW.ZONDERVAN.COM"
"The "NIV" and "New International Version" are trademarks registered in the United States Patent and Trademark Offices by Biblica, Inc.™

Manufactured in the U.S.A.

O! when mine eyes did see Olivia first,
Methought she purg'd the air of pestilence.
That instant was I turn'd into a hart,
And my desires, like fell and cruel hounds,
E'er since pursue me.

—Shakespeare, *Twelfth Night*

What sweet herb art thou
   that causeth me
to love thee,
    even now?

—Stephen

Love is as strong as death,
   its jealousy as unyielding as the grave.
It burns like a blazing flame,
   like a fire lit by God.
Many waters cannot quench love;
   rivers cannot wash it away.
If one were to give
   all the wealth of his house for love,
   it would be utterly scorned.

—Song of Songs 8:6–7

(Based on the New International Version, with some lines translated by the author.)

Contents

Acknowledgments / xi

Introduction / xiii

PART 1: ECSTASY AND AGONY, 1:1—3:5

Section 1: The Passion and the People, 1:2–4 / 3

    Day 1: Simply the Best: "Solomon's Song of Songs"—the title, 1:1
    Day 2: Desire and Longing: "Let him kiss me"—Poem 1, 1:2–4
    Day 3: Intimacy: "Like perfume poured out"
    Day 4: Community: "We will praise your love"
    Day 5: Affirmation: "How right they are to adore you!"

Section 2: Hurt and Healing, 1:5—2:7 / 29

    Day 6: Insecurity: "Dark am I, yet lovely"—Poem 2, 1:5–6
    Day 7: Identity: "Do not stare at me"
    Day 8: Misunderstanding: "Like a veiled woman"—Poem 3, 1:7–8
    Day 9: Listening: "If you do not know"
    Day 10: Adornment: "Earrings of gold"—Poem 4, 1:9–11
    Day 11: Friendship: "I liken you, my darling"
    Day 12: Delighting: "Resting between my breasts"—Poem 5, 1:12–14
    Day 13: As It Should Be: "Our bed is verdant"—Poem 6, 1:15—2:2
    Day 14: Transformation: "I am a rose of Sharon"
    Day 15: Contentment: "His fruit is sweet"—Poem 7, 2:3–7

Section 3: Joy and Fear, 2:8—3:5 / 85

    Day 16: Excitement: "Leaping across mountains"—Poem 8, 2:8–17
    Day 17: Renewal: "The season of singing has come"
    Day 18: Disruption: "Catch for us the foxes"
    Day 19: Satisfaction: "My lover is mine and I am his"

Day 20: Restlessness: "All night long on my bed"—Poem 9, 3:1–5
Day 21: Resolution: "I held him"

PART 2: THE HEART OF THE MATTER, 3:6—5:1

Section 4: The Wedding, 3:6–11 / 125

Day 22: The Wedding: "The day his heart rejoiced"—Poem 10, 3:6–11
Day 23: Awe: "Like a column of smoke"
Day 24: Security: "Escorted by sixty warriors"
Day 25: Extravagance: "Made for himself the carriage"

Section 5: The Wasf, 4:1—5:1 / 147

Day 26: Admiration: "How beautiful you are"—Poem 11, 4:1–7
Day 27: Rapture: "There is no flaw in you"
Day 28: Disclosure: "Come with me"—Poem 12, 4:8–9
Day 29: Friendship: "My sister, my bride"
Day 30: Consummation: "Let my lover come"—Poem 13, 4:10—5:1
Day 31: Realization: "I have come into my garden"
Day 32: Contrast: "Broken down walls"

PART 3: LOST AND FOUND 5:2—8:14

Section 6: Fear and Joy 5:2—8:4 / 187

Day 33: Abuse: "They bruised me"—Poem 14, 5:2–8
Day 34: Understanding: "What will you tell him?"
Day 35: Strength: "My lover is radiant and ruddy," 5:9—6:3
Day 36: Confidence: "My lover is mine"
Day 37: Admiration: "You are beautiful"—Poem 15, 6:4–9
Day 38: Transcendence: "Who is this that appears"—Poem 16, 6:10–12
Day 39: Dance: "That we may gaze on you!"—Poem 17, 6:13—7:10
Day 40: Dignity: "His desire is for me"
Day 41: Invitation: "Let us go early"—Poem 18, 7:11–13
Day 42: Yearning: "If only you were"—Poem 19, 8:1–4

Section 7: Desire and Confidence 8:5-14 / 257

    Day 43: Continuity: "Under the apple tree"—Poem 20, 8:5-7
    Day 44: Identity: "Like a seal over your heart"
    Day 45: Love: "As strong as death"
    Day 46: Self-Confidence: "My breasts are like towers"—Poem 21 8:8-10
    Day 47: Freedom: "Mine to give"—Poem 22, 8:11-12
    Day 48: Happily Ever After? "Let me hear your voice!"—Poem 23, 8:13-14

Appendices / 299

    Day 49: Appendix 1—God: The Garden and the Song
    Day 50: Appendix—Redemption: The Son and the Song

Bibliography / 315

Acknowledgments

So many people and events go into the making of a book that it is impossible even for an author to recognize them all. My parents, Ernest and Elizabeth Clark of Kendal, Jamaica, were extraordinary influences on my life, as indeed was the soil on which I was born. Two exceptional Rhodes Scholars, the poet Mervyn Morris and the pastor Earle Thames, taught me at Munro College. From the former I learned to love language and literature, although I hardly knew it at the time. From the latter I immediately grasped the wonders of the Old Testament, and with time, the humility of service and love.

My children, Stephen, Jean-Paul, and Alisha, refuse to be intimidated by the religiously trite and superficial and have inspired me to follow my own passion to bring together faith, Scripture, scholarship, the mind, and the heart. My wife, Olive, never once doubted that this endeavor would and should come to completion, an extraordinary accomplishment in light of the person to whom she is married. This book is largely the result of her unwavering confidence. I am deeply indebted to her. Thank you, Olivia.

A number of communities have helped give birth to this work. The people of Knowlton, Wallace, and Old Cutler all participated in my initial excursions into this territory, and I am grateful to them for their love, support, and encouragement over the years.

I believe it was C. H. Spurgeon who would brag about the famous people he met in his library. It will immediately be obvious that this undertaking has also greatly benefited from keeping company with a group of extraordinary commentators who account for most, if not all, of the value in it. I have sought to give them full credit, but if any of their thoughts pass for my own, it is the result of being so profoundly influenced by them or because this undertaking was produced in the midst of the busy calling of a pastor.

This manuscript would never have been shown to anyone without the help of Meredith Parker, who untiringly and joyfully cleaned it up. Her enthusiasm for the project never once faltered despite her subject's failure to grasp her corrections. He has not, however, neglected to understand how much she has done on his behalf.

Finally, it is my greatest hope that this work will produce some small contribution to the recovery of the vital relevance of the Word of God to all of life. The revitalization of the people of God waits to be discovered in the central place of the Scriptures in the life and worship of God's people.

Introduction

To discover the Song of Songs is to enter what one great thinker called, "The Strange New World within the Bible."[1] It is a land filled with new fragrances and delights that at once seem both strange and wondrous to us. Like C. S. Lewis's famous *Chronicles of Narnia*, which takes its children through the wardrobe and into the splendid new kingdom of Narnia, the Song is a land filled with wonder, brimming with insight and meaning. Once entered, its songs keep playing over and over in our minds and leave their readers forever changed because they dared to enter. Best of all, we discover that it is a garden steeped in passion, a place filled with this tantalizing thing called love—always nearly in grasp, forever slipping through our fingers, but never left forgotten once it is found.

A couple of predicaments face the traveler once we begin to make our way into the Song. We understand it is written to give us insight and understanding, and therefore, we must explain its meaning and draw out its implication. Yet to do so puts us in danger of destroying the nature of its poetry and the beauty of its impression. "The wooden trap of words can never catch the lobster of love, any more than a wooden 'interpretation' of the meaning of a piece of music can capture the music itself."[2] If we lose its beauty, we have lost our way.

Another difficulty comes as we actually find our way through this strange and wonderful land. We expect that there is a beginning, middle, and end to our journey but soon discover that while there is a middle, there is neither a real beginning nor an end.[3] More than a few travelers have undertaken to map their way through the Song,[4] but they always fail if they insist upon forcing a timeline upon the text. We may forgive

---

1. Barth, *Word of God*, 28–50.
2. Kreeft, *Three Philosophies*, 102.
3. Bloch and Bloch, *Song*, 18.
4. See Exum, *Song*, 39.

them for doing so, because there is a wedding at the middle, but as we shall see, the Song is more creative than "before and after the wedding."

A better way to read the Song is to understand it as a collage of pictures. Our family once went for dinner at the home of some new friends. We were immediately intrigued by a set of twenty or thirty prints arranged on the wall around a central picture of their wedding. What was important was not the chronology of the pictures, which sometimes was evident and at other times not; these pictures instead indicated how they centered their love and their life together as represented by their vows to one another. That is exactly what the Song does.

To use a more contemporary image, the Song is not unlike a music video where the director projects image after image almost randomly onto the screen, appearing to have no particular order. They can be haunting, compelling, intriguing, painful, or beautiful. In the end, we may be able to piece together some sort of a story, but that is to miss the point. What matters are the even disparate images the video imprints on our minds and that keep on playing in our heads long after it has ended. So it is with the Song of Songs.[5]

Finally, not a few travelers who find themselves single quickly come to the conclusion that this land is not a place where they live and that they might even be excused for feeling unwelcome. That would be sad not least of all because love belongs to all of us, and relationships permeate every part of all of our daily lives. The lovers in the Song may climb the heights of love between a man and a woman, but how they do so and the obstacles that they find belong to every human being in all of our daily interactions with others. Becoming comfortable where our lovers make us uncomfortable may be necessary if we are ever to be truly at home in relationships. This book, as one philosopher has said, is about "life as love" and "love as a song."[6] Like all of Scripture, it is for all of us.[7]

Welcome to the Song of Songs, some twenty or thirty pictures that are about to remain indelibly imprinted on our hearts and our minds. Welcome to the haunting, compelling, intriguing, painful, beautiful world of love and relationships that, once entered, thankfully never leaves us the same.

---

5. See Longman, *Song*, 43.

6. Kreeft, *Three Philosophies*, 99–103.

7. Cf. 1 Timothy 3:16: "All Scripture is God-breathed and is useful for teaching, rebuking, correcting and training in righteousness, so that the man of God may be thoroughly equipped for every good work."

PART 1

Ecstasy and Agony, 1:1—3:5

We rejoice and delight in you;
  we will praise your love more than wine (1:4).

Section 1

The Passion and the People, 1:2–4

Day 1

Simply the Best: "Solomon's Song of Songs"

The Title (1:1)

Solomon's Song of Songs (1:1).

INTRODUCTION

With these simple words, we encounter a stunning claim. It is what we call a superlative—that is, an almost exaggerated expression of praise. This is the "Song of Songs," which is to say it is the best there is. It is unsurpassed. It is as good as it gets. It is, if you will, "the best of the best." The title asserts that this is the greatest piece of literature that has ever been written, or will ever be read, on the subject of love and relationships.

What is remarkable is that this statement goes virtually unchallenged now as much as 2,900 years after the Song was first written or collected.[1] In fact, over thirty years ago, one noted commentator counted more than a thousand scholarly articles and books on the Song.[2] With some exasperation, he noted, "The relevant literature turned out to be . . . too much to be catalogued completely, to say nothing of any hope of perusing the whole."[3] That, of course, is a trend that has only increased with the passing of time.

---

1. Many scholars believe that the Song may not have a single author or date of composition and that it is actually a collection of songs. Even if this is the case, there is little reason to doubt that much of the original material may date back to the time of Solomon in the tenth century BC or not to regard it as an organic whole. For a discussion of this subject, see Longman, *Song*, 2–7; Exum, *Song*, 33–37.

2. See Carr's reference to Pope in *Song*, 15.

3. Pope, *Song*, ix.

In other words, if we wish to make life, develop relationships, and take delight in this thing called "love," this is the place to which we must go. It is the "Song of Songs" because "love is the greatest in value" and "the greatest in size." It teaches us that "all of life is a love song" and that "love is the meaning of the whole."[4] It does not get any better than this.

REVIEWS

If this were a movie or a theatrical production, then we might read these reviews online or in the entertainment section of our local newspaper:

> ... a literary, poetic exploration of human love that strongly affirms loyalty, beauty and sexuality in all their variety. With tender metaphor and extravagant imagery, the Song writer spins a tale of human love into the cadence of verse ...[5]

> From the aching yearnings for intimacy, to the ecstasy of consummation, from the tensions of separation and the fears of loss, to the relaxed contentment of togetherness, from coquetry and flirtation, to the triumphalism of passion; all these are traced out in the ebb and flow of a growing relationship of mutual love.[6]

> ... the most tender and inimitable expression of passionate yet graceful love that has come down to us.[7]

THE AUTHOR

At first, it seems fairly obvious that Solomon wrote the Song of Songs. After all, the first verse reads, "Solomon's Song of Songs." It would seem to suggest that the book must have been written by Solomon, the third king of Israel (c. 971–931 BC), in celebration of one of the women he loved.

Of course, some people immediately object. "How could Solomon, who reflected the cultural attitudes of the kings of his day, and who had seven hundred wives and three hundred concubines,[8] possibly know

---

4. Kreeft, *Three Philosophies*, 103, 105, 104.
5. See the back cover of Gledhill, *Song*.
6. Ibid., 13.
7. Goethe, quoted by Exum, *Song*, 30.
8. First Kings 11:3.

anything about love and what it takes to have successful relationships?" We might well reply that his failure would hardly preclude the fact that he had an enormous amount of experience, at least in what not to do! More to the point, it could be the very occasion for his coming to an understanding of what love really has to be if we are to arrive at any measure of success in our relationships.

When we take a closer look at the book, it does not appear to be a history or even a story about Solomon and his love. The theme of a king does appear more than once,[9] but so does that of a shepherd and a woman at one point identified as the Shulammite.[10] Some commentators even suggest that Solomon is an antagonist in the book.[11] They see him as either trying to steal the woman from the shepherd or as a foil against which to contrast the simple beauty and faithful love of the shepherd.[12]

In that case, what the text suggests is that the simplicity of love that is available to the average person is much to be preferred to the extravagant opulence associated with the celebrities of our culture. Good point!

Regardless, when Solomon does appear in the Song,[13] he is described not as its subject but as a person apart. He brings literary coloring to the song. In any event, the question is moot. There is good linguistic reason to believe that the title "Solomon's Song of Songs" may well be a later editorial ascription given to the book,[14] much like "A Psalm of David" appears before many of the Psalms.[15] Even if it is not, it might mean nothing more than this was Solomon's favorite book and that it took a place of pride in his collection. It could have been dedicated to him or simply become a part of the great body of literature that is to be associated with the wisdom of Solomon.[16]

---

9. Song of Songs 1:4, 12, 7:5.
10. Song of Songs 6:13.
11. See the discussion in Gledhill, *Song*, 24–26.
12. See the discussion in Carr, *Song*, 51.
13. Song of Songs 1:5; 3:9, 11; 8:11, 12.
14. The title uses a different and purportedly later relative pronoun than the rest of the Song. See, for example, Longman, *Song*, 87; Gledhill, *Song*, 92; Exum, *Song*, 89.
15. Bloch and Bloch, *Song*, 137.
16. See the discussion in Longman, *Song*, 2–7.

A GREAT BOOK

Whoever the human author or editor is, undoubtedly this is an outstanding work. The reason is that, like all great literature, it never pretends, and it always deals with the real issues of life and love as we find them to be—not necessarily as we want them to be.[17] We may be disappointed to realize that this is not a paperback romance novel. It is about real life, love, and relationships. That is precisely what we need, even if not always what we want.

On the one hand, it celebrates the magnificence of love and even the intoxicating nature of human sexuality. It understands that as human beings we are designed for love, and that our most fundamental emotional need is for satisfying relationships. On the other hand, it does not shrink from facing the fact that human relationships are incredibly difficult and that even the best of them can quickly become mired in conflict, suspicion, and antagonism. The Song knows what it means to be human, to be overcome by love and upended in conflict. It is entirely in keeping with human experience, extraordinarily helpful, and above all truthful.

Yes, we will have to grow accustomed to its imagery, but it will not be impossible once we understand its context. Given our present culture, we may not wish to say to the one whom we love, "Your teeth are like a flock of sheep just shorn," but we might find ourselves saying, "Your lips are like a scarlet ribbon, your mouth is lovely."[18] In the end, we discover that the book is a thing of beauty, and understanding and appreciating its imagery will be more of a pleasure than a task.

The Song is filled with beauty because this is a magnificent subject. If we are going to talk about love, then it has to be dealt with in a lovely way. The form of a thing already tells us something about its very nature.

REFLECTION

Equally, we can say it is a thing of beauty because beauty can live only where faith exists. If we don't believe that human relationships can exist with any measure of joy, then life necessarily becomes ugly. If we do not

---

17. Kreeft points out, "The Bible is about real life . . . it is the most realistic book ever written." *Three Philosophies*, 99.

18. Song of Songs 4:2–3.

believe in forgiveness and understand the need for reconciliation, then an "amazing grace" will have entirely escaped us. If we understand that we are designed for love, that we are loved and that we are truly capable of love, then beauty begins to fill our lives and eventually comes to characterize our love and our relationships. This is as good as it gets!

MEDITATION

The Beauty of God and of the Love He Gives

One thing I ask of the LORD,
  this is what I seek:
that I may dwell in the house of the LORD
  all the days of my life,
to gaze upon the beauty of the LORD
  and to seek him in his temple (Ps 27:4).

Let love and faithfulness never leave you;
  bind them around your neck,
    write them on the tablet of your heart (Prov 3:3).

He who loves me will be loved by my Father, and I too will love him and show myself to him (John 14:21).

Dear friends, since God so loved us, we also ought to love one another (1 John 4:11).

PRAYER

Lord, you are to be praised because you have filled your world with beauty, made us capable of love, and given us life as a love song. You are the "best of the best," and in you all things come together and have their meaning.

Please forgive me for all the times that I have failed to reflect your beauty, neglected to enjoy the life that you have given me as a song, and worst of all, failed to believe that life can be lived with beauty and joy.

Teach me this day to live my life in a lovely way and as a song given by you, for you, and unto you. Amen

Day 2

Poem 1 (1:2–4) A

Desire and Longing: "Let him kiss me"

Woman
A. Let him kiss me with the kisses of his mouth—
   for your love is more delightful than wine.
Pleasing is the fragrance of your perfumes;
   your name is like perfume poured out.
   No wonder the maidens love you!
Take me away with you—let us hurry!
   Let the king bring me into his chambers.

Friends
We rejoice and delight in you;
   we will praise your love more than wine.

Man
How right they are to adore you!

SHOCK AND AWE

Imagine for a moment that you have come to see a theatrical performance that is said to be unsurpassed for its drama and beauty, and especially for its insights into love, life, and relationships. You have brought your whole family with you. After all, it is a "religious" production, and you have heard that it has been recommended by pastors, priests, and rabbis. You know that it is reputed to have more than its fair share of passionate moments, but nothing has prepared you for what is about to take place.

As the curtains pull back, standing on the stage is a beautiful young woman, and the first words out of her mouth are, "Let him kiss me with the kisses of his mouth." The program notes tell you that there are various forms of kissing in the Ancient Near East[19] where the drama is set, but what is in view here is clearly meant to be both sensual and passionate.

The next words out of her mouth are even more shocking, "For your love is more delightful than wine." It is not that her references are to wine and not to tea. You understand that she is referring to the heady and intoxicating power of love[20] and realize that she longs for her lover's kisses to linger over her palate like good wine. Politely put, that would be fine. However, the program notes suggest that the original text of "your love is more delightful than wine" indicates lovemaking, foreplay, and sexual intercourse.[21] In fact, there can be little doubt about it. After less than half a dozen lines, her passionate outburst is brought to an end only by her insistence that she needs to be taken away to her lover's bed to fulfill her longing and desire.

> Take me away with you—let us hurry!
> Let the king bring me into his chambers.

Now you understand why it was that the rabbis apparently gave the Song of Songs a PG-13 rating![22] You wonder what is yet to come. After all, the play has only just begun. Perhaps you would not have been as surprised if you had read the review by Origen (185–232) who, after all, was one of the early fathers of the church:

> "I advise and counsel everyone who is not yet rid of the vexations of the flesh and blood and has not ceased to feel the passion of his bodily nature, to refrain completely from reading this little book and the things that will be said about it."[23]

Then we are forced to wonder, "Who then could read this book? If that is the case, why was it written? Did Origen ever arrive at the point where he 'ceased to feel the passion of his bodily nature'? And do we even want to get to that place?"

---

19. Nose kissing was also customary. See Fox, *Love Songs*, 97.

20. Keel, *Song*, 40.

21. Carr, *Song*, 73; Fox, *Love Songs*, 97; Gledhill, *Song*, 95; Keel, *Song*, 44. The adulteress in Proverbs 7:18 says, "Come, let's drink deep of love till morning; let's enjoy ourselves with love!" Cf. also Ezekiel 16:8.

22. See the discussion in Pope, *Song*, 116–17.

23. Origen, quoted in ibid., 117.

PURPOSE AND PASSION

In contrast, our reaction is very different. Here at last is a "holy book" that speaks the truth about who we know ourselves to be. It is about passionate longings and desire,[24] something that is at the heart of all human experience. Of course, we have heard that before, but usually from those for whom sexual passion was about their own self-indulgence and pleasure, and not about life and love. Here, in the most holy of contexts, is a book that says that passion is part and parcel of what it means to be human, and that dares to talk about love, sex, passionate longing, friendship, and relationships, and all in the same breath.

We should not be surprised. After all, as human beings we are created "in the image of God," and when God made the world, it was with a passion that declared seven times over in the first chapter of Genesis, the very first book of the Bible, "It is good."[25] We understand that as God takes pleasure in creation, so our lives are to be lived with pleasure in him and in his gifts of life and love, relationship and redemption.

More than that, here is a "holy" book daring to declare that being "spiritual" means embracing body and soul, longing and desire, and affirming both as the way in which we are to live our lives. Here is a "holy" book that from the very beginning is telling us we are not to live our lives nervously hiding away from reality, but we are to purposefully embrace life and love as good.

Already we can sense the power of the book. Yes, this is the passion between a man and woman, but even if that relationship is to be regarded as the very epitome of love, pleasure, rapture, delight, and intimacy, it should still be understood to be representative of how the Creator expects us to take delight in all his creation. As in the case of Jesus, it is possible that marriage may not be intended to be a part of God's plan for our life, but that fact would only increase our belief that life, not merely marriage, is to be lived in the pursuit of love, joy, reconciliation, redemption, and relationship. When the shock of our text wears off, we realize that "it is good" and that all life is to be embraced with that same passion.

---

24. Keel, *Song*, 40; Gledhill, *Song*, 93.
25. Genesis 1:26–27; 1:4, 10, 12, 18, 21, 25, 31.

Section 1: The Passion and the People, 1:2–4   13

REFLECTION

This is a very different way of looking at life. What our Song seems to be saying to us poetically is that there is a proper way to approach the reality of passion in our lives. Of course, the daily grind of making ends meet demands sheer hard work and even duty. When we go passionately at life because of fear of want, blind ambition to get ahead, an attempt to fill a void in ourselves, or to prove that we are something that we fear we are not, then we are missing the point. In that scenario, our lives may be lived with purpose—but they are being lived on terms that are contrary to the Song of Songs. They end up not with the rapture, joy, and excitement that we have just witnessed, but with the opposite: namely, the depression that comes with self-absorption, the destruction that accompanies self-indulgence, or sheer exhaustion.

More than that, we are already upended by the Song because when we speak about spiritual life with religious people, it seems to be that it is abstinence and self-discipline, not passion and love, that tend to first to come to their minds. Yet the apostle Paul makes a very pointed remark in this regard, suggesting that while spiritual regulations may appear to be a helpful approach to life, on their own they are entirely lacking.

> Since you died with Christ to the basic principles of this world, why, as though you still belonged to it, do you submit to its rules: "Do not handle! Do not taste! Do not touch!" These are all destined to perish with use, because they are based on human commands and teachings. Such regulations indeed have an appearance of wisdom, with their self-imposed worship, their false humility and their harsh treatment of the body, but they lack any value in restraining sensual indulgence (Col 2:20–23).

The apostle doesn't stop there. He indicates that a negative view of the spiritual life that prizes performance and is absent of the relationship of grace ends up missing what could be best described as vital relationship.

> Therefore do not let anyone judge you by what you eat or drink, or with regard to a religious festival, a New Moon celebration or a Sabbath day. These are a shadow of the things that were to come; the reality, however, is found in Christ. Do not let anyone who delights in false humility and the worship of angels disqualify you for the prize. Such a person goes into great detail about what he has seen, and his unspiritual mind puffs him up with idle notions. He has lost connection with the Head, from whom the

whole body, supported and held together by its ligaments and sinews, grows as God causes it to grow (Col 2:16–19).

We have looked at less than half a dozen lines in the Song, but already we understand that passionate and positive lives are about love and relationships—or what the older theologians called "union and communion."[26]

MEDITATION

The Goodness of God Leads to a Passionate and Purposeful Life

God saw all that he had made, and it was very good (Gen 1:31).

My soul yearns, even faints,
    for the courts of the LORD;
my heart and my flesh cry out
    for the living God (Ps 84:2).

Taking the five loaves and the two fish and looking up to heaven, he gave thanks and broke the loaves. Then he gave them to the disciples, and the disciples gave them to the people. They all ate and were satisfied, and the disciples picked up twelve basketfuls of broken pieces that were left over (Matt 14:19–20).

So then, just as you received Christ Jesus as Lord, continue to live in him, rooted and built up in him, strengthened in the faith as you were taught, and overflowing with thankfulness (Col 2:6–7).

Prayer

Lord, you are good, and so is this world and this life as you intend it. Thank you for making it and recreating it in this way.

Please forgive me for all the times that I have been bitter, negative, and unbelieving.

Help me to live this day with the passion and purpose that you intended and in such a way that others may see your goodness at work in my life. Amen.

---

26. The phrase has been very widely used in discussions on the doctrine of the Trinity and the believer's relationship to Christ and the church. For example, *The Larger Catechism*, Q.65. See also, Taylor, *Union and Communion*.

Day 3

Poem 1 (1:2–4) B

Intimacy: "Like perfume poured out"

Woman
Let him kiss me with the kisses of his mouth—
   for your love is more delightful than wine.

B. Pleasing is the fragrance of your perfumes;
   your name is like perfume poured out.
   No wonder the maidens love you!
Take me away with you—let us hurry!
   Let the king bring me into his chambers.

Friends
We rejoice and delight in you;
   we will praise your love more than wine.

Man
How right they are to adore you!

INTIMACY

Having made our way past the initial shock and passion of the first lines of our poem, we recover just quickly enough to realize that we have not yet even arrived at the heart of our first song. At the very center of the poem are these lines on the lips of the woman, which at first may seem a little strange to us:

> Pleasing is the fragrance of your perfumes;
>   your name is like perfume poured out.
> No wonder the maidens love you!

In the Hebrew culture of the Song, one's name was not simply a designated label by which a child was to be identified or the romantic fancy of one's parents. As the names of God represent the character and personality of God, so the name parents gave a child was usually understood to be a designation, or at least a hope for, or even a prophecy of that person's character and self. Names were about reputation and person,[27] much in the way in that contemporary nicknames like "Rock" or "King" can represent exactly that in our own culture.[28]

The fact that the woman delights in her lover's name, which she describes as being like perfume poured out, indicates that she loves the person she has come to know. More than that, she delights in the fact that he has shared who he is with her. "There is more, then, than chemistry at work here. There is character—character she respects."[29]

As the nature of God is to communicate himself both in creation and in Christ, and as "God is love," so the sharing of our selves is the place where intimacy and passion are to be found. Here the man's name and nature is poured out over and into the woman. There can be no lasting love or passion where the sharing of one's self does not take place.

The joy that exudes from the woman is in the fact that not only is her "king" interested in her, but also in that he wants to share his life with her. The power of the "perfume poured out" is in the intimacy of the sharing of one's self with another. When this happens, as the woman points out, it leaves a fragrance that is delightful and that cannot help but be noticed by all who are around.

There can be no intimacy until we share ourselves with others. Passion is born when the tenderness of that moment is received, cherished, shared, identified with, and then affirmed by the other.

The passion in our song comes from the intimacy that exists between our lovers. In the midst of a world in which shepherds have sheep to find and feed, and kings have terrorists to discover and destroy, like a bottle of good wine, the lovers take time to savor each other, and to share themselves with each other. "Lovers," someone has said, "love to whisper each other's names because the name stands for the person, the individual."[30]

27. Carr, *Song*, 74.
28. Glickman, *A Song for Lovers*, 30.
29. Thomas, *A Biblical Guide*, 19.
30. Kreeft, *Three Philosophies*, 123.

At one level or another, we already realize that successful relationships are about being truly interested in someone besides ourselves. They are about listening, caring, and understanding. Of equal importance, they are about sharing ourselves and who we are with others. The sharing of our self is a gift and not the demand or burden of self-absorption. Perhaps it is to state the obvious, but love finds its fulfillment through the abandonment of one's self to the other.[31]

REFLECTION

This is the way that it has to be because our lovers, along with the community of faith in ancient Israel, already know that we are created male and female and in the image of God. We are created like Adam and Eve to walk with God and each other in the original intimacy of the Garden.[32] We are capable of intimate relationships because we are made in the image of God, and God is one in the perfect union and communion of Father, Son, and Holy Spirit. What this means is that the longing of our souls for intimacy is the way God made us, and its absence is always a part of our alienation.

MEDITATION

God Shares Who He Is with Us, and Intimacy and Love Are Born

> Then God said, "Let us make man in our image, in our likeness..."
> (Gen 1:26).

> The man and his wife were both naked, and they felt no shame
> (Gen 2:25).

> I will exalt you, my God the King;
>   I will praise your name for ever and ever.
> Every day I will praise you
>   and extol your name for ever and ever....

> The LORD is gracious and compassionate,
>   slow to anger and rich in love.

---

31. Gledhill, *Song*, 94–95.
32. Genesis 3:8–11.

> The LORD is good to all;
> he has compassion on all he has made. . . .
>
> The LORD is near to all who call on him,
> to all who call on him in truth.
> He fulfills the desires of those who fear him;
> he hears their cry and saves them (Ps 145:1–2, 8–9, 18–19).

Then he turned toward the woman and said to Simon, "Do you see this woman? I came into your house. You did not give me any water for my feet, but she wet my feet with her tears and wiped them with her hair. You did not give me a kiss, but this woman, from the time I entered, has not stopped kissing my feet. You did not put oil on my head, but she has poured perfume on my feet. Therefore, I tell you, her many sins have been forgiven—for she loved much. But he who has been forgiven little loves little" (Luke 7:44–47).

We loved you so much that we were delighted to share with you not only the gospel of God but our lives as well, because you had become so dear to us (1 Thess 2:8).

PRAYER

Lord, your name is awesome in all the earth. You are powerful, compassionate, loving, and just. You have shown yourself to us in your world and in your word.

Please forgive me for not taking the time to get to know you and to enjoy who you are and what you have done for me.

Give me the courage today to share who I am with others, the wisdom to know when to do so, and the opportunity to be a blessing to others. Amen.

Day 4

Poem 1 (1:2–4) C

Community: "We will praise your love"

Woman
Let him kiss me with the kisses of his mouth—
    for your love is more delightful than wine.
Pleasing is the fragrance of your perfumes;
    your name is like perfume poured out.
    No wonder the maidens love you!
Take me away with you—let us hurry!
    Let the king bring me into his chambers.

Friends
C. We rejoice and delight in you;
    we will praise your love more than wine.

Man
How right they are to adore you!

CELEBRATION

The initial shock of the very first words of the Song has worn off, and our meditation on the intimacy of the friendship between this man and woman has sunk in. Now we are left to make sense of the whole moment that surrounds our first song.

The first thing that we realize is these are not two secret lovers sneaking off to share a sexual tryst when no one is looking. In fact, the excitement of the moment appears to be happening in the company of a chorus of friends, who exclaim:

> We rejoice and delight in you;
>   we will praise your love more than wine.

Wine and oil were a part of the key ingredients of public festive moments in ancient Israel.[33] It is the chorus of friends who help to locate the actual occasion for us. They form, as happens elsewhere in the Scriptures, a public celebration of the woman going off to the king's rooms.[34] They are to be found pronouncing a blessing on the woman as she hurries her lover away to bed. This is in keeping with other biblical references where this sort of "blessing" is used in the context of a marriage.[35]

As we look at this more closely, we realize that the setting is intended either to invoke the bringing of the bride to the house of the groom or as a response to the bridegroom's invitation to move in with him.[36] In any event, the picture circulates around their coming together as man and woman, bride and groom.[37]

As we hear the song, we get the impression of attending their wedding feast, and for a moment being allowed to hear the lovers as they whisper to each other. They just can't wait for everyone to be gone so that they can be alone with each other! This is their royal moment and she longs to be taken off to his bed.

In the ancient world, the bride and groom were honored as a "king" and "queen" at their wedding. They would often crown each other.[38] This public honor and celebration is still something with which we are familiar. Even now it is not unusual for the bride to wear a tiara or for a garland of flowers to be placed around the necks of the couple. In fact, it is that very theme of being "crowned" at one's wedding that will reappear in the Song[39] as a major part of what is taking place. He is her "king," her very own "Solomon."[40]

More than that, the chorus of friends functions as a mirror of the woman's feelings.[41] They echo back to her the approval of the community in regard to what is taking place. It indicates that the woman is confident in her love. She has reason to fear neither condemnation nor competi-

---

33. Keel, *Song*, 44.
34. Cf. Joel 2:16. Longman, *Song*, 93.
35. See the discussion in ibid., 94. For example, see Psalm 45 and Proverbs 5:18.
36. See the discussion in Murphy, *Song*, 127.
37. This will be repeated in 3:6—5:1, which forms the central section of the Song.
38. See Longman, *Song*, 92.
39. Song of Songs 3:11.
40. Bloch and Bloch, *Song*, 137.
41. Longman, *Song*, 94.

tion. There is no jealousy on the part of her friends,[42] only the joyful celebration of the community.

COMMUNITY

Ironically, the capacity for intimacy, and a life and love lived with passion, is never lived alone as a stranger or together as aliens, but always in the midst of community. Sociological studies have shown that successful lives are built in the midst of supportive communities. Families of faith, which secular psychologists once wanted to characterize as toxic, have now been shown to be healthy and good for us.[43]

These two lovers, however passionate and intimate their relationship, are never alone in the book. Their friends are integral to the Song not merely as a clever literary device to cause us to meditate, reflect, and be drawn back into the action, but also as the context in which life and love is to be lived. Celebration and affirmation both require community.

The ability of the lovers to function in the midst of community is itself a significant indicator of the health of their passion and the security of the love that they have found in each other. Intimacy hidden and kept in the corner away from the knowledge of others nearly always ends up being obsessive, dark, and destructive. Love affirmed by others is usually a passion that is to be pursued because as oppressive as community can be, and we will see this later in the Song,[44] the affirmation of friends is most often a sure indication of both character and compatibility. Relationships by their very nature find their expression in community. In isolation, they turn inward and die.

It is important to understand this concept, because while passion may be good, it is a form of desperate longing. It has already made its appearance in our text, and it is going to suffuse our whole Song. It is a yearning after what we have called "union and communion." It is a powerful impulse after both intimacy and affirmation that when it finds its time and place, as in this moment, will fill our lives with exuberance and celebration. Equally, as we know from experience and will soon discover in our Song, when its course fails to find its path, it will turn inward in self-doubt and outward in fear, anxiety, and alienation.

---

42. Gledhill, *Song*, 96.
43. See, for example, Hall, "Religious Attendance," 103–9.
44. Song of Songs 5:7.

REFLECTION

We may as well be honest. This book was written for Israelites who lived in the wildly explicit context of Canaan and the pagan Ancient Near East. It belongs to that library of books we call "the Scriptures," and as such, has always been mandatory reading for Jews and Christians in places like Corinth and in times like the first century when it was rumored by some that a thousand prostitutes plied their trade at the temple of Aphrodite.[45] We discover that it is written for those of us who live in the real world where sex sells shoes, and relationships that work are the exception, not the rule. The Song is written for those who are not in denial but who want to understand the genius of love, sex, friendship, passion, marriage, life, and relationships.

The friends in our text function to tell us this. "The invitation to the women of Jerusalem to participate in the lovers' bliss is also an invitation to the reader. The women's presence is always a reminder that what seems to be a closed dialogue between two perpetually desiring lovers is addressed to us . . ."[46]

The Song shouts that passion is a powerful human impulse. It comes right out and tells us that intimacy and longing are a part of the human experience, and in the midst of everything else that may be going on, when love finds its times and place in the presence of others, it fills our life with exuberance and joy. The chorus of friends makes sure that we hear this and invites us to experience the common joys and aspirations of life brought now to royal heights in the midst of the community of faith. What we are being told is that love and passion are about life and living.

MEDITATION

In the Communion of Father, Son, and Holy Spirit, God Is Perfect in His Oneness. In Union with Others, Love Is Found.

> Let them give thanks to the LORD for his unfailing love
> and his wonderful deeds for men.

---

45. See the discussion in Fee, *First Epistle to the Corinthians*, 2–3.
46. Exum, *Song*, 7.

Let them exalt him in the assembly of the people
and praise him in the council of the elders (Ps 107:31–32).

Now a man named Lazarus was sick. He was from Bethany, the village of Mary and her sister Martha. This Mary, whose brother Lazarus now lay sick, was the same one who poured perfume on the Lord and wiped his feet with her hair. So the sisters sent word to Jesus, "Lord, the one you love is sick."
   When he heard this, Jesus said, "This sickness will not end in death. No, it is for God's glory so that God's Son may be glorified through it." Jesus loved Martha and her sister and Lazarus (John 11:1–5).

And let us consider how we may spur one another on toward love and good deeds. Let us not give up meeting together, as some are in the habit of doing, but let us encourage one another—and all the more as you see the day approaching (Heb 10:24–25).

PRAYER

Lord, you are wise, and you are wonderful, placing us in families who have nurtured us and in communities that have supported us.
   Forgive us for failing to recognize this, for grumbling against others and being ungrateful for all we have been given by our parents, teachers, and friends.
   Help me this day to enjoy those who surround me in family and workplace, and to live my life in support of others rather than for myself. Amen.

Day 5

Song 1 (1:2–4) D

Affirmation: "How right they are to adore you!"

Woman
Let him kiss me with the kisses of his mouth—
   for your love is more delightful than wine.
Pleasing is the fragrance of your perfumes;
   your name is like perfume poured out.
   No wonder the maidens love you!
Take me away with you—let us hurry!
   Let the king bring me into his chambers.

Friends
We rejoice and delight in you;
   we will praise your love more than wine

Man
D. How right they are to adore you!

PRAISE

There is just one more thing that we must say about our first song. Integral to this moment is that both the lovers and their friends strike a note that will become one of the central themes of the Song. Indeed, it will carry the melody of the book even through its most turbulent moments. It is a key not only to intimacy and passion, but also to relationships as a whole. To use a common word, it is *affirmation*. To use a religious word, it is *praise*.

Woman
Pleasing is the fragrance of your perfumes;
   your name is like perfume poured out.
   No wonder the maidens love you!

We can hardly miss the point because the chorus of friends will repeat it for us:

> Friends
> We rejoice and delight in you;
> > we will praise your love more than wine.

And our lover will not miss a beat as he comes right back at the woman with his line:

> Man
> How right they are to adore you!

Our poem is from beginning to end about praise. The woman tells her lover what she likes about his lovemaking, as she says, "Let him kiss me with the kisses of his mouth." Then she explains the effect of his love upon her, "Your love is more delightful than wine." She shares the effect that he has upon her when she is around him: "Pleasing is the fragrance of your perfumes." She delights in the quality of his character and his person: "Your name is like perfume poured out." And she reinforces how others feel about him: "No wonder the maidens love you!"

It is precisely in the response of praise and the context of affirmation that we find ourselves able to share ourselves with others. Praise is the air that intimacy breathes, and without which passion is soon lost.

One of the most sobering moments in my life as a pastor came after the funeral of a stranger. I had been asked by his wife to visit him on his deathbed, and in the intimacy of that moment, he indicated how good his wife had been to him. As I shared this with her after his funeral, she turned to me with sadness in her eyes and responded, "But he never once told me!" How much was lost in life and in death because of the absence of praise.

In contrast, our poem is vibrant and alive with joy, life, passion, and praise. It is not morbid, introspective, or alone. Instead, the community has gathered to sing its praise.

> Woman
> Pleasing is the fragrance of your perfumes;
> > your name is like perfume poured out.
> > No wonder the maidens love you!
> Take me away with you—let us hurry!
> > Let the king bring me into his chambers.

Friends
We rejoice and delight in you;
  we will praise your love more than wine.

Man
How right they are to adore you!

What we are discovering here is that the key to intimacy and the sharing of ourselves with others is praise both given and received. It opens and unlocks doors, and until we can loosen our tongues in admiration of others, we will never know the delights of intimacy or the corresponding physical expressions that accompany such love. As long as we greet each other first with criticism, and then with unrealized expectations on our lips, we will forever remain alienated and alone.

WHAT IT'S ALL ABOUT

Passionate longing has made itself known everywhere in our text. We are tempted to think it must be all about sex, but in fact, as the Christian tradition has insisted in the resurrection of the body, body and soul are entirely bound together. It is impossible to rip one from the other except with the most disastrous of consequences.

In the end, passion is about intimacy. When we share our lives and ourselves with others in the context of praise, appreciation, affirmation, and community, the music begins to be heard in our lives, and the genius of the Song becomes ours. By learning, however tentatively at first, to express praise and affirm the qualities that we see in each other, we create the climate for intimacy, and we begin to build successful relationships.

REFLECTION

What this all means is that we are created for worship and praise in the midst of the community, and when exuberant affirmation is no longer to be found on our lips, all passion is spent and all intimacy is lost. True praise always spills over into taking time to be with others. One needs the other. It is the reason the Christian community begins each week with a service of praise. It is here that we learn to live our lives, express our love, sing our praise, and be a part of a community in which encouragement becomes the norm in the midst of relationships that are forged in the support of one another.

"Love is, simply, superior. It belongs on a throne. It rightly brags, praises, exults, celebrates, sings it Song of Songs, its nonordinary song, its Greatest Song. It deserves silver and gold and robes and crowns. Heaven will be full of it (if the symbolism in Revelation means anything at all); had we not better practice living with it?"[47]

MEDITATION

The Praise of God Is the Beginning of Happy Relationship

I will extol the LORD at all times;
    his praise will always be on my lips.
My soul will boast in the LORD;
    let the afflicted hear and rejoice.
Glorify the LORD with me;
    let us exalt his name together (Ps 34:1–3).

When Jesus heard this, he was astonished and said to those following him, "I tell you the truth, I have not found anyone in Israel with such great faith" (Matt 8:10).

Praise be to the God and Father of our Lord Jesus Christ, who has blessed us in the heavenly realms with every spiritual blessing in Christ (Eph 1:3).

I commend to you our sister Phoebe, a servant of the church in Cenchrea. I ask you to receive her in the Lord in a way worthy of the saints and to give her any help she may need from you, for she has been a great help to many people, including me. . . .

Greet Ampliatus, whom I love in the Lord.

Greet Urbanus, our fellow worker in Christ, and my dear friend Stachys.

Greet Apelles, tested and approved in Christ.

Greet those who belong to the household of Aristobulus.

Greet Herodion, my relative.

Greet those in the household of Narcissus who are in the Lord.

---

47. Kreeft, *Three Philosophies*, 131.

> Greet Tryphena and Tryphosa, those women who work hard in the Lord.
>
> Greet my dear friend Persis, another woman who has worked very hard in the Lord.
>
> Greet Rufus, chosen in the Lord, and his mother, who has been a mother to me, too.
>
> Greet Asyncritus, Phlegon, Hermes, Patrobas, Hermas and the brothers with them.
>
> Greet Philologus, Julia, Nereus and his sister, and Olympas and all the saints with them.
>
> Greet one another with a holy kiss. All the churches of Christ send greetings. Rom 16:1, 8–16.

PRAYER

Father, I praise you because you are awesome, wonderful, and splendid. You are the giver of all life, beauty, joy, and happiness. Everything in all creation sings your praises and shouts your marvelous name.

I have been slow to recognize this and even slower to sing your praises. Forgive me when my prayers have been all about myself and not enough about you.

Teach me this day to spend time singing your praises. Show me how to do the same for others so that they may know the joy that is to be found in you. Amen.

Section 2

Hurt and Healing, 1:5—2:7

Day 6

Poem 2 (1:5–6) A

Insecurity: "Dark am I, yet lovely"

Woman
Dark am I, yet lovely,
  O daughters of Jerusalem,
  dark like the tents of Kedar,
  like the tent curtains of Solomon.
Do not stare at me because I am dark,
  because I am darkened by the sun.
My mother's sons were angry with me
  and made me take care of the vineyards;
  my own vineyard I have neglected.

A PERFECT LOVE AFFAIR

A new section of our book is about to begin, and as we look at what is now the second song in our collection that is the Song of Songs, the mood suddenly changes. Clouds begin to appear.

For one bright, shining moment, we thought that we had stumbled upon the perfect love affair. The woman is every man's dream. She is passionate: "Let him kiss me with the kisses of his mouth." She is warm and intimate: "Take me away with you—let us hurry, let my king bring me into his chambers." She is also filled with praise: "Your love is more delightful than wine, your name is like perfume poured out, no wonder the women love you."

He appears to be everything she could possibly want. He loves her. He is interested in her, and even more importantly, he shares himself with her. She understands who he is. Not only has he shared his "name," his person, his character, and his life with her, but he has also come right out in the midst of the community and unmistakably said so. And yes, she finds him physically and sexually attractive.

All the right ingredients are there. What could possibly go wrong? At last, every man's dream and every woman's hope seem to have come together in that passionate moment when everything explodes and we know that we are "in love" and that this is "happily ever after."

INSECURITY

Now, almost immediately, we begin to discover that all is not well in Camelot. Despite the fact that everything seems to be going so perfectly, or perhaps precisely because everything is going so well, suddenly deep insecurities and doubts begin to intrude into their relationship. Even though she is apparently a stunningly beautiful woman, and at one level knows it, she suffers from what we today would call low self-esteem and of all things in regard to her appearance!

As she describes it for us, when other women, "the daughters of Jerusalem," look at her, she is filled with insecurity and even anxiety. She believes her appearance betrays the fact that she has been forced to work out in the fields and in the heat of the sun. "Do not stare at me," she says, "because I am dark, because I am darkened by the sun."

Her feeling about herself is summed up in the phrase, "Dark am I, yet lovely." This is not about race or color;[1] it is about the fact that she has had to work out in the sun tending the vineyard, in the process ruining her complexion. It might also indicate her poor social position, making her the object of the scorn of the city girls, at least in her own imagination.[2]

On the one hand, she believes that her complexion has become rough and hardened like the nomadic tents of the desert tribes, made as they were of goats' hides,[3] and yet at the same time she understands that she naturally shares the beauty of Solomon's finest curtain hangings.[4]

> Dark am I, yet lovely,
> O daughters of Jerusalem,
> dark like the tents of Kedar,
> like the tent curtains of Solomon.

1. See Murphy, *Song*, 128.
2. Fox, *Love Songs*, 101.
3. Gledhill, *Song*, 103.
4. Carr, *Song*, 78.

Her self-deprecation may be unfounded, but the real problem is that her swarthy complexion represents the abuse that she has suffered. The clue to her insecurity is probably seen in the fact that she feels it necessary to distance herself from her brothers.[5]

> My mother's sons were angry with me
> and made me take care of the vineyards;
> my own vineyard I have neglected.

She has been doubly burned—by the anger of the sun and by the anger of her brothers.[6]

Here, as throughout the Song, "the vineyard" represents herself and perhaps especially herself in terms of her sexuality as a woman.[7] It may be too much to read into the text and say that she has been sexually abused except in the broadest sense of the word,[8] but at the very least we have to say that her overbearing, angry brothers, of all people, have not allowed her to develop independently as a woman.[9]

Clearly, there are deep hurts here. For the first time, she gives voice to her insecurities, her fears, and her self-doubts. She is defiant, even petulant,[10] but only now as she speaks out does she seem to be coming to terms with her past, especially her passive acceptance of the abuse she suffered at the hands of her "mother's sons." This is the first of a number of incidents that will betray a certain passive-aggressive strain in her personality. "Love, as the poet presents it, may be delight and exquisite pleasure, but it is not without complications."[11]

REFLECTION

The human condition, as the Scriptures insist, is deeply rooted in its history.[12] More than that, we understand that the nature of Israel as the people of God cannot be understood apart from its story of covenant,

---

5. Longman, *Song*, 98.
6. Carr, *Song*, 79.
7. Longman, *Song*, 98.
8. See the discussion in Fox, *Love Songs*, 102.
9. Ibid., 100.
10. Gledhill, *Song*, 101.
11. Exum, *Song*, 105.
12. Compare the discussion of the apostle Paul in Romans 5:12–19.

exodus, and exile. It is there that God meets her in election, redemption, and reconciliation and shows her his grace.

In the same way, something remarkable is taking place here. The hurts of the past that have held her captive are being shared with someone she can trust. It is the necessary prelude to everything that is to come. The expression of our need is the first door that opens to grace.

MEDITATION

The Lord Knows All About Us, and He Cares

> I sought the LORD, and he answered me;
>   he delivered me from all my fears.
> Those who look to him are radiant;
>   their faces are never covered with shame.
> This poor man called, and the LORD heard him;
>   he saved him out of all his troubles. . . .
>
> The righteous cry out, and the LORD hears them;
>   he delivers them from all their troubles.
> The LORD is close to the brokenhearted
>   and saves those who are crushed in spirit (Ps 34:4–6, 17–18).

"Come to me, all you who are weary and burdened, and I will give you rest. Take my yoke upon you and learn from me, for I am gentle and humble in heart, and you will find rest for your souls. For my yoke is easy and my burden is light" (Matt 11:28–29).

And the God of all grace, who called you to his eternal glory in Christ, after you have suffered a little while, will himself restore you and make you strong, firm and steadfast (1 Pet 5:10).

PRAYER

Father, I thank you that you made me and you know all about me. Most of all, I thank you that you care for me and your heart goes out to a broken world.

Forgive me for trying to think I really don't need you and that I am supposed to cope with the hurts of my past all by myself. That, Lord, has been my pride, and I repent of it.

Help me to understand all the tangled emotions knotted in my head, and teach me to share my life with others. Show me how to be transparent so all the ways you will bring healing into my life will cause others to also know your grace and find your help and healing. Amen.

Day 7

Poem 2 (1:5–6) B

Identity: "Do not stare at me"

Woman
Dark am I, yet lovely,
   O daughters of Jerusalem,
dark like the tents of Kedar,
   like the tent curtains of Solomon.
Do not stare at me because I am dark,
   because I am darkened by the sun.
My mother's sons were angry with me
   and made me take care of the vineyards;
   my own vineyard I have neglected.

As the woman has presented her past to us, we have been a given a "loose thread" that, as someone has suggested, "Teases and tantalizes the reader to find connections where they are lacking . . ."[13] It is the nature of great literature to do that. "The events the lovers speak about are not restricted to a particular time and place but rather belong to the lyrical domain of desire and to the realm of the senses, where space and time are effortlessly traversed by lovers."[14] We may be legitimately reminded that "what seems to be a closed dialogue between two perpetually desiring lovers is addressed to us, for our pleasure and possibly our enlightenment."[15]

Despite the fact that our song is poetry rather than historical narrative, and as such, it is highly evocative, we do need to be careful with our observations, because we don't have all the facts, and it is easy to say too much. Our text, however, has too many important insights into

---

13. Exum, *Song*, 105.
14. Ibid., 103.
15. Ibid., 7.

the nature of self-identity to quickly pass over. Our reactions to the text will necessarily imply some conjecture, but at the same time, there is a certain poetic license that allows us to do so if we are ever going to discover its meaning.

THE HUMAN EXPERIENCE

We must begin by observing how thoroughly "modern" our text is with its representations of the challenge of not only relationships but also of dysfunctional families. We are tempted to take the reference to "my mother's sons" as being a reference to step-brothers and blended families, but in fact, the phrase probably represents the closest of family.[16] In a way, this makes it all the more powerful. The ones we expect to be closest to us in our families often end up being the very source of dysfunction.

Even more than that, this is the first of a number of songs that are deeply psychological in the exploration of the self. It reminds us that the more things change, the more they remain the same. There is "nothing new under the sun,"[17] not least of all because we share a common humanity. As we read the text and enter the lives of its characters, even across a vast span of time and culture, we find we share a common human experience. The song is ripe with insight into what it means to be a human being and especially what it means to enter into relationship with others. Not least of all, we realize intuitively, but also because of the working of the Spirit, that here God is speaking truth to us.

FATHERS

We should also note that the woman's mother is repeatedly present in the Song,[18] but her father will be found everywhere to be absent. He may have abandoned the family physically or emotionally, or more likely in the ancient world, he may have died of disease or been killed in war. In any case, like too many fathers, he is missing from the action.

Our relationship to our father is a key factor in understanding our insecurities. Mom, with her ties to the child of her womb, appears to be

---

16. Bloch and Bloch are convincing especially with their references to Judges 8:19; Genesis 43:29; and Psalms 50:20; 69:9 in *Song*, 141.

17. Ecclesiastes 1:9.

18. Song of Songs 1:6; 3:4, 11; 6:9; 8:1, 2, 5.

almost always there, as the young men in our jails will attest. But they, like us with our text, are left with the unspoken question, "Where is my father?" It must surely be for this reason of easily absent fathers that Scripture places a particular accountability upon husbands and fathers, not as a right but as a responsibility.[19]

DYSFUNCTIONAL FAMILIES

On one level or another, we have here what we would today call a "dysfunctional family." Perhaps at some level we all have a dysfunctional family. We can at least say that each of us needs to be self-consciously aware of the things that have shaped our lives in the tender moments of our growing up. In the woman's case, it was the bullying she received at the hands of those who should have been closest to her and who apparently resented something about her status in the family.

By way of passing, we must say that it is something that Jesus would experience also. There are hints, of course, about the legitimacy of Joseph as his father and Joseph's apparent absence by the time of the cross, not to mention siblings eager to put him down and parents not always in tune with his mission.[20] Siblings and parents are an essential part of our identity and self-understanding and play a key part in our ability to enjoy healthy relationships. The woman intuitively understands this. It comes bursting out because more than anything else, she needs to find someone to whom she may pour out her heart and find acceptance, love, and understanding.

GENDER

It also appears that the abuse she has received is somehow related to her being a woman. There is clearly a social and physical vulnerability that accompanies her place in the culture as a woman,[21] and it is something that the man in our song will have to take into account if he is ever going to be able to transcend the hurts of her past. The problematic history of

---

19. "Submit to one another out of reverence for Christ. Wives, submit to your husbands as to the Lord. For the husband is the head of the wife as Christ is the head of the church, his body, of which he is the Savior. . . . Husbands love your wives Christ loved the church and gave himself up for her . . ." (Eph 5:21–23, 25).

20. John 8:19; John 19:26–27; Mark 3:31–35; John 7:3–5; Luke 2:48–50.

21. Recent reports make this observation as relevant as ever. See "The War on Baby Girls: Gendercide," 13, 77–80, 104.

man and woman in relationship to one another is a fact that Scripture recognizes from the very beginning of time[22] and that will be addressed by both Jesus and Paul as requiring a distinct response on the part of the gospel.[23] The native tension between men and women is something that simply has to be taken into account if we are ever going to be able to forge healthy relationships between the sexes.

IDENTITY

In the end, this is about identity and where we find it. Physical attractiveness is notoriously shifting sand, especially upon which to build one's sense of self and worth.[24] What the woman longs for is to be understood in terms of her history and accepted in spite of her sometimes deep sense of a lack of worth.

REFLECTION

The good news always rejects any sense of one's own merit as a foundation upon which to find one's righteousness or build one's identity. The woman desires to be held in the hands of grace that will understand and accept everything about her. Only then can love be found and a relationship forged into a thing of worth and beauty.

MEDITATION

The Lord Gives Us Our Identity, and in It We Find Freedom

Praise the LORD, O my soul;
all my inmost being, praise his holy name.

---

22. Scripture represents this as a function of the curse (Gen 3:16). Compare the much-maligned assertion of 1 Peter 3:7, which speaks of the woman as a "weaker partner." This should be understood not only in general terms of relative physical strength but also in regard to "social entitlement and empowerment," leading to the husband's need to offer deference and respect. See Jobes, *1 Peter*, 209.

23. Compare Jesus's example in John 4:9, and Paul's revolutionary model in Romans 16.

24. See Proverbs 31:30, "Charm is deceptive, and beauty is fleeting; but a woman who fears the LORD is to be praised."

> Praise the LORD, O my soul,
>   and forget not all his benefits—
> who forgives all your sins
>   and heals all your diseases,
> who redeems your life from the pit
>   and crowns you with love and compassion,
> who satisfies your desires with good things
>   so that your youth is renewed like the eagle's.
>
> The LORD works righteousness
>   and justice for all the oppressed. . . .
>
> for he knows how we are formed,
>   he remembers that we are dust (Ps 103:1–6, 14).

> Just then his disciples returned and were surprised to find him talking with a woman. But no one asked, "What do you want?" or "Why are you talking with her?"
>   Then, leaving her water jar, the woman went back to the town and said to the people, "Come, see a man who told me everything I ever did. Could this be the Christ?" (John 4:27–29).

> What does the Scripture say? "Abraham believed God, and it was credited to him as righteousness." Now when a man works, his wages are not credited to him as a gift, but as an obligation. However, to the man who does not work but trusts God who justifies the wicked, his faith is credited as righteousness
> (Rom 4:3–5).

PRAYER

Father, I thank you that you have always been present in my life even (perhaps especially) when I thought you were not there. I thank you that you are the one who really knows all about me and understands how frail I am. I am glad that you work righteousness and love justice.

Forgive me for being bitter and resentful about the things that have happened to me in my childhood and in my family.

Now help me to find my identity in you so that I might be a source of strength and joy in my family and in all of my relationships. Make me sensitive to when I am hurting others, and teach me how to bring healing to all of my relationships. Amen.

Day 8

Poem 3 (1:7–8) A

Misunderstanding: "Like a veiled woman"

Woman
Tell me, you whom I love, where you graze your flock
    and where you rest your sheep at midday.
Why should I be like a veiled woman
    beside the flocks of your friends?

Man
If you do not know, most beautiful of women,
    follow the tracks of the sheep
and graze your young goats
    by the tents of the shepherds.

TENSIONS ARISE

For the first time in our Song, there is a real problem between our lovers. Deep insecurities have manifested themselves in the previous poem, and not without significance, in this, our very next text, there is alienation, misunderstanding, and miscommunication. They grow out of the man's absence, and perhaps we may even say they grow out of male abandonment and abuse on the part of her brothers.[25] The elements of uncertainty, tension, and shame that the woman felt in regard to her brothers, her companions, and herself now reappear in regard to her lover and his companions.[26]

---

25. Keel, in *Song*, 51, indicates, "The relative clause used to describe the lover in 1:7 ('whom I fervently love') is used three times in 3:1–3 to speak of him precisely when he is absent."

26. Gledhill, *Song*, 107.

On the one hand, she is loving and even passive. "Tell me, you whom I love, where you graze your flock and where you rest your sheep at midday." On the other hand, she is prickly and aggressive. "Why should I be like a veiled woman beside the flocks of your friends?" In other words, "Why are you treating me like a prostitute?"[27]

Deep feeling permeates the text. The phrase "you whom I love" could be translated more literally, "You for whom my throat thirsts."[28] Yearning and desire have returned to our text, but this time it is not turned outward in appreciation but inward in fear, insecurity, and anxiety. Such is the problem with passionate longing. When turned inward, it goes in search of what it can never find.

It is possible to take this section of the Song as a playful tease, as the woman suggesting a rendezvous and midday tryst and the man's reply as a coy response intended to arouse deeper desire.[29] Even if this is the case, the mood quickly turns dark. The man's response suggests that he sees a certain "willful element in her ignorance."[30] His reply might be taken to mock more than to tease.[31]

In reality, as can often be the case in matters of the heart, an appreciative tease and a mocking taunt are probably going on at the same time. She is concerned that she will be seen as a loose woman, even a prostitute, out soliciting business from the shepherds. Just as easily, she could have said, "It was a mistake on my part that I did not ask."[32] We take his response to be kind and loving while at the same time not without a note of rebuke. "If you do not know, most beautiful of women, follow the tracks of the sheep . . ."

In any event, the multiple uses of the verb "to shepherd" and the text itself have rich poetic suggestions of having "lost her way."[33]

---

27. Fox, *Love Songs*, 103. See Genesis 38:14–15. Pope, in *Song*, 331, suggests she did not want to resort to the same device that Tamar used.

28. See Keel's suggestions, *Song*, 52.

29. Longman, *Song*, 100, 101.

30. Fox, *Love Songs*, 103.

31. Keel, *Song*, 53.

32. Ibid., 52.

33. Bloch and Bloch, *Song*, 142.

WHAT'S A SHEPHERD TO DO?

The real question is, "What is his advice for resolving this situation?" On the surface of things, he appears to be telling her to follow the sheep path until she finds him, and then they will be able to graze their goats together while enjoying each other's company. This suggestion hardly addresses her concerns.[34] In fact, he does not tell her a location. He gives her only a strategy of pursuit. She is to take her flocks with her so that the onlookers will think that she is simply taking care of her goats.

Nevertheless, it seems to be implying more than that. In search of love and of her lover, she will have to go where she did not want to go. That is the nature of love! "If her desire is as great as she claims, she cannot avoid this consequence."[35]

That may be what is going on here, but at the same time, we need to stick close to what the poetry is suggesting, not least of all in its unanswered questions. She wants to be with him all of the time. He has work to do and acquaintances of his own who will appear not only to intrude but also to misunderstand her desire to have him for herself. In fact, he has a life of his own. He is left with the delicate task of pointing that out to her while at the same time wanting to share the presence of the one he loves and encourage the passion that she exudes.[36] Love has its balances to be weighed. If all this is confusing, it is because it is the nature of love to be so.

In any event, she gets her desire. Scattered on the hillsides of ancient Israel are makeshift "tents" or huts that the shepherds have made to shelter them from the elements. It is to the shepherd's hut that he takes her.

Gentleness and Strength

It is tempting to take the part of the shepherd in our story. Suddenly he finds himself being accused of treating her like a woman to be used and discarded. What has happened? It is just as easy to retort that men are notorious for their lack of ability to communicate, and many an unpleasant situation could be avoided if they would only do so more clearly.

Instead, gentleness and strength play themselves out in our text. The shepherd refuses to take advantage of her vulnerability. Once again,

---

34. Carr, *Song*, 81.
35. Keel, *Song*, 53.
36. Gledhill, *Song*, 109–10.

as in our last poem, we find the woman, precisely because of her place in the culture, vulnerable in the presence of the "stronger" men who surround her. They populate the landscape of her family and now of her lover's environment. The shepherd's friends tending their flocks, at least in her imagination, are characterized by their menacing looks.

We are impressed that our shepherd does not say, "Look, girl (putting her down in the same way that she has been belittled previously), you are just going to have to get over what your brothers did to you, take responsibility for yourself, and not speak to me that way again. Do you want this relationship or not?"

To the contrary, he is gentle, caring, and complimentary, but also strong. "If you do not know, most beautiful of women . . ." Or as it is famously expressed in Proverbs:

> A gentle answer turns away wrath,
>   but a harsh word stirs up anger.
> The tongue of the wise commends knowledge,
>   but the mouth of the fool gushes folly (Prov. 15:1–2).

As irrational as her outburst may at first seem to be, it represents a legitimate longing that is, in fact, well intentioned and yet able to produce a happy result.

Boundaries and Borders

At the same time, the woman is to be complimented. She has not allowed the anxieties and insecurities that may have come from the absence of a parent and the abuse of her siblings to obliterate her boundaries and rob her of dignity. Falling in love necessarily involves the opening of borders and the tearing down of boundaries. She is being careful to preserve her sense of self-worth and dignity, and because of his love, she is glad to do so.

REFLECTION

We can learn from both the shepherd and the shepherdess. Likewise, the story of Israel, the church, is the history of God's sheltering protection and of the faithfulness and love of the Shepherd of Israel who is ever looking for his people and achieving his purposes. Where we stumble, he is gentle, wise, constant, and ever true.

MEDITATION

The Lord Is My Shepherd, I Shall Not Want

In the shelter of your presence you hide them
   from the intrigues of men;
in your dwelling you keep them safe
   from accusing tongues.

Praise be to the LORD,
   for he showed his wonderful love to me
   when I was in a besieged city.

In my alarm I said,
   "I am cut off from your sight!"
Yet you heard my cry for mercy
   when I called to you for help (Ps 31:20–22).

But his bow remained steady,
   his strong arms stayed limber,
because of the hand of the Mighty One of Jacob,
   because of the Shepherd, the Rock of Israel . . . (Gen 49:24).

I am the good shepherd; I know my sheep and my sheep know me—just as the Father knows me and I know the Father—and I lay down my life for the sheep. . . . The reason my Father loves me is that I lay down my life—only to take it up again. No one takes it from me, but I lay it down of my own accord. I have authority to lay it down and authority to take it up again (John 10:14–15, 17–18).

Love is patient, love is kind. . . . It is not rude, it is not self-seeking, it is not easily angered, it keeps no record of wrongs. . . . It always protects, always trusts, always hopes, always perseveres (1 Cor 13:4, 5, 7).

PRAYER

Lord, you are the Good Shepherd. I praise you for your wise care, tenderness, gentleness, and protection. I am grateful that you always come to look for your people and that you never leave until you find them. I am glad that you communicate your ways and your will so clearly to me in your Word and through your Spirit.

Forgive me for all the times I have doubted your love and concern for me and behaved in ways that showed my impatience and foolishness.

This day, make me wise, gentle, and caring. Teach me to protect and preserve those boundaries that are good and for the well-being of all your children. Amen.

Day 9

Poem 3 (1:7–8) B

Listening: "If you do not know"

Woman
Tell me, you whom I love, where you graze your flock
   and where you rest your sheep at midday.
Why should I be like a veiled woman
   beside the flocks of your friends?

Man
B. If you do not know, most beautiful of women,
   follow the tracks of the sheep
and graze your young goats
   by the tents of the shepherds.

IN THE SHEPHERD'S HUT

There can be little doubt about what the woman has in mind. The references to "graze" in the Song always have playful sexual connotations.[37] We should not be surprised. Anxiety and insecurity often seek to find release in a sexual consummation that will bring an assurance of being found desirable. As we have seen before, this is an integral part of the nature of passion and of "desperate longing."

The text leaves us in little doubt as to where our lovers end up. She is to graze her flock by the shepherds' tents so they may, presumably, spend time together in the shepherd's hut. It is a place of shelter from the sun and the storms, a place of intimacy where they may spend time together.

---

37. For example, see Song of Songs 6:2–3.

If the first verse of our poem is characterized by tension, the second suggests contentment and consummation. The resolution of both the passion and the anxiety in our text clearly comes from the return of intimacy. How is this to be achieved in the face of crisis and conflict?

We have seen that gentleness, reassurance, and even strength are present in the response of the shepherd, but it is clear that there is something more. They have been spending time together, and rather than being inordinately defensive, he is hearing what she says, and he is listening to her.

Listening

I can still remember the first person who came to my office for help. I was a very young pastor, and she was a woman who stood at the door trembling like a leaf. Her very first words were, "You don't know this, but I have been seeing a psychiatrist for six years, and he has gone on leave for six months." I panicked while desperately trying to remember the basics of Counseling 101. The only thing that I could recall was, "Listen!"

It was great advice. She started into the history of her life, and every time I stopped her to give my opinion, she would say, "Please, let me finish, and when I am done, you can tell me what you think." She told me that she was left alone with her father who was an alcoholic, she was being robbed of her life, and she had come to the conclusion that her care for him was only facilitating his behavior. Was it appropriate for her to accept a job that would mean leaving home? I explained to her why she was not being selfish and suggested that it might only do him good. After praying with her, she got to her feet, sighed a great sigh of relief, and exclaimed, "Thank you so much for your help!"

It was the best thing that ever could have happened to a young pastor. Instead of always feeling the need to give advice and to control and of course, to be right, I learned to listen. On a hundred occasions since then, when wisdom has failed me and I have been mercifully at a loss for words, I have listened, prayed, and shared the burdens of others, and it has been enough.

Yes, there is a time to speak the truth in love,[38] and in his own way, the shepherd has done just that. Somehow in the midst of it all, he managed to listen and to share in their common humanity and longings.

---

38. Ephesians 4:15.

He did so long enough to understand and not to feel that he had to straighten her out and correct everything that she said. She came to realize that he understood, that he cared, and that he listened.

This is first time that the man is introduced to us as a shepherd. Now we understand why. In listening to her, he has shepherded her heart. That is love, and it ends up in the shepherd's hut.

REFLECTION

It is of the very nature of love to listen and to understand. When we think of the love of God, we are amazed to realize that he did not remain in his glory and give instructions about how to straighten ourselves out. Instead, the eternal Son of God "became flesh and 'pitched his tent' among us."[39] He walked where we walked and was spared no part of being fully human. He was subject to the totality of the human experience in all its extremes. Indeed, his love would cause him to lay down his life, not as a tragedy that overcame him, but as a sacrifice that he made out of love for his bride. He listens, and he understands.

MEDITATION

The Lord Understands and Hears Us

Hear us, O Shepherd of Israel,
   you who lead Joseph like a flock;
you who sit enthroned between the cherubim, shine forth
   before Ephraim, Benjamin and Manasseh.
Awaken your might;
   come and save us.

Restore us, O God;
   make your face shine upon us,
   that we may be saved (Ps 80:1–3).

When he saw the crowds, he had compassion on them, because they were harassed and helpless, like sheep without a shepherd (Matt 9:36).

---

39. This is the literal translation of John 1:14.

> For we do not have a high priest who is unable to sympathize with our weaknesses, but we have one who has been tempted in every way, just as we are-yet was without sin. Let us then approach the throne of grace with confidence, so that we may receive mercy and find grace to help us in our time of need (Heb 4:15–16).

PRAYER

Thank you, Lord, for caring for me, and for listening to me when I pour out my heart to you. I am grateful to you for your Son, who knows all about me.

Forgive me for being such a poor listener and for always being ready to give advice before I know and understand the hurts of others.

Teach me this day to listen long enough to be of help in bearing the burdens of others. When all else goes wrong this day, please remind me once again to listen, to care, and to love. And Lord, help me to listen to you today! Amen.

Day 10

Poem 4 (1:9–11)

Adornment: "Earrings of gold"

Man
I liken you, my darling, to a mare
 harnessed to one of the chariots of Pharaoh.
Your cheeks are beautiful with earrings,
 your neck with strings of jewels.
We will make you earrings of gold,
 studded with silver.

IN OUR LAST TWO poems, we went from what at first appeared to be the perfect love affair to a deeply troubled relationship hovering, it seemed, on the brink of disaster. Now there comes a burst of at least five poems in which the lovers banter back and forth, poems of praise and admiration.

Placed as they are after the tensions and ambiguities of the last two poems, they have the effect of laying aside the anxiety and misunderstanding, and dissolving them, at least for the moment, in mutual admiration and praise.[40] In the face of the troubled obstacles that the lovers have just encountered, they bring praise and compliments to bear upon the tattered relationship. In so doing, we are brought into a new dimension of this thing called love.

A ROYAL RELATIONSHIP

The scene shifts, at least in the lover's imagination, from the simple world of the shepherds to the magnificent world of kings and princes, pharaohs, and their horses and chariots.[41] The mention of extravagant

40. Gledhill, *Song*, 110–11.
41. Keel, *Song*, 56.

jewelry heightens the royal motif[42] associated with the bride and groom. Love and admiration transform the ordinary and mundane to cause the lovers to inhabit an exotic world to which they would otherwise have little by way of access.

COMPLIMENT

It is the shepherd who begins the barrage of compliments, admiration, and praise, likening the woman to a mare among the chariots of Pharaoh. Horses are, of course, magnificent creatures, and a beautiful mare would well represent grace, beauty, and nobility.[43] But even if we take this to be the case, his first lines might still sound like little more than a typical male, telling his girlfriend that she is like his favorite Porsche, curves and all.

Actually, he is doing better than that. Solomon had traded in magnificent Egyptian horses, but also in the stallions that were used to drive the chariots of the time. Inhabitants of the ancient world, including the rabbis of Israel, were well aware of a battle near Kadesh (c. 1450 BC) in which the enemy released a mare among the Egyptian chariots to disrupt and overturn the stallions.[44] In effect, the shepherd looks the deeply insecure woman in the eyes and says, "Lady, a man could no more keep his composure in your presence than Pharaoh's stallions could pursue the enemy in the presence of a mare."

COMMITMENT

"Flattery," it is said, "will get you everywhere." Indeed, that is true. It is heady stuff and quite intoxicating. Flattery is used to devastate others by first disarming them and then taking advantage of their stupor for selfish ends. Praise and affirmation are also heady stuff. They are equally intoxicating. The difference is that while flattery is used to disarm and take advantage, praise is used to build up and adorn. It is a commitment to show off the glory of the other and to set that person in his or her best light.

That is exactly what our shepherd does now. He traces his finger, as it were, down the cheeks of the woman, imagining earrings that

---

42. Longman, *Song*, 102.
43. Balchin, "The Song of Songs," 621.
44. Pope, *Song*, 338–39.

hang there, complementing her face. He gently touches the neck of the woman, seeing it strung with pearls, and then compliment turns to commitment.

> We will make you earrings of gold
> studded with silver.

His desire is not to change her but to make sure that her natural beauty is heightened by her jewelry.[45] He intends to make her yet more royal. He wants her to be seen at her best advantage.[46] In other words, the shepherd is making a commitment to provide for her in such a way that he will enhance the person she really is and show her off in the very best light.

True love does not seek to possess for one's own glory. The shepherd does not wear the woman on his arm to show off his trophy. He extends his arm to her so that she can be seen in all her glory. That is his commitment, and it is love.

REFLECTION

Love discovers the one who is hurting and commits itself to helping that person look resplendent, shine again, and prosper. It wants the one we love to be seen at his or her best advantage.

We learn from our shepherd that when someone takes time to compliment us, especially when we have been rattled by insecurity and overturned by anger, the poison begins to drain away. The apostle Paul put it this way: "We who are strong ought to bear with the failings of the weak and not to please ourselves. Each of us should please his neighbor for his good, to build him up" (Rom 15:1–2).

Relationships recover when we can look past the hurt, and right at the moment when we could be striking the winning blow of condemnation, we share compliments instead. As the apostle says again, "Do not be overcome by evil, but overcome evil with good" (Rom 12:21).

We learn that even our children do not exist to adorn us, nor our parents simply to provide for us. Love is a commitment to build others up not for our adornment but for their good, and in so doing, we discover that it brings us joy.

---

45. Longman, *Song*, 104.
46. Gledhill, *Song*, 112–13.

Our ability to adorn others implies a need for us to do so. It is a part of the redemption of our world. The amazing thing is that it is what the Lord does for his people. We are given his own adorning beauty and righteousness.

MEDITATION

The Lord Makes His People Beautiful

Great is the LORD, and most worthy of praise,
   in the city of our God, his holy mountain.
It is beautiful in its loftiness,
   the joy of the whole earth (Ps 48:1–2).

I clothed you with an embroidered dress and put leather sandals on you. I dressed you in fine linen and covered you with costly garments. I adorned you with jewelry: I put bracelets on your arms and a necklace around your neck, and I put a ring on your nose, earrings on your ears and a beautiful crown on your head. So you were adorned with gold and silver; your clothes were of fine linen and costly fabric and embroidered cloth. Your food was fine flour, honey and olive oil. You became very beautiful and rose to be a queen. And your fame spread among the nations on account of your beauty, because the splendor I had given you made your beauty perfect, declares the Sovereign LORD. (Ezek 16:10–14).

When they came to Jesus, they found the man from whom the demons had gone out, sitting at Jesus' feet, dressed and in his right mind. . . . (Luke 8:35).

David says the same thing when he speaks of the blessedness of the man to whom God credits righteousness apart from works:
  "Blessed are they
    whose transgressions are forgiven,
    whose sins are covered.
  Blessed is the man
    whose sin the Lord will never count against him"
(Rom 4:6–8).

PRAYER

Lord, you are glorious and worthy of all our praise. I thank you for clothing me with the righteousness of your Son. There is no adornment more beautiful than this.

Forgive me for taking my identity from my failure and refusing to believe that I am who you have made me to be in your Son.

Help me this day to forget myself and my needs and instead to show the beauty of Christ in my life. Make me to be a reflection of your grace. Amen.

Day 11

Poem 4 (1:9–11) B

Friendship: "I liken you, my darling"

Man
I liken you, my darling, to a mare
   harnessed to one of the chariots of Pharaoh.
Your cheeks are beautiful with earrings,
   your neck with strings of jewels.
We will make you earrings of gold,
   studded with silver.

COMPANIONSHIP

EVEN THOUGH IT BEGINS the poem in our English translation, we have saved the best for last. It is friendship and companionship.

As we have just seen in the previous poem, in times of trouble, it may be compliment and commitment that bring back companionship. It is also true to say that in this poem, compliment and commitment spring from companionship. Clearly, they are interdependent.

"I liken you, my darling..." says the shepherd. The word *darling* in our translation is fine, but we get a better sense of the word if we translate it simply as *friend*. This is not an ancient word, but yes, it literally means *girl-friend*. However, given the context in our culture of it being used of frivolous friendship, it is too weak a word to be satisfactory in this context. Jerome (c. 340–420), in his famous Latin translation, used the word *amica*.[47]

---

47. Keel, *Song*, 58.

This is the first of some nine appearances of the word.[48] It is therefore an important theme that implies the priority of close relationship.[49] At the root of the verb, it suggests "to guard, care for, or tend, with an emphasis on the delight and pleasure which attends that responsibility."[50]

In the world of the shepherd, the woman is his best friend and companion. As someone has suggested, she is not:

> A plaything, to satisfy his every whim or fancy . . . a kind of living doll, who flatters and praises him in public, soothes his bruised ego in private, and whose life revolves so remorselessly around the centre of gravity of his career, profession, social standing and total well-being. . . . Their "togetherness" is not mutual self-absorption, not an egotism of two but a relaxed harmony of two distinct and very different personalities.[51]

This is wisdom literature intended to teach the faithful in Israel how to live their lives with both success and blessing. These poems are the first of a number of references that form an attack intended in part to undermine the corrupted extravagance of the royal court with its wives, concubines, and women. They suggest that life may be better lived, and royally so, by ordinary men and women who know the extravagant, even exotic, nature and language of love. Nine times we will be reminded of the friendship and companionship that is at the heart of their bantering back and forth.[52]

REFLECTION

The Scriptures are replete, of course, with references to friendship and companionship: David and Jonathan; Peter, James, and John; Jesus and John; Jesus, Mary, Martha, and Lazarus; Paul and Barnabas; Priscilla and Aquila. It all comes, of course, from being made in the image of God, the Father, Son, and Holy Spirit.

Friendship is about having someone who will share our joys without having to be competitive and with whom we can form a bond to take on the common obstacles of life that confront us. A friend is someone

---

48. See also Song of Songs 1:15; 2:2, 10, 13; 4:1, 7; 5:2; 6:4.
49. Keel, *Song*, 58
50. Carr, *Song*, 82.
51. Gledhill, *Song*, 111.
52. Longman, *Song*, 103.

with whom we share our life and who will be there for us. It is someone against whom, to whom, and with whom we live this thing called life.

With that person we share our stories and bare our soul. That someone is found with us on the road. It is what the Lord intended in marriage when we read, "The LORD God said, 'It is not good for the man to be alone. I will make a helper suitable for him'" (Gen 2:18).

When that is no longer the case, then it is time to make a visit to the shepherd's hut. It is there that instead of accusing, we listen. We talk about what it is in our past that causes us to overreact rudely and accusingly, and we begin to put things back together, however haltingly at first, by complimenting. We say what it is that we like about each other and learn to compliment and adorn each other. Our friendship is renewed by committing ourselves to helping the one who hurts to be seen in his or her best light, to adorn that person, show him or her off to his or her best advantage, and help him or her to prosper. Then we begin to rediscover the intimacy of companionship and learn again to face the world together in our joys and in our sorrows.

MEDITATION

The Friendship of God

The LORD would speak to Moses face to face, as a man speaks with his friend (Exod 33:11).

Two are better than one,
   because they have a good return for their work:
If one falls down,
   his friend can help him up.
But pity the man who falls
   and has no one to help him up!
Also, if two lie down together, they will keep warm.
   But how can one keep warm alone?
Though one may be overpowered,
   two can defend themselves.
A cord of three strands is not quickly broken (Eccl 4:9–12).

My command is this: Love each other as I have loved you. Greater love has no one than this, that he lay down his life for his friends. You are my friends if you do what I command. I no longer call you servants, because a servant does not know his master's business. Instead, I have called you friends, for everything that I learned from my Father I have made known to you. You did not choose me, but I chose you and appointed you to go and bear fruit—fruit that will last. Then the Father will give you whatever you ask in my name (John 15:12–16).

Tychicus, the dear brother and faithful servant in the Lord, will tell you everything, so that you also may know how I am and what I am doing. I am sending him to you for this very purpose, that you may know how we are, and that he may encourage you (Eph 6:21–22).

PRAYER

Father, I thank you for your friendship and love. It is amazing to me that you share my life! You really are extraordinary.

Please forgive me when it is not your presence that I have sought but only your help so that I may succeed in building my own little kingdom.

Teach me to be a friend of your purposes. Help me this day to cultivate relationships and to be there for others as you are always there for me. Amen.

Day 12

Poem 5 (1:12–14)

Delighting: "Resting between my breasts"

Woman
While the king was at his table,
  my perfume spread its fragrance.
My lover is to me a sachet of myrrh
  resting between my breasts.
My lover is to me a cluster of henna blossoms
  from the vineyards of En Gedi.

THE SETTING

In our last poem, we were treated to a description of love, a thing of beauty, an illustration of friendship, and a song of praise and admiration from the lips of our shepherd. He forged before our very eyes a royal relationship. Now the woman does not miss a beat. She picks up the theme, heaps on the praise, and declares, as she reclines with him, that she is at the table with her king.

She imagines a royal banquet[53] in which the king reclines between her breasts. Her reference to nard also evokes the courtly realm.[54] The poem is a rapturous soliloquy in which the woman responds to her lover's praise with three erotic similes[55] that describe what the beloved means to the woman.[56]

Our English text describes the man in verse thirteen as the "lover." In fact, the word *lover* equally means *beloved*. The term is used thirty-one

---

53. Carr, *Song*, 84.
54. Longman, *Song*, 105.
55. Carr, *Song*, 84.
56. Keel, *Song*, 64.

times in the Song to refer to the man. The word originally was used of a close relative, but in the world of the Song, cousins could become lovers.[57] In other words, there is a mutuality here that must not be missed. Once again, as in the previous poem, we see that love is about closeness of relation. Without there being such intimacy, there can be no real love or lasting passion.

SACHET

Here the woman imagines her beloved lying between her breasts like a sachet of rare and valuable spices. The word *resting* in our translation is rather weak. It usually means to spend the night. Clearly, that is what she intends for him to do.[58]

The sachet indicates his "sure and intimate solidarity with her."[59] In other words, it is he who is her sachet, and as such, its ingredients are a description of whom he is in relation to her and what he means to her.[60]

The perfume to which she refers is nard or spikenard. It was a plant native to India, exotic and expensive, known for its erotic connotations.[61] Myrrh also was understood to have a sensual aroma, but it also contained certain sacred associations. Its pleasant fragrance signaled a divine presence.[62] In the springtime, henna was covered with clusters of tiny yellow-white flowers of a very pleasant odor,[63] but probably more significantly, it was thought of as containing life and therefore suggested a life-giving quality.[64]

It is clear that "the perfumes symbolize the pleasure which their mutual presence brings to them."[65] For the woman, being with him was nothing short of a royal occasion. Such a relationship is rare, exotic,

---

57. Ibid., 64–65.
58. Gledhill, *Song*, 116; Pope, *Song*, 351.
59. Keel, *Song*, 66.
60. Ibid., 64.
61. Origen, who earlier warned us to be careful of the Song, indicated that the plant emitted its scent only when it hairy stem was rubbed. See Gledhill, *Song*, 115.
62. Keel, *Song*, 65.
63. Gledhill, *Song*, 116.
64. Keel, *Song*, 67.
65. Murphy, *Song*, 135.

pleasant, life giving, and even divine. Such intimacy could not help but be filled with an erotic fragrance.

WHO SHE IS TO HIM

What comes next is a description of who she wishes to be for him. He is a cluster of henna blossoms not *from* En Gedi (as in our translation) but *in* En Gedi.[66] In other words, in the same way that he is the sachet between her breasts, he is also the henna blossoms to be found in En Gedi. Of course, it is she who is the garden of En Gedi where he is to be found. Once again, as it will be throughout the book, the vineyard is her and her sexuality as a woman.

From the end of the seventh century BC, En Gedi was a carefully tended royal garden.[67] It was "an oasis on the western boundary of the Dead Sea, set among inaccessible cliffs, in the suffocatingly hot area of the Rift Valley. The oasis was a luscious land of freshness and fertility in an area of incredible barrenness and heat."[68] The major crops of the area were exotic spices.[69]

This is a particularly compelling picture of love. In the midst of the suffocating heat and rough terrain through which the lovers must often travel and in which at times they are even forced to live, it is an incredible gift to have someone's love as an oasis, a place of retreat, a luscious land, fresh and fertile. She is confident that she can not only be that for him but already is that for him.

Once again, the text gives a very sensual description of their intimacy and their relationship to one another. It is not merely, of course, that their sexuality is an indication of their intimacy, which, of course, it is. It is that their sexuality is, in turn, a token of the love for life that is given to them precisely because they have found in each other a sure source of love, comfort, encouragement, and passion. All five senses—touching, tasting, smelling, seeing, and hearing—are at play in the Song[70] because in the end, love is about life.

---

66. Gledhill, *Song*, 116.
67. Keel, *Song*, 67.
68. Gledhill, *Song*, 116.
69. Carr, *Song*, 85.
70. Glehill, *Song*, 117.

THE REAL THING

The passion that the man and the woman feel in our text is entirely related to the intimacy, the love, and the friendship that they have found in each other. The loss of passion in our lives is entirely about a loss of intimacy, acceptance, appreciation, and time spent in the presence of each other.

Our lovers show us that it is in the giving away of our lives that we find it. Not least of all, all of life is to be lived with passion and delight, for and in the presence of the other.

REFLECTION

As passionate as our text is, it is filled with a divine beauty and fragrance that the spices signal to us is everywhere present. Being in each other's presence is so sacred to them that they come about as close as is possible to Adam and Eve, who once walked in the Garden in the presence of God and each other.

The man and the woman are together as one flesh, each rediscovering the joys of being male and female, echoing Adam's first poetic exclamation:

> "This is now bone of my bones
>   and flesh of my flesh;
> she shall be called 'woman,'
>   for she was taken out of man."
>
> For this reason a man will leave his father and mother and be united to his wife, and they will become one flesh. The man and his wife were both naked, and they felt no shame (Gen 2:23–25).

There is a redemptive theme here. It is as close as we can come in this life to a return to paradise, where the divine presence permeates everything. More than that, the union of the man and the woman as body and soul, in which the delights of their passion are entirely linked to the intimacy of their friendship, helps us to understand the gospel. The grace that comes to them in our text, in the midst of their emotional need, is real, even physical. And so it is with us.

This grace is not merely cognitive, a matter of the mind—or worse, a divorce of the soul from the body. For our lovers, soul and body are but two aspects of the whole person. For grace to be real and redemption to be true, the soul and the body must come together in joyous rapture. So it is, "The Word became flesh and made his dwelling among us. We have seen his glory, the glory of the One and Only, who came from the Father, full of grace and truth" (John 1:14). It is there we discover that the divine presence and joys of love come to their fragrant fruition.

MEDITATION

Delighting in the Presence of God Spreads Pleasant Fragrance Everywhere

Your throne, O God, will last for ever and ever;
  a scepter of justice will be the scepter of your kingdom.
You love righteousness and hate wickedness;
  therefore God, your God, has set you above your companions
  by anointing you with the oil of joy.
All your robes are fragrant with myrrh and aloes and cassia;
  from palaces adorned with ivory
  the music of the strings makes you glad.
Daughters of kings are among your honored women;
  at your right hand is the royal bride in gold of Ophir
  (Ps 45:6–9).

While he was in Bethany, reclining at the table in the home of a man known as Simon the Leper, a woman came with an alabaster jar of very expensive perfume, made of pure nard. She broke the jar and poured the perfume on his head.

Some of those present were saying indignantly to one another, "Why this waste of perfume? It could have been sold for more than a year's wages and the money given to the poor." And they rebuked her harshly.

"Leave her alone," said Jesus. "Why are you bothering her? She has done a beautiful thing to me. The poor you will always have with you, and you can help them any time you want. But you will not always have me. She did what she could. She poured perfume on my body beforehand to prepare for my burial. I tell you the truth, wherever the gospel is preached throughout the world, what she has done will also be told, in memory of her" (Mark 14:3–9).

I have received full payment and even more; I am amply supplied, now that I have received from Epaphroditus the gifts you sent. They are a fragrant offering, an acceptable sacrifice, pleasing to God. And my God will meet all your needs according to his glorious riches in Christ Jesus.

To our God and Father be glory for ever and ever. Amen.

Greet all the saints in Christ Jesus. The brothers who are with me send greetings. All the saints send you greetings, especially those who belong to Caesar's household.

The grace of the Lord Jesus Christ be with your spirit. Amen (Phil 4:18–23).

Be imitators of God, therefore, as dearly loved children and live a life of love, just as Christ loved us and gave himself up for us as a fragrant offering and sacrifice to God (Eph 5:1–2).

PRAYER

Father, there is a fragrance to your presence and love that makes our hearts glad. We rejoice in your royal extravagance.

Lord, I have become so accustomed to the ordinary. Forgive me for taking your presence for granted as if it were nothing special.

Take my life this day as an offering given to you and grant that my presence in the life of others may likewise be a source of pleasure and delight. Amen.

Day 13

Poem 6 (1:15—2:2) A

As It Should Be: "Our bed is verdant"

Man
How beautiful you are, my darling!
  Oh, how beautiful!
  Your eyes are doves.

Woman
How handsome you are, my lover!
  Oh, how charming!
  And our bed is verdant.
The beams of our house are cedars;
  our rafters are firs.
I am a rose of Sharon,
  a lily of the valleys.

Man
Like a lily among thorns
  is my darling among the maidens.

THIS POEM[71] REPRESENTS ONE of the great moments in the Song. There are, of course, many such occasions, but few are of greater significance. On the surface, it appears to represent nothing more than one more mutual interchange of admiration between our lovers. Then something remarkable takes place in the second half of the poem, and it has everything to do with the continued banter of praise that has characterized the Song. Before we can get there, we must see how the stage has been set and what it is that is the necessary preamble to transformation.

---

71. We have followed Carr in making 2:2 the end of the poem. Gledhill ends at 2:3. Longman, Keel, and others end it at 1:17. In any event, as Fox points out, 1:9–17 and 2:1–7 belong to the same scene. Fox, *Love Songs*, 107.

YOUR EYES ... YOU ARE ...

It is the man who opens our exchange, once again calling her his love[72] (*amica*), with an emphasis on the fact that *you* are my love. She is the one who it is a delight and pleasure to tend, care for, and love.

Her eyes, he says, are doves, a statement that may be easier to understand intuitively than to define descriptively. Clearly, eyes can be things of extraordinary beauty. David's beauty was on more than one occasion said to be in his eyes.[73] In a number of places in the Old Testament, it is the sparkle of the eyes that is singled out for comment.[74] Leah's disadvantage with her sister Rachel was said to be the lack of luster in her eyes.[75] More than all of that, eyes are to be understood as reflective of one's mood or personality.[76] They can speak of vivacity or sadness or anger.

We are still not sure we have fully understood what it means to say, "Your eyes are doves." Jesus speaks of being as innocent as a dove.[77] Even more likely, as in other parts of the ancient world, the descent of the dove upon him was what we might describe as the "eye of love." It looked down upon him at his baptism, and the voice from heaven declared, "You are my Son, whom I love ..."[78] In this sense, the lover would be saying that a look or even a glance from her eyes would be a messenger of love to his heart.

She immediately matches his reply with a reference to his own beauty and once again with the emphasis on *you*.[79] We have already seen that this reciprocal going back and forth with praise is integral to the nature of love and affirmation. What is equally instructive is that in the world of the Old Testament, comments on beauty and seductiveness were not only spoken of women, but also given without embarrassment to men.[80] As we see everywhere in the Song, the sexual stereotypes that

---

72. cf. Song of Songs 1:9.

73. First Samuel 17:42; 16:12. Many English translations do not indicate this clearly. See the discussion in Keel, *Song*, 69.

74. Proverbs 23:31; Ezekiel 1:7; Daniel 10:6.

75. Genesis 29:17. Keel, *Song*, 69.

76. Carr, *Song*, 86.

77. Matthew 10:16.

78. Mark 1:10–11. Keel, *Song*, 69–71.

79. Ibid., 68, 71.

80. Ibid., 71; 1 Samuel 16:12; 17:42; 2 Samuel 14:25; Genesis 39:6–7.

belong to legalistic religions and Victorian cultures are entirely absent. Passion and sexual attraction are the equal prerogative of the man and the woman in the Song, with the woman, if anything, being the more aggressive.

The ambiance of the Song is delightfully refreshing, allowing young men and women to equally explore the delights of love and passion. It is also essential to the breaking of counterproductive stereotypes that, while pretending to be the guardians of purity, actually pollute the beauty of love. When sexuality is understood as "boys are made of frogs and snails and puppy-dogs' tails and girls are made of sugar and spice, and all things nice,"[81] we already have a perversion of what it means to be male and female.

GOING GREEN

Now the woman asserts without embarrassment, "And our bed is verdant." As far as she is concerned, their life together is to be understood as a garden of pleasure. She describes their bed as being a canopy of leaves: lush, green, and filled with life-giving vitality.[82] It is poetry, of course, but the description of their bed and their home is not merely about their lovemaking in the outdoors but once again, of their life together understood as a garden of paradise.

The mutual double emphasis on *you* is not to be overlooked. The delight of love is to know that *you* are someone's special treasure. The bantering back and forth with expressions of praise and appreciation are essential to the liveliness, strength, and vigor of the relationship. This is what keeps their lives together "green," verdant, growing, strong, and filled with life and energy. And it is of course the place from which their family will grow.[83]

GROWING FRAGRANT AND STRONG

At the same time, the woman suggests that there is a certain "divine fragrance" to their relationship.

> The beams of our house are cedars;
> our rafters are firs.

---

81. "What Are Little Boys Made Of?" Early nineteenth-century nursery rhyme.
82. Keel, *Song*, 75.
83. Murphy, *Song*, 136.

The word "house" is actually in the plural in the Hebrew. The places where they share their intimacy are pictured as being in the midst of nature. As they look up at the trees, they appear to be protected by the strength of the limbs that provide shelter and privacy, but even more than that, made as they often are of cedars and firs, they exude a wonderful fragrance.[84]

Inhabitants of ancient Israel regarded the cedar as being the mightiest of trees, and because it was of such great value, it was used for the building of temples and palaces. It is, however, probably going too far to import pagan notions of the mountains of cedars as being the dwelling place or garden of the gods.[85] Nevertheless, their love, set as it is in the midst of the strength and fragrance of nature, suggests that this is how it is meant to be. There is a divine fragrance to love. It is beautiful, precious, and secure.

REFLECTION

The going back and forth with praise is integral to the nature of love. It is fragrant and even divine. It is the spirit that characterizes their relationship, and it is the antidote to brittleness, dryness, and weariness. As someone has said, "There is no physical perpetual motion machine, but there is a spiritual perpetual motion machine: love. Love is perpetually reinforcing: the more we love, the more we are loved, and the more we are loved, the more we love. There is no necessary limit to this process."[86]

Most importantly, it is the necessary prelude of what is to come, and of the incredible transformation that is about to take place. What is true of their love is true of the realm of the Spirit. One is a reflection of the other, a promise of life that is growing strong in grace, fragrant with the presence of the divine.

---

84. Longman, *Song*, 108.
85. Keel, *Song*, 75.
86. Kreeft, *Three Philosophies*, 106.

MEDITATION

In the Praise of God, New Life Is Found

The righteous will flourish like a palm tree,
 they will grow like a cedar of Lebanon;
planted in the house of the LORD,
 they will flourish in the courts of our God.
They will still bear fruit in old age,
 they will stay fresh and green,
proclaiming, "The LORD is upright;
 he is my Rock, and there is no wickedness in him"
(Ps 92:12–15).

Even youths grow tired and weary,
 and young men stumble and fall;
but those who hope in the LORD
 will renew their strength.
They will soar on wings like eagles;
 they will run and not grow weary,
 they will walk and not be faint (Isa 40:30–31).

Jesus answered her, "If you knew the gift of God and who it is that asks you for a drink, you would have asked him and he would have given you living water."

"Sir," the woman said, "you have nothing to draw with and the well is deep. Where can you get this living water? Are you greater than our father Jacob, who gave us the well and drank from it himself, as did also his sons and his flocks and herds?"

Jesus answered, "Everyone who drinks this water will be thirsty again, but whoever drinks the water I give him will never thirst. Indeed, the water I give him will become in him a spring of water welling up to eternal life" (John 4:10–14).

Then the angel showed me the river of the water of life, as clear as crystal, flowing from the throne of God and of the Lamb down the middle of the great street of the city. On each side of the river stood the tree of life, bearing twelve crops of fruit, yielding its fruit every month. And the leaves of the tree are for the healing of the nations (Rev 22:1–2).

PRAYER

Lord, I praise you because we awaken each morning to the fragrance and strength of your love, which is always making all things new.

Forgive me for thinking that this new life is something I must produce. Lord, that is a part of my arrogance, pride, and self-will.

Allow me this day to enjoy the renewing grace of your Holy Spirit. Cause my love to spring up from the well spring of your love. May it be to the praise of your glory and grace, and for the blessing of all with whom I come into contact. Amen.

Day 14

Poem 6 (1:15—2:2) B

Transformation: "I am a Rose of Sharon"

Man
How beautiful you are, my darling!
  Oh, how beautiful!
  Your eyes are doves.

Woman
How handsome you are, my lover!
  Oh, how charming!
  And our bed is verdant.
The beams of our house are cedars;
  our rafters are firs.
B. I am a rose of Sharon,
  a lily of the valleys.

Man
Like a lily among thorns
  is my darling among the maidens.

A ROSE OF SHARON

Now comes our extraordinary moment. It is an epiphany, a remarkable revelation that leads to transformation. Out it comes, utterly unexpected and with complete spontaneity.

> I am a rose of Sharon,
>   a lily of the valleys.

First we must understand what it is she says. The conventional wisdom is that the woman, with characteristic modesty, describes herself as being like the lilies of the valley, common enough but not without beauty. Others suggest that she is probably fishing for a compliment,[87] an expedition that turns out to be wildly successful, as her lover quickly showers her with the effusive praise that we have come to understand as characteristic of the Song.

Her beauty, he says, is not only totally unexpected in the harsh surrounding of their lives[88] but also is absolutely without comparison when held up against the rest.

> Like a lily among thorns
> is my darling among the maidens.

At least one commentator proposes that it is not the common lily that is in mind here but the lotus of the plains, which has ancient and strong associations with love's regenerating powers.[89] The lotus certainly is more in keeping with the surrounding descriptions of the luxurious and verdant growth that is to be understood as the garden of their love.

In any event, we surely need to remark, "Commonplace flowers can be extraordinarily beautiful."[90] Even more to the point, Jesus picked up on the legendary beauty of the lily by remarking, "Not even Solomon in all his splendor was dressed like one of these."[91]

In this case, she asserts the comparison to the lilies not with characteristic modesty, but with uncharacteristic confidence. The emphasis that we need to highlight is surely that the woman for the first time in the Song has come out and said what everyone else already knows, "Yes, I am beautiful. Thank you very much."

TRANSFORMATION

Now consider what a remarkable transformation this is. When we first met the woman and praise was poured upon her by her lover, she was both unable and unwilling to accept it.

> Do not stare at me because I am dark,
>   darkened by the sun.
> My mother's sons were angry with me

---

87. Fox, *Love Songs*, 107.
88. Gledhill, *Song*, 122.
89. Keel, *Song*, 80.
90. Gledhill, *Song*, 122.
91. Matthew 6:29.

> and made me take care of the vineyards;
> my own vineyard I have neglected.

Not unexpectedly, the abuse, which had been a part of the harsh environment in which she had been raised and was the way she was accustomed to being treated by men, not only made her unable to receive praise but also caused her to be characterized by a prickly sensitivity in her relationships to others.

> Why should I be like a veiled woman
> beside the flocks of your friends?

Now, as a result of his listening to her, of their sharing their lives together, and particularly as a result of the way in which he treats her royally, showering her with compliments, commitment, and companionship, she has made her first giant step forward. As he praises her beauty in the present song, instead of saying, "I am not beautiful" and then pushing him away by insisting, "You are treating me like some sort of a loose woman," she begins to return the compliments.

> How handsome you are, my lover!
> Oh, how charming!

She is filled with a deep realization that what they have is alive and vibrant ("our bed is verdant"), and that their life together is beautiful, precious, and secure ("the beams of our house are cedars; and our rafters are firs").

Then comes the final signal of their success. Instead of saying, "Do not stare at me, I have been abused by my brothers," this time she declares:

> I am a rose of Sharon,
> a lily of the valleys.

"The girl has now moved away from her earlier self-consciousness. The king's love for her causes her to have a new self-esteem. She sees herself as a beautiful flower."[92] The chains of the past that have bound her and made her incapable of receiving and sustaining love have been broken. At last, love has been set free to take its course. She is filled with a confidence that she is beautiful, desirable, and ready to both give and

---

92. Balchin, "Song of Songs," 621.

receive love. "It is a very beautiful thing how being truly loved can bring about a transformation in the view you have of yourself."[93]

THE KEY TO THE BOOK

When I first began to read this book called the Song of Songs, I was keenly aware that there was something extraordinarily important going on in the book that was eluding me. I applied all the buzzwords that have to do with relationships, like *communication*, and still could not come up with it. Then one day while driving, deep in thought about this very point, the news on the radio ended with this human-interest line, "It has always been thought that communication is the most important ingredient in a good marriage, but a recent survey has shown that the key to good relationships is affirmation."

There it was! It had been staring me in the face all along. If there is one thing that characterizes this book, it is affirmation. Nothing else even comes close. It may take time for this to revolutionize the way that we relate to others, but until it does, we will find ourselves alone, embattled, and unready to love and be loved.

What we have witnessed in this song is that remarkable moment of transformation, apart from which we will limp through life, succeeding only in heaping guilt on and alienating others. This is the very essence of friendship and every positive relationship. What our song shows us is that the deforming absence of praise and affirmation in our lives need not be the end of our song. Instead, in love we are transformed, and in loving we become life-transforming.

REFLECTION

We know this is true. It has to be true, because this exactly is the good news. It is what God has done for his people, and he has told us so.

He has showed his commitment to us by sending his only Son to die for our sins and clothe us in his righteousness. He has taken all our past upon himself and canceled the debt that was against us. He has returned us to the Father, made us his children, and taken *us* as his bride, perfect in his eyes.

His biggest "problem" right now is to convince his bride just how much he loves us, delights to be with us, and is committed to us. The

---

93. Ibid.

lover in our Song has persisted, and he has "won." No less true is this of the One who pursues Israel, the church, with his love, wins her back to himself, and brings her to delight in his presence.

Our greatest challenge is to get from saying, "Do not stare at me because my sins make me ugly," to realizing, "Therefore, there is now no condemnation for those who are in Christ Jesus" (Rom 8:1). When we finally come to the place where we accept and believe the gospel, not just once but all the time, then everything changes. We begin to say, "Do you know what, Lord? I like being with You. You are awesome, wondrous, and good." Then the songs of praise begin, and the music never stops.

MEDITATION

God Has Made Us to Be Beautiful

The desert and the parched land will be glad;
    the wilderness will rejoice and blossom.
Like the crocus, it will burst into bloom;
    it will rejoice greatly and shout for joy (Isa 35:1–2).

For he has rescued us from the dominion of darkness and brought us into the kingdom of the Son he loves, in whom we have redemption, the forgiveness of sins. . . . and through him to reconcile to himself all things, whether things on earth or things in heaven, by making peace through his blood, shed on the cross.

    Once you were alienated from God and were enemies in your minds because of your evil behavior. But now he has reconciled you by Christ's physical body through death to present you holy in his sight, without blemish and free from accusation
(Col 1:13–14, 20–22)

Let us rejoice and be glad
    and give him glory!
For the wedding of the Lamb has come,
    and his bride has made herself ready.
Fine linen, bright and clean,
    was given her to wear."
(Fine linen stands for the righteous acts of the saints.)

Then the angel said to me, "Write: 'Blessed are those who are invited to the wedding supper of the Lamb!'" And he added, "These are the true words of God" (Rev 19:7–9).

PRAYER

Lord, your love is awesome. You find me beautiful in your sight! You have loved me, told me so, and shown me that it is true. Thank you so much!

Forgive me for my pride, which keeps on trying to prove to you that I am good enough to be loved by you. Lord, it is making me ugly, self-righteous, proud, and despairing, and all at the same time.

Allow me to be so filled with the confidence of your love this day that I will be able to love and be loved because of what you have done for me. Amen.

Day 15

Poem 7 (2:3–7)

Contentment: "His fruit is sweet"

Woman
Like an apple tree among the trees of the forest
   is my lover among the young men.
I delight to sit in his shade,
   and his fruit is sweet to my taste.
He has taken me to the banquet hall,
   and his banner over me is love.
Strengthen me with raisins,
   refresh me with apples,
   for I am faint with love.
His left arm is under my head,
   and his right arm embraces me.
Daughters of Jerusalem, I charge you
   by the gazelles and by the does of the field:
Do not arouse or awaken love
   until it so desires.

We have already come in our last song to that wonderful moment when the transforming power of grace and the exhilarating realization of love have finally dawned upon the woman. It is that realization immortalized in the children's story of the ugly duckling that comes to exclaim, "A swan! What, me a swan?" The answer is of course, "Yes, you a swan, loved and lovely."[94]

---

94. Adapted from Hans Christian Andersen's fairly tale, "The Ugly Duckling," 1843.

UNDER THE APPLE TREE

Now we begin a new song. It is that fresh new moment in which she wastes no time in continuing the compliments and praise and then making what just about amounts to the swearing of a public oath of affirmation.

> Like an apple tree among the trees of the forest,
>   is my lover among the young men.
> I delight to sit in his shade,
>   and his fruit is sweet to my taste.

Once again, we find our lovers out in the fields, in the midst of apple trees and forests, vineyards, and mountainsides. They have been enjoying the freedom that comes from frolicking together out in the countryside. They have stopped, as it were, under an apple tree, and they are going nowhere in a hurry.

We can only characterize these lines, as she says herself, as words of delight. In the past, he has rested with her and spent the night between her breasts. Now it is he who is the tree, and it is she who is being protected by his shade, an image in itself of shelter, security, and safety.[95]

The ancients often regarded the apple as an erotic symbol,[96] and she will later explain to us on more than one occasion that his fruits are, at the very least, "the kisses of his mouth."[97]

THE BANQUET HALL

Not surprisingly, the intoxicating power of wine returns.

> He has taken me to the banquet hall,
>   and his banner over me is love.

What our English version politely terms "the banquet hall" is quite literally "the house of wine." Wine in our song is always associated with the delights of love,[98] and in the ancient world, for them to be seen drinking together would have erotic associations that would be unavoidable.[99] The "house of wine" was used "presumably for a wed-

---

95. Keel, *Song*, 82.
96. Carr, *Song*, 90.
97. Song of Songs 5:16; 7:10. Fox, *Love Songs*, 108.
98. Song of Songs 1:2, 5:1, 7:9, 8:2
99. Keel, *Song*, 85.

ding or for some sacral celebration,"¹⁰⁰ but here it is probably one more picture of the places in which they meet and share their love. No, this is not their wedding, but it is their marriage, and she is overwhelmed by the taste of his fruit and the intoxicating power of his love and of course, their relationship.

Next, she imagines a banner flying over her tent. It is best understood as a military image, with all of the romantic passion associated with a young, virile soldier. It also reflects a royal dignity. The "king" has won her love.¹⁰¹ It is a public display of his love that implies belonging, inclusion, and commitment.¹⁰² His flying the flag indicates his intention. It is a flag of love, perhaps best represented with a dove,¹⁰³ and his intention is to make love.¹⁰⁴

The food on the table is apples and raisin cakes. In the world of the Ancient Near East, they were understood to be aphrodisiacs.¹⁰⁵ With his left arm under her head and his right arm embracing her, she lies in what was regarded as a classic position in the ancient world,¹⁰⁶ and in all probability, it should be understood as a sexual embrace.¹⁰⁷ She is overwhelmed by the power of love.¹⁰⁸ Basking as she is in the afterglow of his love, she is exhausted. Paradoxical as it may be, she must be strengthened with the food and fuel of love.¹⁰⁹

> Strengthen me with raisins,
>   refresh me with apples,
>   for I am faint with love.
> His left arm is under my head,
>   and his right arm embraces me.

---

100. Fox, *Love Songs*, 108.
101. Murphy, *Song*, 136.
102. Longman, *Song*, 113.
103. Keel, *Song*, 85.
104. Carr, *Song*, 91; Longman, *Song*, 113.
105. Keel, *Song*, 88.
106. Ibid., 89.
107. Longman, *Song*, 115.
108. Ibid., 114.
109. Murphy, *Song*, 137.

A WARNING

Finally comes her rather enigmatic statement:

> Daughters of Jerusalem, I charge you
>   by the gazelles and by the does of the field:
> Do not arouse or awaken love
>   until it so desires.

This is often taken, especially by those who impose a narrative timeline on the text and who think the lovers are not yet married, as a request not to stir up sexual desire until the time is right. But from the opening verses of the Song, we have seen she is already willing and partaking in their making love.

This verse is more appropriately taken as a wish that is already the case. It would be better to say that she is hanging out the "Do Not Disturb" sign![110]

More to the point, it should be noted that this is a characteristic refrain that comes in the Song after love has been fulfilled.[111] It is, therefore, better understood as a warning to the other girls not to rush into love and lovemaking until the time is right. The "Daughters of Jerusalem" are surrogates for those who listen to the music of the song. What she does is to warn us that it is easy to envy what she has, but in fact, love with its attendant sexual passion is not a passing fling but a demanding and exhausting relationship. Let it blossom, but let the time be right.[112] Only when the time is right in "the sight of God and man" can the participants truly handle it and enjoy it.

She accompanies her charge with an oath of sorts. It functions to emphasize the importance of what she has just said, but rather curiously it is sworn "by the gazelles and by the does of the field." Gazelles are animals noted for their sexual potency,[113] and became associated with the goddess of love.[114] More to the point, it is nearly always noted that in the original Hebrew the name for "gazelles" and "does of the field" bear a remarkable resemblance to the names of God.[115]

---

110. Fox, *Love Songs*, 109.

111. Song of Songs 2:7; 3:5. Keel, *Song*, 89.

112. Longman, *Song*, 115–16.

113. Fox, *Love Songs*, 109.

114. Keel, *Song*, 92.

115. "The reference to the gazelles and hinds seems to be an imitation of an invocation of God." Murphy, *Song*, 137.

Perhaps it is a way of avoiding the use of the name of God in a secular or erotic context.[116] In the ancient world, one did not always swear by the deity but by its attributes, so one could swear by heaven as the throne of God and earth as his footstool.[117] Perhaps it is best to understand this as "a playful allusion to the divine name, while at the same time evoking a pastoral image in keeping with the tenor of the book."[118]

The oath also functions to summarize what has gone before and perhaps even to bring our section to an end.[119] Love is personified as a power here.[120] It has its own laws and is not to be tampered with. It reminds us of the sacredness of love and of lovemaking.

REFLECTION

When all is said and done, the passion simmers throughout our song, so much so that the woman is keenly aware how exhausting it can be, but of course in a way that is at the same time both satisfying and exhilarating. She warns of its power while delighting in its presence.

That such ardor belongs to our lovers is not a factor of their youth or even of the discovery of their sexuality, as true as both of these things may be. Its power lies in the freedom that they have found in the praise, affirmation, delight, admiration, and acceptance that they have discovered in each other. It is explored in the shelter and security of their relationship. Their flag flies for all to see.

We would be foolish not to understand the difference between their passion and our promiscuity as a culture. The latter pretends to be married to freedom but is better understood as the desperate craving of an anxious culture. Its reckless pursuit is best understood as a longing after both security and acceptance. It is hoping, against all odds, that sex is an end in itself and that the giving of one's self sexually will necessarily end at the point where affirmation and love comes together in the sort of praise, passion, and commitment that we see in our song.

Our lovers know better. They understand that this passion is the fruit of a physical but mature relationship where growth has taken place

---

116. Fox, *Love Songs*, 110.
117. cf. Matthew 5:34–35. See Keel, *Song*, 92–94.
118. Longman, *Song*, 116.
119. Gledhill, *Song*, 131–32.
120. Murphy, *Song*, 137.

in the context of commitment and shelter. It is sworn by an oath that is sacred and divine, plain for all to see.

MEDITATION

God Flies the Flag of His Love Over Us for All to See

I will be like the dew to Israel;
  he will blossom like a lily.
Like a cedar of Lebanon
  he will send down his roots;
  his young shoots will grow.
His splendor will be like an olive tree,
  his fragrance like a cedar of Lebanon.
Men will dwell again in his shade.
  He will flourish like the grain.
He will blossom like a vine,
  and his fame will be like the wine from Lebanon
(Hos 14:5–7).

On the third day a wedding took place at Cana in Galilee. Jesus' mother was there, and Jesus and his disciples had also been invited to the wedding. When the wine was gone, Jesus' mother said to him, "They have no more wine."

"Dear woman, why do you involve me?" Jesus replied, "My time has not yet come."

His mother said to the servants, "Do whatever he tells you."

Nearby stood six stone water jars, the kind used by the Jews for ceremonial washing, each holding from twenty to thirty gallons.

Jesus said to the servants, "Fill the jars with water"; so they filled them to the brim.

Then he told them, "Now draw some out and take it to the master of the banquet."

They did so, and the master of the banquet tasted the water that had been turned into wine. He did not realize where it had come from, though the servants who had drawn the water knew. Then he called the bridegroom aside and said, "Everyone brings out the choice wine first and then the cheaper wine after the guests have had too much to drink; but you have saved the best till now."

This, the first of his miraculous signs, Jesus performed in Cana of Galilee. He thus revealed his glory, and his disciples put their faith in him (John 2:1–11).

PRAYER

Father, thank you for publicly swearing your love to me in the sacraments of baptism and the Lord's Supper. I am grateful that you feed me there with the bread of your Son and the wine of your Spirit.

Forgive me for neglecting your presence and failing to remember all that you have done for me in the love of Christ.

Make me bold today to affirm my love for you. Let it be an expression of gratefulness for all that you have given to me. In the knowledge that you own me, give me the confidence to share your love with others. Amen.

Section 3

Joy and Fear, 2:8—3:5

Day 16

Poem 8 (2:8–17) A

Excitement: "Leaping across the mountains"

Woman
A. Listen! My lover!
   Look! Here he comes,
leaping across the mountains,
   bounding over the hills.
My lover is like a gazelle or a young stag.
   Look! There he stands behind our wall,
gazing through the windows,
   peering through the lattice.
My lover spoke and said to me,
   "Arise, my darling,
my beautiful one, and come with me.

B. See! The winter is past;
   the rains are over and gone.
Flowers appear on the earth;
   the season of singing has come,
the cooing of doves
   is heard in our land.
The fig tree forms its early fruit;
   the blossoming vines spread their fragrance.
Arise, come, my darling;
   my beautiful one, come with me."

Man
C. My dove in the clefts of the rock,
   in the hiding places on the mountainside,
show me your face,
   let me hear your voice;
for your voice is sweet,
   and your face is lovely.

Woman
Catch for us the foxes,
   the little foxes
that ruin the vineyards,
   our vineyards that are in bloom.

D. My lover is mine and I am his;
   he browses among the lilies.
Until the day breaks
   and the shadows flee,
turn, my lover,
   and be like a gazelle
or like a young stag
   on the rugged hills.

THE POEM

This is one of the longest of our poems in the Song, and it begins our third section of part 1. It is a segment that is characterized, like all love, by "joy and fear."

We are able to identify this song with some certainty since it has a clearly defined literary structure. It begins with mountains, a gazelle, and a young stag, and in chiastic fashion, it turns things around to end with a young stag, a gazelle, and mountains.[1] We will break it into three sections (8–10, 11–13, 14–17), the first two ending with "arise, come," and the last ending with resolution and consummation as she invites him to return.

ANTICIPATION

The scene, as someone says, "Drips with the woman's excited anticipation of the arrival of her lover."[2] The text is marvelously alive.[3] Although the woman is narrating something from the past, she uses the present tense to convey a sense of immediacy and excitement.[4] Her sense of anticipation is almost tangible, and his exhilaration is equally contagious!

The song begins with the sound of his coming, "Listen!" even as she invites us to "Look!" He is not simply walking or even running; he

---

1. See Longman, *Song*, 117.
2. Ibid., 119.
3. Gledhill, *Song*, 132.
4. Fox, *Love Songs*, 112.

is leaping and bounding with all the beauty, swiftness, agility, grace, and sensual appeal of a gazelle.

He comes bounding in from the countryside, which throughout the Song is a place of freedom, exhilaration, energetic enthusiasm, and adventure. It has the potential for new growth, fresh experiences, and unexplored pathways.[5]

When the gazelle finally arrives, the woman makes a point of remarking:

> Look! There he stands behind our wall,
> gazing through the windows,
>   peering through the lattice.

As one commentator points out, "The intensity of his gazing is emphasized by using the plural forms for both the windows and lattices ... the brief clauses constructed in strict parallelism, betray the excitement of the woman who has been sought so fervently and watched so intently."[6]

Most scholars suggest that the wall through which he gazes from the outside in is her mother's home. That is the place where on two later occasions she will choose to give herself to him.[7] But there is no good reason why "our wall" or "our home" may not, in fact, be their own. The last verse may suggest that it is late at night and just before dawn,[8] and on a later occasion the shepherd will come home late at night ready to make love, his hair dripping with dew, presumably from tending the sheep in the countryside. That occasion will also begin with an excited invitation, "Listen! My lover is knocking..."[9]

Of course, it a lover's playful tease. He is anxious to make love, but at the same time there is much more going on here. Yes, the scene "evokes a sense of excitement and eagerness," but the real point is that "the lover overcomes obstacles in his desire to reach his beloved. This is an indication of his loving commitment, his determination to make a

---

5. Gledhill, *Song*, 132.
6. Keel, *Song*, 98.
7. Ibid., 96.
8. Fox, *Love Songs*, 112.
9. Song of Solomon 5:2.

rendezvous."[10] The Hebrew word for *bounding* at its root suggests that he is closing the distance,[11] bridging the gap.

Walls and lattices get in the way of intimacy and communication, and peering in from the outside suggests distance and a desire to be closer. If the countryside is the place of freedom, then the wall, windows, and lattices suggest safety, security, convention, dullness, decay, drab conformity, and even suffocating domesticity. They are a barrier that must be penetrated both emotionally and psychologically. Poetically, she is being asked to abandon her former undemanding securities for a life of mutual exploration, new delights, and trembling uncertainties.[12]

REFLECTION

There is, as we have said, enormous excitement in this poem. It is bursting with virility. This is about young lovers, but it is about more than that. There is a determination to keep the passion and excitement.

There is a sense of intentionality here as well. It is about a way of living our lives with determined purpose, going for it with passion, and being willing to enter into relationships with others.

The woman cannot but help respond to his excitement. "Listen," she says, "Look . . . Look!" She is excited by his commitment to come searching for her. She understands that he is saying to her that love knows no obstacles, that she is worth it to him, and that overcoming obstacles is a pleasure and a passion for him, not a trouble or burden.

I once asked an extraordinarily successful music teacher what the secret was to her students winning so many national competitions. Without hesitation, she replied, "My father told me when I was a student, 'Do the hard work. Master the notes and the technique. Then when you have done that, play the music with feeling and passion.'"

Leaping over obstacles and bounding over the hills may require technical expertise and hard work. We understand that, "Love is not passive. Love is singing a duet, and that is work. Joyful work, but work none the less."[13] But our lover knows what it is to play the music and sing the song. He puts feeling and passion into it.

---

10. Longman, *Song*, 119–20.
11. Carr sees this at the root meaning of the word, *Song*, 95.
12. Gledhill, *Song*, 133.
13. Kreeft, *Three Philosophies*, 110.

The whole song comes to us in the form of the woman reminiscing[14] and recounting, as well as remembering with pleasure. His love, excitement, and commitment are not lost on her as she remembers and recalls. It never is.

MEDITATION

God's Love Fills Us with Joy, Strength, Healing, and Life

You, O LORD, keep my lamp burning;
   my God turns my darkness into light.
With your help I can advance against a troop;
   with my God I can scale a wall. . . .

It is God who arms me with strength
   and makes my way perfect.
He makes my feet like the feet of a deer;
   he enables me to stand on the heights (Ps 18:28–29, 32–33).

Then will the eyes of the blind be opened
   and the ears of the deaf unstopped.
Then will the lame leap like a deer,
   and the mute tongue shout for joy. . . .

They will enter Zion with singing;
   everlasting joy will crown their heads.
Gladness and joy will overtake them,
   and sorrow and sighing will flee away (Isa 35:5–6, 10).

When Elizabeth heard Mary's greeting, the baby leaped in her womb, and Elizabeth was filled with the Holy Spirit. In a loud voice she exclaimed: "Blessed are you among women, and blessed is the child you will bear!" (Luke 1:41–42).

And Jesus, when he came out, saw much people, and was moved with compassion toward them, because they were as sheep not having a shepherd: and he began to teach them many things (Mark 6:34 KJV).

Rejoice with those who rejoice; mourn with those who mourn (Rom 12:15).

---

14. Murphy, *Song*, 140.

PRAYER

Father, I thank you that your love for me is no academic enterprise but the intentional expression of your mercy, compassion, and grace. I rejoice in the passion with which you pursue your people. Thank you for overcoming the obstacles and breaking down the barriers that once separated us from each other.

Please forgive me for all of the times when I have woodenly plodded along in my relationship with you, lacking the passion with which you have pursued me.

Teach me this day to be intentional in living my life for you and to be willing and able to overcome the obstacles that will come in the way of loving others. Amen.

Day 17

Poem 8 (2:8–17) B

Renewal: "The season of singing has come"

Woman
A. Listen! My lover!
   Look! Here he comes,
leaping across the mountains,
   bounding over the hills.
My lover is like a gazelle or a young stag.
   Look! There he stands behind our wall,
gazing through the windows,
   peering through the lattice.
My lover spoke and said to me,
   "Arise, my darling,
my beautiful one, and come with me.

B. See! The winter is past;
   the rains are over and gone.
Flowers appear on the earth;
   the season of singing has come,
the cooing of doves
   is heard in our land.
The fig tree forms its early fruit;
   the blossoming vines spread their fragrance.
Arise, come, my darling;
   my beautiful one, come with me."

Man
C. My dove in the clefts of the rock,
   in the hiding places on the mountainside,
show me your face,
   let me hear your voice;
for your voice is sweet,
   and your face is lovely.

> Woman
> Catch for us the foxes,
>   the little foxes
> that ruin the vineyards,
>   our vineyards that are in bloom.
>
> D. My lover is mine and I am his;
>   he browses among the lilies.
> Until the day breaks
>   and the shadows flee,
> turn, my lover,
>   and be like a gazelle
> or like a young stag
>   on the rugged hills.

INTRODUCTION

We are in the middle of a poem that begins with mountains, a gazelle, and a stag and ends in chiastic fashion with a stag, a gazelle, and mountains. The first section has sizzled with intention and excitement. It has been about the joy of being found and wanted. Buried just beneath the surface is the realization that making sure that we know where something is to be found implies not least of all a fear of something precious being lost. In fact, our whole poem (vs. 8–17), like this entire section of the Song (2:8—3:5) is about being found, lost, and found.[15]

In the first section of our poem, the excitement was on the lips of the woman. Now the beauty, rhythm, and cadence of the relationship are maintained as the man invites his lover to explore the enchantment of the changing seasons of life and fresh beginnings.

It is springtime in our text, and from the lips of the lover comes a poem of extraordinary beauty, filled with life, grace, hope, and love.

> See! The winter is past;
>   the rains are over and gone.
> Flowers appear on the earth;
>   the season of singing has come,
> the cooing of doves
>   is heard in our land.
> The fig tree forms its early fruit;
>   the blossoming vines spread their fragrance.

---

15. Carr, *Song*, 95.

> Arise, come, my darling;
> my beautiful one, come with me.

THE RETREAT OF THE COUNTRYSIDE

We are forced to pause and simply reflect on the beauty of our poem. It is time to stop and smell the roses, lest we become so obsessed with trying to understand what it means for our relationships that we fail to simply absorb, enjoy, and relish what it is that we are hearing. As we have said, if we lose the beauty of the Song, then we have lost our way.

This poem has been praised as the "most beautiful nature song in the Old Testament" and celebrated for its "lyrical and sensitive observation of nature."[16] It is to be savored and delighted in not least of all because it is once again a reminder of God's sevenfold pronouncement that everything coming from his hand is good and that we are meant to find satisfaction in it and revel in its pleasures.[17] It is in this soil that we grow, mature, and learn to love.

There are deep ties in our poem, not only to nature but also to the earth, and in particular to "our land."[18] The individual spirit is tied into the environment, not just with the renewed joy and purpose that seems to come with the spring, but also from having its own sense of place and of being connected to the soil in which it has grown. It is not just that our lovers are from the countryside; it is that we must return to the land from which we came, not least of all because we are created out of the dust of the earth.[19] Love and health seem to thrive in the midst of the natural world. The shepherd invites his lover to escape with him into the countryside, where landscape and geography are at their splendid best. It is something that all lovers need, and of which we must be reminded, especially with the frantic pace of life in the city and suburb.

The ability to bask in the goodness of God given to us in the splendors of his creation is somehow all tied up in what it means to be able to enter into love and friendships. We are, it turns out, all part and parcel of the created order, and we need each other.

---

16. See Keel, *Song*, 100.
17. Genesis 1:4, 10, 12, 18, 21, 25, 31.
18. Fox, *Love Songs*, 113.
19. "The LORD God formed the man from the dust of the ground and breathed into his nostrils the breath of life, and the man became a living being" (Gen 2:7).

THE RENEWAL OF THE SEASONS

But our lover also understands the present moment in our text to be a time of unparalleled opportunity. The winter is past, the heavy rains of April are over, the flowers are out, the birds can be heard, the early fruit has appeared, and the fragrance of the blossoming vines has made itself known. A favorable time has arrived,[20] or as our poem puts it so poignantly, "The time for singing has come."

And of course we understand that in the meaning of its poetry, this song about the vineyards is understood as a metaphor of their own selves. The poem is to be understood as their lives together. The lover grasps this moment of opportunity, realizing full well that it is not to be taken for granted. We understand that winter has its place, and the rainy season, as drenching and confining as it may be, has its necessary purpose. But it is the joys of what have been previously grasped and what we know is yet once again to come that carry us through the confining seasons of life. The changing seasons and cycles of life—of winter, spring, summer, fall, winter, spring, summer, fall—are not the mechanical turnings of a tiring wheel called life. They are, as we shall see, about love and grace, because they are about renewal, growth, beauty, and desire.

THE RECREATION OF LIFE

Even more fundamental to what our text is saying is the understanding that the "lovers are part and parcel of this explosion of new life and new hope."[21] The renewal of nature mirrors the replenishment of life, love, and relationships. Our lovers need not succumb to winter or be overwhelmed by the torrential rains of spring. Instead, each season may become the occasion to see life replenished and relationships renewed.

The lover's urgent request is nothing less than an invitation for them to participate together in the gift of new life that is everywhere bursting out around them. To miss this grace is nothing less than to succumb to a loss of hope and despair. It is to fail to emerge from the wintry past or else to succumb to the rains. To be left behind is to remain at home and rot. It will leave him on the outside, longing for her to come and join him in the riotous outburst of life and love that is everywhere to be seen in the blossoming of spring. As one commentator suggests, "The boy's

---

20. Keel, *Song*, 100–01.
21. Gledhill, *Song*, 133.

invitation is a model of literary construction.... There is a strong sense of temporal movement in the poem from the past through the present into the future."[22]

Whatever challenges there may be in our poem in terms of obstacles to be overcome and walls and lattices to be penetrated, the sure new life of spring and the splendor of the countryside and of the created order fill the poem with joy, confidence, and anticipation.

REFLECTION

In the pagan world that surrounded our lovers in the Ancient Near East, the renewal of nature was seen as death and rebirth, the latter brought about by the sexual intercourse of the gods and the worshipers at their altars. In the world of Israel and of the wisdom literature that was populated by our lovers, the Creator was instead the giver and sustainer of life. Consequently, we can say with confidence, "The way he works in the cycle of the seasons is a mirror of his workings in the lives of his people: from the secret growth in days of darkness, to the exuberance of new life."[23] Our lover understands the grace being given in this moment and calls on his beloved to take ahold of it with him. This really is about faith, hope, and love.

In our present spiritual context, faith is often understood as our turning on the switch rather than our being turned on by the grace that God gives to us. In such a setting, relationships become mechanical, and success gives way to self-righteousness, or else failure gives way to despair. What is to be understood as an organic relationship becomes ten things to do rather than life lived together in affection, trust, and joyful expectation. We would do better to understand the organic nature of grace in which faith is invited and grace is initiated. It is what the older theologians used to refer to as an *effectual calling*.

The beautiful lines that end this section of the poem say exactly that. They express the friendship of our lovers and the delight they find in coming into each other's presence.

> "Arise, come, my darling;
> my beautiful one, come with me."

---

22. Ibid.
23. Ibid., 134.

Thus all the images for love in the poem, as in most love poems, are images of living, growing things.... Love grows like a plant. It does not merely grow in us, with us, as a function of us; we grow in it, with it, as a function of it. It has a life of its own—ultimately because it is a seed of God planted in our lives. "He who lives in love, lives in God, and God in him" (1 John 4:16).[24]

MEDITATION

God's Love Is Making All Things New

Be exalted, O God, above the heavens;
    let your glory be over all the earth....

    I will sing and make music.
Awake, my soul!
    Awake, harp and lyre!
    I will awaken the dawn.

I will praise you, O Lord, among the nations;
    I will sing of you among the peoples.
For great is your love, reaching to the heavens;
    your faithfulness reaches to the skies.

Be exalted, O God, above the heavens;
    let your glory be over all the earth (Ps 57:5, 7–11).

As the rain and the snow
    come down from heaven
and do not return to it
    without watering the earth
and making it bud and flourish,
    so that it yields seed for the sower and bread for the eater,
so is my word that goes out from my mouth:
    It will not return to me empty,
but will accomplish what I desire
    and achieve the purpose for which I sent it.
You will go out in joy
    and be led forth in peace;
the mountains and the hills
    will burst forth before you,

---

24. Kreeft, *Three Philosophies*, 108.

and all the trees of the fields
   will clap their hands (Isa 55:10–13).

... being confident of this, that he who began a good work in you will carry it on to completion until the day of Christ Jesus.

... for it is God who works in you to will and to act according to his good purpose (Phil 1:6, 2:13).

PRAYER

Father, I praise you for the changing seasons of life and the renewing grace of your Holy Spirit. May this new life fill my heart with faith, hope, and love.

Forgive me for when I have allowed myself to begin to rot and become mildewed with time, obscuring the beauty of your life that beats within me.

This day please cause your new life to come bursting forth in my person and self. May the new creation you have begun in me spread its life and beauty to all with whom I come into contact. Amen.

Day 18

Poem 8 (2:8–17) C

Disruption: "Catch for us the foxes"

Woman
A. Listen! My lover!
   Look! Here he comes,
leaping across the mountains,
   bounding over the hills.
My lover is like a gazelle or a young stag.
   Look! There he stands behind our wall,
gazing through the windows,
   peering through the lattice.
My lover spoke and said to me,
   "Arise, my darling,
   my beautiful one, and come with me.

B. See! The winter is past;
   the rains are over and gone.
Flowers appear on the earth;
   the season of singing has come,
the cooing of doves
   is heard in our land.
The fig tree forms its early fruit;
   the blossoming vines spread their fragrance.
Arise, come, my darling;
   my beautiful one, come with me."

Man
C. My dove in the clefts of the rock,
   in the hiding places on the mountainside,
show me your face,
   let me hear your voice;
for your voice is sweet,
   and your face is lovely.

Woman
Catch for us the foxes,
   the little foxes
that ruin the vineyards,
   our vineyards that are in bloom.

D. My lover is mine and I am his;
   he browses among the lilies.
Until the day breaks
   and the shadows flee,
turn, my lover,
   and be like a gazelle
or like a young stag
   on the rugged hills.

DISCLOSURE

In this third section of our poem, the man's continued invitation to his lover to come to him begins to take on a new urgency. Here they are, and it is as if she is separated and hidden from him.[25] His pining for her may be no more than that of any lover aching to be with the object of his desire, and their separation may be of his own imagining, but these lines represent a longing for her to disclose herself more intimately and fully to him.

> My dove in the clefts of the rock,
>   in the hiding places on the mountainside,
> show me your face,
>   let me hear your voice;
> for your voice is sweet,
>   and your face is lovely.

At the heart of these lines is a yearning to share, disclose, and communicate. It is the lover's wish to discover all about the person who is the object of his affection. "No detail seems too trivial to be related. No mood or feeling of one is unimportant to the other."[26] "The man's invitation calls her out of hiding. Her inaccessibility heightens his desire. His excitement rises as he waits for his first glimpse of her. . . . He wants her to come out so that he might see her. . . . In the process of the invitation he also compliments her. She is a pleasure of sight and sound. Her form

---

25. Longman, *Song*, 122.
26. Glickman, *Song*, 47.

and her voice are attractive."[27] One might say that he pries her out of hiding with his praise. That, indeed, is the best way to do it.

DISRUPTION

As it turns out, there are very real dangers lurking in the background. The scenery changes abruptly from doves and the sweetness of her voice to foxes that ruin the vineyards. The only connection to the larger poem is the vineyards that were in bloom, at least, before the foxes appeared. The very abruptness of what takes place illustrates the uncertainties that have been just under the surface all the time and that, perhaps, have been the very cause of the man's urgent invitations to come out and be with him.

Still, it is an intrusion, and it catches us by surprise just as the foxes would. We take it that the verses are spoken by the woman.

> Catch for us the foxes,
>   the little foxes
> that ruin the vineyards,
>   our vineyards that are in bloom.

The meaning of the verse is plain enough. There are pesky creatures that have a way of getting in under the wall and tearing up one's vineyards. What is not so clear is what the woman has in mind.[28] It is, of course, futile to speculate what is in view by way of the foxes. In fact, to do so destroys the poetic sensibility that understands that foxes represent those things, whatever they may be, that have a way of creeping in upon us unexpectedly and disrupting or even destroying our relationships.

We have to remember the context of our song (2:8—3:5), with its themes of found and lost and found.[29] He begs her to come out and be with him, to let him see who she is, and to allow him to hear her voice. The forces that keep her hidden away and reluctant to disclose herself may be more than a shy reluctance or a lover's tease. It is entirely possible that they are, in fact, deeply psychological, not necessarily in some deep, dark way, but at least in the sense that her shyness and reluctance might already have suggested. Or it may be, of course, that there are even minor, but as yet unresolved, conflicts that have caused her to withdraw.

---

27. Longman, *Song*, 123.
28. See the discussion in Exum, *Song*, 128–30.
29. Carr, *Song*, 95.

The lover's urgent invitation has perhaps been suggesting that there are things that have a way of appearing and reappearing, suddenly coming into sight after having been hid in the deep recesses of the mind. The unseen secrets of the soul and the unresolved conflicts of the self must be shared if they are not to come back like the foxes to haunt, torment, and destroy.

Given the context of these lines in our poem, it is important to understand that these sentiments are not the musings of a nervous hypochondriac always looking inward and never able to move upward or outward. They represent the tenderness and sensitivity of a lover's heart and conscience, always wanting to be perfectly in tune with the other, but still aware of the larger relationship, which is one of confidence, joy, and celebration.

REFLECTION

What is true of our lovers is no less true of us in all our relationships. Things have a way of creeping in, which in turn are able to bring disruption before we know it. There is a vigilance that belongs to the lover's heart that is no less true in the realm of the spirit. It is not ours alone to discover, it is no less tenderly shown to us by the Lord.

MEDITATION

The Lord Brings Everything to Light for Healing

> Search me, O God, and know my heart;
>   test me and know my anxious thoughts.
> See if there is any offensive way in me,
>   and lead me in the way everlasting (Ps 139:23–24).

> Just then a woman who had been subject to bleeding for twelve years came up behind him and touched the edge of his cloak. She said to herself, "If I only touch his cloak, I will be healed."
>   Jesus turned and saw her. "Take heart, daughter," he said, "your faith has healed you." And the woman was healed from that moment (Matt 9:20–22).

> My conscience is clear, but that does not make me innocent. It is the Lord who judges me. Therefore judge nothing before the

appointed time; wait till the Lord comes. He will bring to light what is hidden in darkness and will expose the motives of men's hearts. At that time each will receive his praise from God
(1 Cor 4:4–5).

PRAYER

Father, I thank you that you know all about me in ways in which I cannot even understand myself.

Please forgive me for often not being sensitive enough to know when things are eating away at my relationships or wise enough to understand them.

Give me this day a tenderness and sensitivity of heart to understand my motives. Root out my sins, and carefully guard my relationships, both with you and with others. Amen.

Day 19

Poem 8 (2:8–17) D

Satisfaction: "My lover is mine and I am his"

Woman
A. Listen! My lover!
  Look! Here he comes,
leaping across the mountains,
  bounding over the hills.
My lover is like a gazelle or a young stag.
  Look! There he stands behind our wall,
gazing through the windows,
  peering through the lattice.
My lover spoke and said to me,
  "Arise, my darling,
my beautiful one, and come with me.

B. See! The winter is past;
  the rains are over and gone.
Flowers appear on the earth;
  the season of singing has come,
the cooing of doves
  is heard in our land.
The fig tree forms its early fruit;
  the blossoming vines spread their fragrance.
Arise, come, my darling;
  my beautiful one, come with me."

Man
C. My dove in the clefts of the rock,
  in the hiding places on the mountainside,
show me your face,
  let me hear your voice;

for your voice is sweet,
  and your face is lovely.

Woman
Catch for us the foxes,
  the little foxes
that ruin the vineyards,
  our vineyards that are in bloom.

D. My lover is mine and I am his;
  he browses among the lilies.
Until the day breaks
  and the shadows flee,
turn, my lover,
  and be like a gazelle
or like a young stag
  on the rugged hills.

WALLS, LATTICES, HIDING PLACES, AND FOXES

As we look back over the expanse of our present poem, there has been great excitement as the beloved comes, leaping over mountains and bounding over hills. There is an exhilaration that comes from drawing near and coming close together. In the end, despite his coming close, he is to be found standing behind the wall, gazing through windows, peering through the lattice, and inviting her to come out to be with him.

No matter how exciting the relationship and how close the lovers are becoming, he is still left, on some level, on the outside looking in. All the barriers that exist between us never quite disappear, and we never fully understand all that is going on inside of the other.

The apostle Paul's reminder remains not simply a fact but a pursuit that can be both exhilarating and frustrating. "For this reason a man will leave his father and mother and be united to his wife, and the two will become one flesh" (Eph 5:31). As he suggests elsewhere, there is still a "not yet" to our experience. "Now we see but a poor reflection as in a mirror; then we shall see face to face. Now I know in part; then I shall know fully, even as I am fully known" (1 Cor 13:12).

SATISFACTION

Yet when all is said and done, our song remains highly optimistic. There is a deep sense of satisfaction that allows the woman to declare with confidence, "My lover is mine and I am his." Despite the ominous factors that appear to have been lurking beneath the surface, we are reminded that after all, "Love is patient, love is kind. . . . it is not easily angered, it keeps no record of wrongs. Love does not delight in evil but rejoices with the truth. It always protects, always trusts, always hopes, always perseveres. Love never fails" (1 Cor 13:4, 5–8).

There is also more going on here than at first meets the eye. The line, "My lover is mine and I am his" will be repeated on two more occasions in 6:3 and 7:10. It indicates their belonging to each other, and not merely in a casual way. It has been rightly pointed out that this line "has a rough parallel in the covenant formula, 'I will be their God, and they will be my people.'"[30]

There is a sense of belonging here that comes from the swearing of one's self to the other. It is not an obsessive possessiveness because it is mutually shared one with the other. They have entered into a covenant relationship, and it gives our lovers a confidence that encourages abandonment to each other and causes the simmering passion to flare up once again. It allows the lovers to move from anxious reflection to strong affirmation and then finally to passionate consummation.

CONSUMMATION

The passion comes back with a vengeance. One commentator has pointed out that the first of our songs in this broader collection (vs. 2–7), "fades away in a haze of passion."[31] If that is the case, then we will have to say that the last of these three sections in our poem ends again in a blaze of passion.

> My lover is mine and I am his;
>   he browses among the lilies.
> Until the day breaks
>   and the shadows flee,
> turn, my lover,

---

30. Longman, *Song*, 125. Cf. Jeremiah 7:23, 11:4; Ezekiel 34:40. Also Pope, *Song*, 405.

31. Gledhill, *Song*, 129.

> and be like a gazelle
> or like a young stag
> on the rugged hills.

"Browsing among the lilies" has already been used in the Song. In 4:5, it refers to her breasts, and in 5:13 to his lips. Here, combined as it is with an invitation to be like a gazelle and a young stag, it is an invitation to make love all night long, "Until the day breaks and the shadows flee." This is yet another example of the way in which "The poetry of The Song of Songs is an exquisite balance of ripe sensuality and delicacy of expression and feeling."[32] But it cannot be missed.

Our poem ends then not with the voice of despair but with a deep sense of satisfaction. Passion speaks not only of deep needs being expressed, but also, as in this case, of those needs being met in the context of a covenant relationship. It is a passion born not only of covenant faithfulness but also of union, of love, and of an exchange of selves. It is an understanding that "When I love you, I no longer possess myself; you do. I have given it away. But I possess yourself." The gift of the giver is the very giver. The hand that gives holds itself in itself as its own gift. "The ordinary relationship between giver and gift, subject and object, cause and effect, is overcome here. The simple-sounding truism that in love you give your very self to your beloved is a high and holy mystery."[33]

We understand that relationships are at the heart of what it means to be a human being. We are created in the image of God—Father, Son, and Holy Spirit. That is, we are created with the need to reveal ourselves to others and especially to give and to receive love in the bond of covenant oneness. In the end, this is about the movement inherent in this whole section of the Song (2:8—3:5) of being found, lost, and found.[34]

REFLECTION

Once again, our human relationships echo all that we know about our spiritual life, but especially of our life hid in Christ with God. Already Christ has been victorious. He reveals himself to us. There is great excitement even in creation at his coming. He takes his disciples to a wedding and makes the finest of wine to drink. He heals the sick, and the lame

---

32. Bloch and Bloch, *Song*, 119.
33. Kreeft, *Three Philosophies*, 128.
34. Carr, *Song*, 95.

are made to walk. His love has laid ahold of us, and the wedding ring of faith brings us into relationship with him. Our relationship with him has its ups and downs, but we are a part of a new creation, even if it has not yet fully come.[35]

Spiritually, we understand that we are called to walk with the Lord. The spiritual life is at its essence a pilgrimage in which the Lord is constantly revealing himself to us and we are learning to delight in him.

At the same time, we have to say that the elusiveness of mastering love—our inability to tie it down, distill its properties, and come up with Ten Principles of Success—is born of our insecurities. There remains an elusive nature to love and relationships that cannot ultimately be tied down and formularized for success. To say this is to be delivered not only from false expectations and perfectionism but also from what is even worse in a relationship: unrealized expectations.

In the end, our native insecurity, born of our need for the gospel, never entirely disappears. That is good and as it should be. It forces us back to the realization that we are never without the need for grace and that love is about relationship.

MEDITATION

God in his Grace Is Always at Work in Our Lives

> This is what God the LORD says—
> he who created the heavens and stretched them out,
>   who spread out the earth and all that comes out of it,
> who gives breath to its people,
>   and life to those who walk on it:
> "I, the LORD, have called you in righteousness;
>   I will take hold of your hand.
> I will keep you and will make you
>   to be a covenant for the people
>   and a light for the Gentiles,
> to open eyes that are blind,
>   to free captives from prison
>   and to release from the dungeon those who sit in darkness
> (Isa 42:5–7).

---

[35]. "Therefore, if anyone is in Christ, he is a new creation; the old has gone, the new has come!" (2 Cor 5:17).

"I will not leave you as orphans; I will come to you. Before long, the world will not see me anymore, but you will see me. Because I live, you also will live. On that day you will realize that I am in my Father, and you are in me, and I am in you. Whoever has my commands and obeys them, he is the one who loves me. He who loves me will be loved by my Father, and I too will love him and show myself to him" (John 14:18–21).

Therefore, if anyone is in Christ, he is a new creation; the old has gone, the new has come! All this is from God, who reconciled us to himself through Christ and gave us the ministry of reconciliation: that God was reconciling the world to himself in Christ, not counting men's sins against them. And he has committed to us the message of reconciliation. We are therefore Christ's ambassadors, as though God were making his appeal through us. We implore you on Christ's behalf: Be reconciled to God. God made him who had no sin to be sin for us, so that in him we might become the righteousness of God (2 Cor 5:17–21).

PRAYER

Father, thank you for swearing yourself to me in your covenant of grace. I am grateful you come searching for us, finding us, revealing yourself to us, and making us one with you.

Forgive me for thinking it was I who found you and made myself one with you and for always believing that our relationship is up to me.

This day, in the confidence that I belong to you and that you belong to me, fill me with grace and strength to give myself away in service to others. Amen.

Day 20

Poem 9 (3:1–5) A

Restlessness: "All night long on my bed"

Woman
A. All night long on my bed
   I looked for the one my heart loves;
   I looked for him but did not find him.
I will get up now and go about the city,
   through its streets and squares;
I will search for the one my heart loves.
   So I looked for him but did not find him.
The watchmen found me
   as they made their rounds in the city.
   "Have you seen the one my heart loves?"
Scarcely had I passed them
   when I found the one my heart loves.

B. I held him and would not let him go
   till I had brought him to my mother's house,
   to the room of the one who conceived me.
Daughters of Jerusalem, I charge you
   by the gazelles and by the does of the field:
Do not arouse or awaken love
   until it so desires.

THE GALLERY

As we begin a new poem, it is easy for us to lose our way among the multiplicity of the striking images that have been presented to us. This especially happens if we are looking for a simple narrative line. Instead, let us imagine for a moment that we have entered a gallery and come to view an exhibition of photographs that everyone has been talking about.

They are brilliantly done and stunningly effective. We are not quite sure if every picture was taken by the same photographer, but it really doesn't matter because they share everything in common. The gallery has put together a collection that comprises a number of perspectives on love, life, and relationships.

Certain themes begin to appear, and as we make our way around the room, we take note of the different angles, perspectives, locations, and subjects. Each has a different effect upon us. Some are shocking, passionate or exciting, and some are all three at the same time.

We are delighted by the lovers frolicking in the fields, but we notice that the images are never entirely or perfectly romantic. Instead, we are left wondering about the fox in the corner of at least one of them, digging away at the roots of a vine in full bloom. We are fascinated by the beauty of the woman, while at the same time we sometimes notice a certain haunting quality that seems to lie lurking just below the surface. We wonder just what is going on inside her head.

As we make our way around the room, the collection seems to have certain common themes and even some particular lovers who keep appearing, but it is difficult for us to piece together the narrative of an actual love story. It hardly matters. Each perspective has drawn us deep into the subject that it studies, lingers over, delights in, and wonders about.

OUR POEM

Now we have come to what by one count is the ninth of our pictures.[36] This one stops us dead in our tracks. As we look at our exhibition notes, we notice that one critic has suggested that this picture "shares with the preceding one the theme of night time search. On this occasion it is the girl who goes in search of her lover. The point seems to be that each is willing to face the dangers of the night."[37]

We are forced to pause, wonder, and reflect. Of all of the studies that we have lingered over so far, this one is the most emotionally disturbing. We might even describe it as haunting. It strikes us as very modern and deeply psychological. The elements of the picture seem to be confused and even collapsed into one another. As another commentator suggests,

---

36. Longman, *Song*, 127.
37. Fox, *Love Songs*, 117.

the "speed of the action seems too compressed to represent an actual event."[38] We might even describe it as surreal.[39] Of all the pictures, it is the one that has managed to get deepest into the inner recesses of the mind. It appears to be a dream, but it also has the qualities of a nightmare.

The woman is seen tossing on her bed all night long. And then superimposed upon it is a collage of images in which we see her restlessly wandering the streets at night—seeking and searching, but not finding.

RESTLESSNESS

Restlessness leads to risky behavior. In this song, it appears to revolve around a single line that is repeated for emphasis and effect: "I sought him but could not find him."

Risky business and the deep disturbance of the soul go hand in hand. It appears, the poem suggests, to be deeply rooted in a native insecurity best understood as a seeking after something that we have not entirely found, at least to our satisfaction.

"People of the Book" understand that it is born of having been thrown out of the Garden, and as Genesis describes it, wandering "east of Eden."[40] It is first discovered in troubled relationships with our parents, nurtured in the difficult bonds we often share with our siblings and our peers, and then reinforced by the failure of friendships and the loss of love. "On a human level, there is the terrible but very real possibility that the beloved will not freely return our love. Love is terribly vulnerable, easily misunderstood, or rejected. There is plenty to fear."[41]

Perhaps, for the sake of wisdom, we also need to remember that in the fear of losing something important to us, the imagination has a way of dwelling on the possibility. And, "The imagination seems more vivid and the possibility even more real at night."[42]

THE WATCHMEN

As the woman goes in search of her love, she encounters the watchmen who keep guard over the city at night. The authorities apprehend her,

38. Gledhill, *Song*, 144.
39. Longman, *Song*, 127.
40. Genesis 3:23–24; 4:10–14.
41. Kreeft, *Three Philosophies*, 127.
42. Curtis, *Song*, 74.

and we are left wondering whether to be fearful or relieved. It is risky business for a woman to be roaming the streets at night, and those who guard the city are no help to her at all.

The fact is that watchmen, although they should know what is going on, do not always appreciate matters of the heart. They recognize the thieves who break in and the enemies who come over the wall. What they understand is that we should be in bed at night and not wandering the streets. Those who are the authorities and keep the structures of reality in place, no matter how important their function, do not always understand the dark night of the soul—or at least what to do with it.

In a sense, it doesn't matter. Our taxes pay the watchmen to keep guard over us at night, but the responsibility to find rest, to procure love, and to secure resolution is very much our own. There is, of course, a sense in which no one else can do it for us. It is ours to go through.

No sooner do the watchmen turn out to be unhelpful than she finds her lover, clings to him, and takes him home to her mother's bed, of all places, while all at the same time addressing her friends in the background. Perhaps it is significant that no sooner have the watchmen been unable to help her that she finds her love herself. The finding seems to be in the seeking.

REFLECTION

Jesus comes immediately to mind.

> Ask and it will be given to you; seek and you will find; knock and the door will be opened to you. For everyone who asks receives; he who seeks finds; and to him who knocks, the door will be opened. Which of you, if his son asks for bread, will give him a stone? Or if he asks for a fish, will give him a snake? If you, then, though you are evil, know how to give good gifts to your children, how much more will your Father in heaven give good gifts to those who ask him! (Matt 7:7–11).

As with love, so it is with life. The dark night of the soul, the failure of the watchmen, the seeking, the searching, the knocking, the opening, the receiving, and the finding are all part and parcel of experiencing this thing called grace.

We are not strange because we know restless nights, risky behavior, the dark night of the soul, the fear of failure, and disappointment with our counselors. Pain is a part of the process. The Lover is found in the searching.

There is no easy sanctification or instant gratification. There is no lottery ticket that we scratch off and win "happily ever after." Grace comes to us in the need and in the searching for the One whom we need. But the need never entirely goes away, because we are never allowed to forget the gospel or live without the need for grace. Were that to happen, we would soon forget.

MEDITATION

God Uses Our Hurts to Awaken Us to His Grace

> I am worn out from groaning;
>   all night long I flood my bed with weeping
> and drench my couch with tears. . . .
>
> The LORD has heard my cry for mercy;
>   the LORD accepts my prayer.
> All my enemies will be ashamed and dismayed;
>   they will turn back in sudden disgrace (Ps. 6:6, 9–10).
>
> O God, you are my God,
>   earnestly I seek you;
> my soul thirsts for you,
>   my body longs for you,
> in a dry and weary land
>   where there is no water. . . .
>
> On my bed I remember you;
>   I think of you through the watches of the night.
> Because you are my help,
>   I sing in the shadow of your wings.
> My soul clings to you;
>   your right hand upholds me (Ps 63:1, 6–8).

One of those days Jesus went out to a mountainside to pray, and spent the night praying to God. When morning came, he called his disciples to him and chose twelve of them, whom he also designated apostles . . . (Luke 6:12–13).

And the Lord said, "Listen to what the unjust judge says. And will not God bring about justice for his chosen ones, who cry out to him day and night? Will he keep putting them off? I tell you, he will see that they get justice, and quickly" (Luke 18:6–8).

There is no fear in love. But perfect love drives out fear, because fear has to do with punishment. The one who fears is not made perfect in love (1 John 4:18).

PRAYER

Father, I praise you for the perfect love of your Son, Jesus Christ, who has brought me back to you. Thank you for being my Father and that nothing can change that relationship.

Forgive me for thinking that you are an unjust god who will punish me for my sins when your Son has already borne that penalty for me.

In the security of your care and in the sure knowledge of your unconditional love for your children, teach me this day to fear nothing and in so doing, to bless others with freedom, righteousness, and justice. Amen.

Day 21

Poem Five (3:1–5) B

Resolution: "I held him"

Woman
A. All night long on my bed
   I looked for the one my heart loves;
   I looked for him but did not find him.
I will get up now and go about the city,
   through its streets and squares;
I will search for the one my heart loves.
   So I looked for him but did not find him.
The watchmen found me
   as they made their rounds in the city.
   "Have you seen the one my heart loves?"
Scarcely had I passed them
   when I found the one my heart loves.

B. I held him and would not let him go
   till I had brought him to my mother's house,
   to the room of the one who conceived me.
Daughters of Jerusalem, I charge you
   by the gazelles and by the does of the field:
Do not arouse or awaken love
   until it so desires.

MY MOTHER'S HOUSE

We understand the restlessness that characterizes the woman in our poem and have come to realize that the finding is already in the seeking. But what are we to make of this business in verse 4?

> I held him and would not let him go
> till I had brought him to my mother's house,
> to the room of the one who conceived me.

Culturally, something may be going on here that we do not yet understand, but the picture is not without its parallels. In the biblical book of Ruth, Naomi encourages her daughter to seek out her kinsman Boaz as he lies by his threshing floor in the middle of the night; in Genesis, Isaac takes Rebekah back to his mother's tent; and Solomon is "crowned" by his mother in our Song. In the most fascinating parallel of all, some suggest that the apostle John consciously developed the literary structure of his resurrection narrative in such a way as to reflect this passage. Mary, after what must have been a long and restless night, comes to the tomb early in the morning in search of Jesus. Seeking, she does not find him, encountering instead the angelic watchmen, who do not tell her where to find him. Then, quite unexpectedly, she turns to address Jesus, at first mistaking him for the gardener, desiring to cling to him and not let him go.[43]

Isaac's taking Rebekah to his mother's tent would hardly be our choice for a honeymoon. Some scholars suggest it speaks of the mother's role in arranging or blessing a marriage[44] or of the friendship the woman enjoys in sharing her intimate secrets with the one who understands her best, her mother. We can certainly also say that her mother is someone who would herself have already experienced these same passions[45] and that our text is telling us that we are coming full circle and sharing a common humanity. In the sense of that security, her mother's house would appear to her poetically appropriate as a place of resolution and sexual consummation.[46]

It is, of course, hard to pin down all this because poetry does not perfectly represent reality but creates a reality of its own.[47] Nevertheless, when we find someone we love and want to share our life with, we take that person back to our "roots" and to the place of our origin. We take that person home to meet our parents. If the one with whom we are go-

---

43. Ruth 1:8–9; Genesis 24:67; Song of Songs 3:11; John 20:11–18. See Longman, *Song*, 131, 128.

44. Bloch and Bloch, *Song*, 159. See the discussion in Exum, *Song*, 137.

45. Keel, *Song*, 124.

46. Longman, *Song*, 131.

47. Keel, *Song*, 120.

ing to share our life has not been there it is going to be hard for them to understand who we are, where we are coming from, and what the need is that we hope will be met in our lives.

Or put another way, the resolution of our restlessness is somehow tied up in coming to terms with the place from which we come and the person who gave us birth. After all, it is back there that her deep insecurities were first formed in her troubled relationship to her mother's sons.[48] In other words, deeply personal needs and insecurities are not always entirely resolved, no matter how much progress we have made. That is a need that love both meets and seeks to understand.

LOVE AWAKENED

Now comes a sentiment we have met before in 2:7. It is addressed to the chorus of friends who surround the woman.

> Daughters of Jerusalem, I charge you
>   by the gazelles and the does of the field:
> Do not arouse or awaken love
>   until it so desires.

Once again, we must say that although this song is a deeply personal, intimate, and individual moment that has explored the depths of the mind and the recesses of the soul, none of us is an island to himself or herself. There are watchmen who take us into custody as we restlessly wander the streets at night and friends who are all too ready to counsel us. Although both may be a nuisance at times, they remain integral to what it means to be human because we are designed to be a part of community.

Our text suggests, "You can't hurry love." It proceeds at its own pace and if forced, may well be stillborn. As we have seen on the previous occasion where this refrain was first heard,[49] the lesson that she has learned from her experience is "that love is not to be trifled with; its arousal drives one into unanticipated and even unknown experiences."[50] Her warning carries within it an understanding that although love is an unsurpassed joy, it is also a demanding and even exhausting experience.

---

48. Song of Songs 1:6.
49. See day 15.
50. Murphy, *Song*, 147.

REFLECTION

> when I found the one my heart loves.
> I held him and would not let him go . . .

Death, disease, divorce, desertion, depression, abuse, fear of failure, and loss of love may all plunge us into the dark night of the soul and leave us tossing on our beds or wandering the streets at night. Similarly, unfulfilled dreams and fantasies can lead to a desperate fear of isolation and loss.[51]

We take courage from this poem because we discover that the haunting recesses of our soul are common to all human beings. We are not strange. This is what it means to be human and to have been thrown out of the Garden.

Even as Christians, to whom God gives new life, we understand that the footprints of our wretchedness are still to be found in our souls. But we dare to look deep into the soul and we know what we will find there. We understand the great drama of life that began when we discovered ourselves to be naked and we hid from God.[52] We still know what it means to struggle with insecurities and passions and to lie awake restless at night.

Grace, or the breaking of God's love into our life, is often a turbulent and upending matter. New birth is a messy business not because violence is being done but because a new creation is taking place.

There is no instant sanctification, no matter how much Job's comforters told him to pull up his socks, repent of his sins, and get on with it.[53] Yes, there may be a God-shaped void in our life that only he can fill, but it never quite goes away until that time when we shall be perfectly full of God. The slavery of sin may be broken in our lives in terms of its penalty and even its power, but its presence still haunts us. The apostle Paul, ever honest and never afraid to admit his ever-present need for the gospel, says, "The good I want to do, I do not do, and what I do not want to do, I do. . . . What a wretched man I am!" (Rom 7:19–20, 24).

At the same time, we know what it means to ask and to receive, to seek and to find, to knock and to have the door opened to us. We have found the One our soul loves. We cling to him, and we will not let him

---

51. Gledhill, *Song*, 146.
52. Genesis 3:8–11.
53. For example, see Job 26:1–4.

go. And yet even then, like the woman in our Song, it comes with a price, and as Jesus pointed out, we must count the cost.[54]

MEDITATION

God Never Lets Us Go

> Those who sow in tears
>   will reap with songs of joy.
> He who goes out weeping,
>   carrying seed to sow,
> will return with songs of joy,
>   carrying sheaves with him (Ps 126:5–6).

> "I have told you these things, so that in me you may have peace. In this world you will have trouble. But take heart! I have overcome the world" (John 16:33).

> Praise be to the God and Father of our Lord Jesus Christ, the Father of compassion and the God of all comfort, who comforts us in all our troubles, so that we can comfort those in any trouble with the comfort we ourselves have received from God. For just as the sufferings of Christ flow over into our lives, so also through Christ our comfort overflows (2 Cor 1:3–5).

PRAYER

Father, I am grateful for the deep needs in my life that have driven me to find you. Thank you for causing me to always need to be near to you.

Forgive me when I have doubted my daily need for the gospel and your desire that it should be so.

This day teach me to comfort others with the comfort that you have given to me and to share the joy of having found you. Amen.

---

54. Luke 14:25–33.

PART 2

The Heart of the Matter 3:6—5:1

Come out, you daughters of Zion,
  and look at King Solomon wearing the crown,
  the crown with which his mother crowned him
on the day of this wedding,
  the day his heart rejoiced (Song 3:11).

Section 4

The Wedding 3:6–11

Day 22

Poem 10 (3:6–11) A

The Wedding: "The day his heart rejoiced"

Woman
B. Who is this coming up from the desert
   like a column of smoke,
perfumed with myrrh and incense
   made from all the spices of the merchant?

C. Look! It is Solomon's carriage,
   escorted by sixty warriors,
   the noblest of Israel,
All of them wearing the sword,
   all experienced in battle,
each with his sword at his side,
   prepared for the terrors of the night.

D. King Solomon made for himself the carriage;
   he made it of wood from Lebanon.
Its posts he made of silver,
   its base of gold.
Its seat was upholstered with purple,
   its interior lovingly inlaid
   by the daughters of Jerusalem.
Come out, you daughters of Zion,
   and look at King Solomon wearing the crown,
   the crown with which his mother crowned him
on the day of his wedding,
   the day his heart rejoiced.

THE HEART OF THE SONG

With this poem (3:6–11), we have entered into the very heart of the Song of Songs. It is our part 2. It stands quite literally at the middle of the book[1] and is the "central pivot around which the rest of the Song revolves."[2] We can hardly do justice to the Song without this realization.

We would like to call it act 2, but that would give the impression that the book is a narrative drama. In fact, as we look at this poem we discover once again that it is a poet, not a historian, who is at work.[3]

As we have suggested before, we miss the point if we think that *the Song of Songs* is a love story with a beginning, middle, and end. If we were to read the book in that way, we would soon start to wonder how this poem fits into our story.[4] After all, the immediate context that has gone before (3:1–5) contained no suggestion of an impending wedding, and from the beginning, we have seen that such a union has long been presupposed. The previous poems have tended to revolve around a shepherd. Now we are suddenly introduced to a description not just of a wedding, but of Solomon's wedding!

To come to terms with what is going on, it bears repeating that we have to understand the brilliance of the Song. Like all great literature, it is timeless because of its insight into human nature and particularly, of course, because of what we might even call its deeply psychological portrayal of human relationships. It is remarkably modern, but its form is also something with which we are once again familiar. It is, as we have suggested, more like a music video than it is the narrative of a love story.

The images do not appear on the screen in a chronological sequence. We have had a passionate woman, a quarrel between lovers, an adoring man lingering over an anxious beauty, a banquet of wine and raisins, spring time and flowers, foxes digging in a vineyard, and a woman restlessly tossing on her bed at night. Now what we have is a shot of a royal wedding, and around this clip, the whole video revolves.

---

1. Gledhill, in *Song*, 147, indicates that there are 111 lines from 1:2 to 4:15, and 111 lines from 5:2 to 8:14.
2. Carr, *Song*, 106.
3. Longman, *Song*, 135.
4. See Carr, *Song*, 106–7.

A ROYAL WEDDING

What we see as the camera pans out onto the horizon is some sort of royal procession from which there rises a plume of smoke and the fragrance of spices. A rhetorical question makes sure to draw our attention to it.

> Who is this coming up from the desert
> > like a column of smoke,
> perfumed with myrrh and incense
> > made from all the spices of the merchant?

It is a dramatic moment. In the movies, it is not unlike the hero riding into town surrounded by a gang of his cowboys, churning up a great a cloud of dust generated by the horses and their hooves. What we are shown in the Song is a carriage, but it is not just any carriage; it is a royal carriage. And it is not just any royal carriage; it is Solomon's royal carriage!

What it seems to be saying to us through the use of the poetic imagination is that when we see the bride coming down the aisle or the groom waiting at the altar, it is not just any moment; it is a royal moment.[5] The man who is the hero of our love song is being likened to King Solomon on the day of his wedding.[6] In fact, in the Ancient Near East the bride and groom were the king and the queen of the village for their royal wedding week.[7] As such, it stands as the epitome of all relationships, even with the divine.[8]

THE MAIN THING

In the end, we understand that up out of the wilderness comes this marriage scene that is the calm at the eye of the storm. Centered right in the heart of the book, surrounded as it is with all the swirling passions of love, desire, longing, anxiety, and insecurity, is this royal wedding. It is to be understood as the thing, the place, and the event that sums up,

---

5. See Fox, *Love Songs*, 123.

6. Murphy, *Song*, 152.

7. With Psalm 45, this poem forms one of two wedding songs in the Bible. Both are royal in nature. See also Genesis 29:26; Judges 14:12. Also, Longman, *Song*, 92.

8. Compare the observation of the apostle Paul, "'For this reason a man will leave his father and mother and be united to his wife, and the two will become one flesh.' This is a profound mystery—but I am talking about Christ and the church" (Eph 5:31–32).

signifies, and secures the essence of a relationship between a man and a woman.

Poetically we are being told by the song that covenant relationship is to be understood as the eye at the heart of the storm, whether that storm be of life or of love. Here, two people treasure each other and delight in having something that we will see is rare, royal, extravagant, expensive, extraordinary, fragrant, and precious. No matter what forces are swirling around us threatening to crush us in their coming together, or tearing us apart in spiraling away, this love, this royal marriage, this wedding feast is what we are to cherish. It values, protects, and rejoices in love and loyalty.

Like a bride being swept off her feet with all of the extravagance of a wedding with the world's richest and most famous king, King Solomon himself, such is this moment between a man and a woman.

REFLECTION

The wonder of marriage is not that a man and a woman should find each other attractive; that is common enough. It is that they should swear themselves to each other "for better or worse," having already known, as in our Song, what it is going to mean to be there "in sickness and in health."

The genius of marriage is that it is a public covenant, a swearing of one's self to the other in the presence of the community. It is a public affirmation not merely that "you are worth it," but that "You are of such worth to me that come what may, I will be there for you, and in the 'presence of God and these witnesses,' I will celebrate you."

Marriage is a covenant, the seal of which is a man and a woman giving themselves to each other and becoming "one flesh." All meaningful relationships require some sort of covenant context. It may be as simple as an employment contract, as common as a friendship,[9] or as complex as taking the name of another. The bonds of love and care are discovered in Christian communities entered through baptism understood as the covenant initiation ceremony, and renewed with regularity in our participation in Holy Communion. Where covenant fails to exist, there can be no "royal" relationship. Instead, we are simply there at the whim

---

9. "My companion attacks his friends; he violates his covenant" (Ps 55:20).

and fancy of the other, to be taken when useful and disposed of when no longer preferable or practical.

Marriage and covenant begin in the Garden with God's covenant with the man and are soon discovered in the relationship between the man and the woman. The nature of its grace is almost immediately discovered in the need for redemption, reconciliation, and renewal in the relationship between God and his people. It comes, of course, to its height in "the new covenant in my blood, which is poured out for you" (Luke 22:20). Even in the relationship between God and his people, faithfulness, love, and grace are found in covenant relationship and described in terms of the marriage between a man and a woman. And so it is that the wedding is the pivot on which all else turns.

MEDITATION

God Swears His Love to Us So That We Might Be Sure of His Faithfulness

> I will sing of the LORD's great love forever;
>   with my mouth I will make your faithfulness known through
>   all generations.
> I will declare that your love stands firm forever,
>   that you established your faithfulness in heaven itself.
>
> You said, "I have made a covenant with my chosen one,
>   I have sworn to David my servant,
> 'I will establish your line forever
>   and make your throne firm through all generations.'"
>
> The heavens praise your wonders, O LORD,
>   your faithfulness too, in the assembly of the holy ones
> (Ps 89:1–5).

> Later I passed by, and when I looked at you and saw that you were old enough for love, I spread the corner of my garment over you and covered your nakedness. I gave you my solemn oath and entered into a covenant with you, declares the Sovereign LORD, and you became mine (Ezek 16:8).

> In the same way, after the supper he took the cup, saying, "This cup is the new covenant in my blood, which is poured out for you" (Luke 22:20).

> This is the covenant I will make with the house of Israel
> after that time, declares the Lord.
> I will put my laws in their minds
> and write them on their hearts.
> I will be their God,
> and they will be my people.... (Heb 8:10).

PRAYER

O Lord, you are King and Lord over all creation. You are absolutely free to do as you please, and yet you have chosen in your grace to enter into covenant with your people Israel, the church. Thank you for making us one with you.

Forgive me when I have forgotten how royally you have treated me and indeed for my unfaithfulness to you.

This day, please help my covenant relationship with you to be at the very center of my life, the pivot on which all turns, the calm at the eye at the storm. Help me to live with the dignity and purity becoming of one you have taken to be your own. Amen.

Day 23

Poem 10 (3:6–11) B

Awe: "Like a column of smoke"

Woman
B. Who is this coming up from the desert
   like a column of smoke,
perfumed with myrrh and incense
   made from all the spices of the merchant?

C. Look! It is Solomon's carriage,
   escorted by sixty warriors,
   the noblest of Israel,
All of them wearing the sword,
   all experienced in battle,
each with his sword at his side,
   prepared for the terrors of the night.

D. King Solomon made for himself the carriage;
   he made it of wood from Lebanon.
Its posts he made of silver,
   its base of gold.
Its seat was upholstered with purple,
   its interior lovingly inlaid
   by the daughters of Jerusalem.
Come out, you daughters of Zion,
   and look at King Solomon wearing the crown,
   the crown with which his mother crowned him
on the day of his wedding,
   the day his heart rejoiced.

AWE AND WONDER

As we see the royal wedding procession "coming up from the desert," there is a sense of mystery and awe that attends the moment. It appears like a column of smoke and a cloud of incense, and mouths fall open and bystanders gape. We can see crowds rushing to line the streets as this awesome moment parades before them.

The significance of this event is quite unmistakable because the Lord had led his people through the wilderness with a cloud of smoke and the glory of his presence.[10] The aroma of incense that is said to accompany the procession creates an aura of wonder—one might even say of worship.[11] One commentator titles this scene *Tremendum et fascinosum*, or "Fear and fascination." He points out, "In this case, the enchanting allure (*fascinosum*) and awesome magnificence (*tremendum*), radiated by every extraordinary beauty, is not presented by describing the woman herself but by picturing her surroundings—just as clouds and lightning announce the coming of an invisible holiness."[12]

As in this song, there are parallels in the literature of Israel[13] where a poet will ask a question intended to evoke wonder and awe and announce the arrival of majesty. The prophet Isaiah uses it to point to the approach of the Lord.

> Who is this coming from Edom,
>   from Bazrah, with his garments stained crimson?
> Who is this, robed in splendor,
>   striding forward in the greatness of his strength?[14]

The pomp and the circumstance of the procession, located at the very heart of our book, is to be seen as representing the importance and joy associated with the wonders of love and indeed, marriage.[15]

There is a certain wonder and mystery that belongs to the approach of love. The union of a man and a woman, the two becoming one, is something that is to be understood as awesome and quite frankly, a thing

---

10. Exodus 13:21–22.
11. See Pope, *Song*, 426.
12. Keel, *Song*, 129.
13. Murphy, *Song*, 149.
14. Isaiah 63:1.
15. Cf. Longman, *Song*, 133.

of wonder. It is a fact over which lovers have long lingered in surprise and astonishment.

Poetically, it is as if the Lord turns up in the wedding. We are to understand that something extraordinary, even sacred, is taking place when two people become one flesh. It is a matter of wonder and awe.

REFLECTION

What is being celebrated here is the sacredness and awe that belongs to the union of a man and woman, and the sense of mystery that accompanies the idea of two people becoming one. In light of the above, it is not surprising that the relationship of God to his people is described as a wedding,[16] and the coming of Christ and his kingdom is celebrated as a wedding feast.[17] For all of these reasons, marriage is sacred and in its holiness joy is found.

MEDITATION

Seeing the Glory of God Leads to a Life Lived in a New Way

> By day the LORD went ahead of them in a pillar of cloud to guide them on their way and by night in a pillar of fire to give them light, so that they could travel by day or night. Neither the pillar of cloud by day nor the pillar of fire by night left its place in front of the people (Exod 13:21–22).

> Who are these that fly along like clouds,
>   like doves to their nests?
> Surely the islands look to me;
>   in the lead are the ships of Tarshish,
> bringing your sons from afar,
>   with their silver and gold,
> to the honor of the Lord your God,
>   the Holy One of Israel,
>   for he has endowed you with splendor (Isa 60:8–9).

---

16. Isaiah 54:5–6; 62:4–5; Jeremiah 3:14, 20; 31:32; Ezekiel 16:8; Hosea 2:1, 7; Ephesians 5:31–32.

17. Matthew 22:1–14; Luke 14:7–24; John 2:1–11; Revelation 19:7–9; 21:2, 9.

After six days Jesus took with him Peter, James and John the brother of James, and led them up a high mountain by themselves. There he was transfigured before them. His face shone like the sun, and his clothes became as white as the light. Just then there appeared before them Moses and Elijah, talking with Jesus.

Peter said to Jesus, "Lord, it is good for us to be here. If you wish, I will put up three shelters-one for you, one for Moses and one for Elijah."

While he was still speaking, a bright cloud enveloped them, and a voice from the cloud said, "This is my Son, whom I love; with him I am well pleased. Listen to him!"

When the disciples heard this, they fell facedown to the ground, terrified. But Jesus came and touched them. "Get up," he said. "Don't be afraid." When they looked up, they saw no one except Jesus (Matt 17:1–8).

"For this reason a man will leave his father and mother and be united to his wife, and the two will become one flesh." This is a profound mystery—but I am talking about Christ and the church (Eph 5:31–32).

PRAYER

Lord, you are awesome, mysterious, terrifying, and fascinating, and all at the same time. We kneel before you, swept away by the glory of your approach to us.

Lord, I cannot believe the familiar rudeness with which I have treated you. I ask for your forgiveness and pray that you will teach me what it means to love, respect, and worship you in all your awesome holiness.

Help me this day, having seen you, to be fascinated by nothing else! Cause that the gods that clamor for my attention will be seen by me for what they are, wood and stone. And in the strength of this vision, allow me to transcend my circumstances and live my life in light of your wonder, awe, and love. Amen.

Day 24

Poem 10 (3:6–11) C

Security: "Escorted by sixty warriors"

Woman
B. Who is this coming up from the desert
   like a column of smoke,
perfumed with myrrh and incense
   made from all the spices of the merchant?

C. Look! It is Solomon's carriage,
   escorted by sixty warriors,
   the noblest of Israel,
All of them wearing the sword,
   all experienced in battle,
each with his sword at his side,
   prepared for the terrors of the night.

D. King Solomon made for himself the carriage;
   he made it of wood from Lebanon.
Its posts he made of silver,
   its base of gold.
Its seat was upholstered with purple,
   its interior lovingly inlaid
   by the daughters of Jerusalem.
Come out, you daughters of Zion,
   and look at King Solomon wearing the crown,
   the crown with which his mother crowned him
on the day of his wedding,
   the day his heart rejoiced.

THE NOBLEST OF WARRIORS

Here comes the "royal" bride adorned as she is, at least in the poetic imagination, by Solomon's splendid carriage.[18] As she comes riding up out of the wilderness, it is immediately noticed that the carriage is escorted by sixty of Solomon's finest warriors.

> Look! It is Solomon's carriage,
>   escorted by sixty warriors,
>   the noblest of Israel,
> all of them wearing the sword,
>   all experienced in battle,
> each with his sword at his side,
>   prepared for the terrors of the night.

Like a contemporary wedding in which the bride and groom are surrounded by the closest members of their family and the most loyal of their friends, the bridal carriage is surrounded by the noblest warriors of Israel. Soon (v. 11), the whole community of faith will be invited to attend. The "daughters of Jerusalem" will be added to the finest warriors in Israel.

Sixty warriors are twice as many as the guard that accompanied Solomon's father, David.[19] The reference to their being prepared for "the terrors of the night" explains this detail. It may be an allusion to the fact that in the Ancient Near East, it was common to suspect that even the demons were jealous of the joy of newlyweds; therefore, they lay in wait to do the couple mischief.[20]

This is a moment that is to be doubly protected. The king has made sure that they are surrounded by the noblest of warriors who have had experience in battle. No matter what "demons" may seek to undo their relationships, help will never be far from hand in taking the sword to them.

Security is high at the wedding of a king, as it should be in marriage. This is not a private moment in which a promise of protection is made between friends. It is a public declaration stated in the presence of witnesses that "those whom God joins together, let no one tear apart."

---

18. For the reasons why it is best to understand the woman as being the one in the carriage, see Carr, *Song*, 107–8.

19. Second Samuel 23:23.

20. Pope, *Song*, 435.

All that is represented in the wedding is to be surrounded by the experience of friends who have done battle.

Whatever cultural forces would threaten to destroy us, no matter how prevalent may be the death of marriage or the divorce of couples, there is a community of faith in which life is nurtured and love is protected. Marriage requires nothing less than that it should be guarded by the very finest of our warriors and the most faithful of our friends.

The protection that the king brings to the wedding says that his bride is the real jewel in his crown. To be given that gift is to be given the greatest gift of all. What our poem shows us, placed as it is on the lips of the woman, is that the bride exudes an excitement and admiration related to the doubly sure protection of her king and the knowledge that she is valued above all. In other words, what is represented in the wedding will be treasured and held secure. That is the essence of marriage.

THE BRIDESMAIDS

Indeed, the king is presented to us as a Champion, and the woman calls for her bridesmaids to pay attention to what is happening.

> Come out, you daughters of Zion,
>   and look at King Solomon wearing the crown,
>   the crown with which his mother crowned him
> on the day of his wedding,
>   the day his heart rejoiced.

The king's mother places a garland around the neck of her son, not in his coronation as a king, but in honor of his taking his bride to himself. This is his moment of coming into his own. It appears to be a recognition that the time has come for him to take his love and make her the central woman in his life. "For this reason a man shall leave his father and mother, and be united to his wife, and the two shall become one flesh" (Eph 5:31). He is now a champion who joyfully takes that honor unto himself, both as his duty and delight, but also as something that he will protect above all else.

THE MAIN THING

In the end, we understand that out of the wilderness comes this love that is the calm in the eye of the storm. Centered right in the heart of the book, surrounded as it is with all the swirling passions of love, desire, longing, anxiety, and insecurity, is this royal wedding. It is to be understood as the thing, the place, and the event that sums up, signifies, and secures the essence of a relationship between a man and a woman. It is secure. It values, protects, and rejoices in love and loyalty.

REFLECTION

In the Scriptures, marriage is always represented to us as a covenant relationship. It is an oath-swearing ceremony that comes replete with blessings and curses. *Covenant love* is a term that assumes a special meaning not only in the context of marriage, but also of God's love for his bride Israel, the church. Safety is singled out as one of its particular features that are not to be overlooked.[21] We speak about "cutting" a covenant, which comes from the ancient rite of cutting an animal in two, symbolic as it is of the serious implications that come from the breaking of a covenant.[22]

In particular, Christ is also presented in Scripture as the great Champion who disarms the powers of darkness. Theologians call this the *Christus Victor* theme, and we see it not just in the casting out of demons, but also in Jesus's utter defeat of Satan upon the cross.[23] The apostle John will go as far as to say, "The reason the Son of God appeared was to destroy the devil's work."[24]

In fact, the theme of the wedding, the king, and the sword comes together most famously in Psalm 45, a piece of Scripture that the people of God have long seen as analogous to the relationship between Christ and his bride. The apostle Paul would bring these very themes together in his famous line, "But thanks be to God who always leads us in triumphal procession in Christ and through us spreads everywhere the fragrance of the knowledge of him" (2 Cor 2:14).

This love of the Son is the calm at the eye of the storm. As this passage is the pivot on which the Song turns, so is this covenant love that is enacted in the wedding the hinge upon which all turns. No matter what forces swirl around us and threaten to crush us in their coming together,

---

21. For example, Hosea 2:18–19; Exodus 15:3; Ezekiel 34:25.
22. See Genesis 15:7–20; Jeremiah 34:18.
23. Colossians 2:15; Hebrews 2:14–15.
24. First John 3:8. See also Luke 10:17–18, 11:20; Colossians 2:15; Hebrews 2:14.

it is this love, this royal marriage, this wedding feast that we cherish. Our Champion has covenanted it and will hold it sure and secure.

MEDITATION

Christ Having Triumphed over All, We Are Safe in God's Love

My heart is stirred by a noble theme
   as I recite my verses for the king; . . .

Gird your sword upon your side, O mighty one;
   clothe yourself with splendor and majesty.
In your majesty ride forth victoriously
   in behalf of truth, humility and righteousness;
   let your right hand display awesome deeds. . . .
Daughters or kings are among your honored women;
   at your right hand is the royal bride in fold of Ophir
(Ps 45:1, 3-4, 9).

"In that day," declares the Lord,
   "you will call me 'my husband' . . .
In that day I will make a covenant for them . . .
Bow and sword and battle
   I will abolish from the land,
   so that all may lie down in safety.
I will betroth you to me forever . . . (Hos 2:16, 18, 19).

"I will make a covenant of peace with them and rid the land of wild beasts so that they may live in the desert and sleep in the forests in safety. . . . They will live in safety, and no one will make them afraid . . ." (Ezek 34:25, 28).

And having disarmed the powers and authorities, he made a public spectacle of them, triumphing over them by the cross (Col 2:15).

Since the children have flesh and blood, he too shared in their humanity so that by his death he might destroy him who holds the power of death—that is, the devil—and free those who all their lives were held in slavery by their fear of death (Heb 2:14-15).

PRAYER

Thank you, Lord, for your love upon which all my life turns and for your protection, which is my calm amid all of the swirling currents of life. Thank you for Christ, who is my Champion, the one who has defeated sin, death, Satan, and hell on my behalf.

Forgive me for my insecurities and anxieties, which call into question your protection and provision in my life.

This day make me bold and strong in the knowledge of your mighty acts on my behalf. Strengthen me to be of service to your kingdom, to care for the weak, and to do what is right. Amen.

Day 25

Poem 10 (3:6–11) D

Extravagance: "Made for himself the carriage"

Woman
B. Who is this coming up from the desert
   like a column of smoke,
perfumed with myrrh and incense
   made from all the spices of the merchant?

C. Look! It is Solomon's carriage,
   escorted by sixty warriors,
   the noblest of Israel,
All of them wearing the sword,
   all experienced in battle,
each with his sword at his side,
   prepared for the terrors of the night.

D. King Solomon made for himself the carriage;
   he made it of wood from Lebanon.
Its posts he made of silver,
   its base of gold.
Its seat was upholstered with purple,
   its interior lovingly inlaid
   by the daughters of Jerusalem.
Come out, you daughters of Zion,
   and look at King Solomon wearing the crown,
   the crown with which his mother crowned him
on the day of his wedding,
   the day his heart rejoiced.

THE KING'S CARRIAGE

The text describes Solomon's carriage as being made of the finest of woods. They are rare, expensive, and fragrant. The posts are gold and silver, extraordinary, precious, and exceedingly beautiful. The upholstery is done in purple, a color that was rare and of course, royal. The interior is lovingly inlaid with scenes of love. The craftsmanship is a work of art and in itself it is a treasure.

The effect of the whole picture suggests that what we have here is something that is rare, royal, expensive, extraordinary, fragrant, precious, beautiful, and lovingly inlaid.

This is an impulse that is not entirely lost in our own culture. The extravagant expenses associated with a wedding may, in fact, be a flagrant materialism intended only to impress. More properly, the costly nature of the ceremony is a reflection of the importance in which marriage is to be held. It is an understanding that this is a day that is to be truly celebrated because of the value associated with the wonder of the gift. Poetically, "the king" says to his bride, "Nothing is too good for you! I value and treasure you above all else."

It is as good as it gets when each knows that the other is treasured above all else. All that is brought to the wedding is not lost on the bride. She basks in the king's attention, and she makes sure that her friends see it. It is shown off to all "these persons here present." This is not the contrived extravagance of what is really self-congratulation. Before the eyes of love, the shepherd is a king,[25] and on the lips of love, the expression of that sentiment is never lost to silence.

Once again, admiration and affirmation are the currency used in the kingdom of love. As Jesus indicated, "It is more blessed to give than to receive."[26] We spend it, only to receive it back again doubly given. "Give, and it will be given to you. A good measure, pressed down, shaken together and running over, will be poured into your lap. For with the measure you use, it will be measured to you."[27] The Song everywhere shouts the truth of this to us.

---

25. See Fox, *Love Songs*, 127.
26. Acts 20:35.
27. Luke 6:38.

THE MAIN THING

When the poetry is over, this song is left at the heart of the book, as the eye of the storm and as the hinge upon which the book turns. What we are left with are two people who prize each other above all else and delight in having something that is rare and royal. In the midst of all of the swirling currents that surround the man and the woman in the Song, this wedding feast stands for all that is to be cherished. It is fragrant, beautiful, and acquired at great expense. This moment is to be valued above everything else.

REFLECTION

It is with this understanding that the bride is the jewel in the crown, the one who is loved and protected above everything else, that we see mirrored for us the very love of God for his bride. Above all else, that is what is most rare, royal, extravagant, extraordinary, and procured at great cost. To know that we are treasured by Someone is the greatest gift of all.

MEDITATION

Nothing Compares to the Love of God

> I delight greatly in the Lord;
>   my soul rejoices in my God.
> For he has clothed me in the garments of salvation
>   and arrayed me in a robe of righteousness,
> as a bridegroom adorns his head like a priest,
>   and as a bride adorns herself with her jewels (Isa 61:10).

Jesus spoke to them again in parables, saying: "The kingdom of heaven is like a king who prepared a wedding banquet for his son. He sent his servants to those who had been invited to the banquet to tell them to come, but they refused to come.

"Then he sent some more servants and said, 'Tell those who have been invited that I have prepared my dinner: My oxen and fattened cattle have been butchered, and everything is ready. Come to the wedding banquet.'

"But they paid no attention and went off—one to his field, another to his business. The rest seized his servants, mistreated them and killed them. The king was enraged. He sent his army and destroyed those murderers and burned their city.

"Then he said to his servants, 'The wedding banquet is ready, but those I invited did not deserve to come. Go to the street corners and invite to the banquet anyone you find.' So the servants went out into the streets and gathered all the people they could find, both good and bad, and the wedding hall was filled with guests" (Matt 22:1–10).

I saw the Holy City, the new Jerusalem, coming down out of heaven from God, prepared as a bride beautifully dressed for her husband. And I heard a loud voice from the throne saying, "Now the dwelling of God is with men, and he will live with them. They will be his people, and God himself be with them and be their God" (Rev 21:2–3).

PRAYER

Lord, to be treasured by you is the greatest gift of all, especially as we understand the extravagant cost involved in our wedding with your Son. You have given him to us, and he is exquisite, royal, and extraordinary.

Forgive me for thinking that I am not now special in your sight.

Fill me with a sense of being so loved and royally treated by you that I will learn to do the same for the widow, the orphan, and the alien. Amen.

Section 5

The Wasf, 4:1—5:1

Day 26

Poem 11 (4:1–7) A

Admiration: "How beautiful you are"

Man
How beautiful you are, my darling!
  Oh, how beautiful!
    Your eyes behind your veil are doves.
Your hair is like a flock of goats
  descending from Mount Gilead.
Your teeth are like a flock of sheep just shorn,
  coming up from the washing.
Each has its twin;
  not one of them is alone.
Your lips are like a scarlet ribbon;
  your mouth is lovely.
Your temples behind your veil
  are like the halves of a pomegranate.
Your neck is like the tower of David,
  built with elegance;
on it hang a thousand shields,
  all of them shields of warriors.
Your two breasts are like two fawns,
  like twin fawns of a gazelle
  that browse among the lilies.
Until the day breaks
  and the shadows flee,
I will go to the mountain of myrrh
  and to the hill of incense.
All beautiful you are, my darling;
  there is no flaw in you.

We have come to the central section of our book. We have called it the eye of the storm, the place of calm in the midst of the Song of Songs and of love and relationships. It is "the pivot around which the rest of the Song revolves."[1] It is the place of covenant and commitment in which the wedding is described to us in terms of the royal son of David, who lovingly pays attention to the smallest of details and spares no expense to celebrate the importance of this moment.

THE WEDDING FEAST

This is quite literally the wedding feast, and what appears now is one of the two most explicit passages in the Song of Songs. Our lovers are about to head off to the honeymoon, and what we have before us is something that in the Ancient Near East was called a *wasf*. It is an ancient Arabic term that depicts the custom practiced by the bride and groom in which they would each describe the beauties of the other before their guests and as a prelude to their lovemaking.[2]

The song is a rapturous portrayal of the exquisite beauties of the woman. It is a tantalizing description in which he begins with her head and moves teasingly downward over her body. The descriptions may seem far too risqué for a wedding reception given in the Judeo-Christian tradition, but we need to begin by reminding ourselves that this is Scripture. It is the word of God, and this song has been bound into the book we call the Holy Bible. It is holy, and it is good.

YOU ARE SO BEAUTIFUL

This time the imagery is no longer that of a king on his wedding day, but instead it belongs to that of the real people who populate our text and in particular, that of a shepherd. A wedding may be a royal event, but to delight in love and discover passion belongs to all of us.

In the first seven verses, the man is in absolute awe of her beauty. Borrowing, as we said, the sensibilities of a shepherd, the lover describes his bride in terms strange to us but entirely at home in his world. As the cowboy herding cattle sees a beauty in their movement that is lost on the city dweller, so our shepherd draws on the pleasures of his calling and the exotic fruits that populate his terrain to describe his love.

---

1. Carr, *Song*, 106.
2. Longman, *Song*, 140–41.

Her eyes are striking. Like doves, there is a delicacy and softness to them,[3] but perhaps also we might imagine a certain "fluttering timidity" to them.[4] The veil behind which they are hidden suggests a longing to be uncovered and set free. In fact, the veil, rather than hiding her beauty, serves only to heighten his desire to see her. Her dark, curly hair tumbles with all the youthful vibrancy and movement of a herd of black rams and goats descending the side of a mountain.[5] The curls are filled with movement and shimmer with excitement. Closer to home, the poet Longfellow would remark, "Not ten yoke of oxen have the power to draw us like a woman's hair."[6]

Her teeth, in contrast, are strikingly white, reminiscent of festive moments associated with sheep shearing.[7] Their perfect symmetry and whiteness serve to draw attention to the loveliness of her mouth and the passionate redness of her lips. Her cheeks radiate the blushing smoothness and vibrant colors of exotic fruits thought in the ancient world to be aphrodisiacs that stimulate love.[8] Her neck is long, proud, and elegant, and the necklaces that hang around it evoke the excitement that a warrior would feel when he viewed the thousands of magnificent shields hanging in the ancient tower of David.

Before our first section ends, he lingers over her breasts, describing them with graceful and playful images drawn from the excitement of young twin fawns browsing among the lilies that elsewhere are described as lips of the lover.[9] They are warm, lively, delicate, sprightly, soft, and youthful.[10] Immediately, as we would expect, he is swept away in anticipation of the pleasures of making love. This, he imagines, will take all night long.

> Until the day breaks
> and the shadows flee,

---

3. Fox, *Love Songs*, 129.
4. Gledhill, *Song*, 155.
5. Carr, *Song*, 114–15; Keel *Song*, 142.
6. Quoted by Gledhill, *Song*, 156.
7. Keel, in *Song*, 142, suggests that "the unbroken rows of the beloved's teeth, radiantly white and well formed, evoke the full blessing and the friendly and cheerful festivities of a sheepshearing."
8. Carr, *Song*, 116–17.
9. Exum, *Song*, 156. Cf. Song of Songs 5:13.
10. Ibid.

> I will go to the mountain of myrrh
> and to the hill of incense.

Finally, he is able to pull himself back only long enough to exclaim, "You are so beautiful, there is no flaw in you."

REFLECTION

We have said that our text is a *wasf*, an exercise played at the wedding reception where the bride and the groom tell each other, in front of all their guests, what it is that they like about each other.

It is a "game" that I play with couples who come to be married. I ask them what it is that they like about each other, carefully paying attention to how easily it comes off their lips, the light that comes into their eyes, and the joy or the apprehension expressed on their faces as they listen to each other. It says the world about our lovemaking, our insecurities, our hopes, and our fears, and above all, about what it means to love and appreciate another person. Once again, we understand that praise and affirmation are the currency of the kingdom of love.

MEDITATION

We Sing the Praises of God and Learn to Do the Same for Others

> Shout for joy to the LORD, all the earth.
> > Worship the LORD with gladness;
> > come before him with joyful songs.
> Know that the LORD is God.
> > It is he who made us, and we are his;
> > we are his people, the sheep of his pasture.
>
> Enter his gates with thanksgiving
> > and his courts with praise;
> > give thanks to him and praise his name.
> For the LORD is good and his love endures forever;
> > his faithfulness continues through all generations (Ps 100).
>
> You will be a crown of splendor in the Lord's hand,
> > a royal diadem in the hand of your God.
> No longer will they call you Deserted,
> > or name your land Desolate.

> But you will be called Hephzibah (my delight is in her),
>   and your land Beulah (married)
> for the LORD will take delight in you,
>   and your land will be married.
> As a young man marries a maiden,
>   so will your sons marry you;
> as a bridegroom rejoices over his bride,
>   so will your God rejoice over you (Isa 62:3–5).

> We ought always to thank God for you, brothers, and rightly so, because your faith is growing more and more, and the love every one of you has for each other is increasing. Therefore, among God's churches we boast about your perseverance and faith . . . (2 Thess 1:3–4).

PRAYER

Lord, it is a thing of wonder that you should find us beautiful and attractive. We know that it is because of what your Son has done for us. It fills us with joy. Our beauty is not something we have won, but you have given it to us.

Forgive me, Lord, for thinking that I am not delightful in your sight, because in so thinking, I have insulted what you have done for me.

Now, in the confidence of that love and of being desired, use me this day to reach the deserted and desolate with your love that surpasses all description! Amen.

Day 27

Poem 11 (4:1–7) B

Rapture: "There is no flaw in you."

Man
A How beautiful you are, my darling!
   Oh, how beautiful!
   Your eyes behind your veil are doves.
Your hair is like a flock of goats
   descending from Mount Gilead.
Your teeth are like a flock of sheep just shorn,
   coming up from the washing.
Each has its twin;
   not one of them is alone.
Your lips are like a scarlet ribbon;
   your mouth is lovely.
Your temples behind your veil
   are like the halves of a pomegranate.
Your neck is like the tower of David,
   built with elegance;
on it hang a thousand shields,
   all of them shields of warriors.

B. Your two breasts are like two fawns,
   like twin fawns of a gazelle
   that browse among the lilies.
Until the day breaks
   and the shadows flee,
I will go to the mountain of myrrh
   and to the hill of incense.
All beautiful you are, my darling;
   there is no flaw in you.

LOVE, SEX, AND PASSION

As we reflect on this poem, it is easy for us to dismiss it too quickly. After all, we have met this passionate rapture before and commented on it then. We will meet it again. We find ourselves therefore forced to revisit these themes precisely because it is the intention of the Song that we do so. We do justice to the text only when we allow it to have its proper weight. If the emphasis keeps coming back again and again to this passionate rapture, it must be because we need to hear it over and over.

As our poem progresses, the man becomes even more explicit. He visualizes the woman's breasts "in a relatively innocuous pastoral image of fawns grazing," but he savors them as parts of his lover's body that are perfumed, intoxicating, and expensive.[11] As he moves down her body, perhaps he even has more in mind.[12]

If we are taken aback by the passionate nature of this text, we should not be. I suppose there is a place for calm, rational talk about love, sex, and marriage. At the same time, we need to come to terms with the fact that love, sex, and relationships rarely are a calm and rational business. It is more a storm than a science, and it is better to say so than to pretend otherwise. Passionate attraction and appreciation are absolutely normal, and therefore, it is appropriate to talk about making love in a passionate way. To pretend otherwise is to deny the reality that wells up in us as human beings.

The truth is that passion is a swirling storm that is able to drive us to the heights of ecstasy or else totally upend us as human beings. Brought out into the open and properly celebrated, it becomes a thing of beauty.

What is fascinating about sex and passionate rapture is that here, as nowhere else, deeply felt emotions all meet together. A longing for acceptance, powerful expressions of love, aspirations for joy, heights of bliss, and happiness all collide and explode in this place.

The fundamental mistake of our culture is to think that sex is just sex and that it can be covered in Human Plumbing 101. Sex is not unlike the nuclear option. It has incredible power and potential, but it also requires enormous care and protection. It has the potential at once to

---

11. Exum, *Song*, 167.
12. Longman, *Song*, 147.

either raise us to the heights of love and passion or else cause us a meltdown of unparalleled proportions.

The reason these passages simmer with passion and yet never cross over the line into pornography is because they are about the power of anticipation as yet unrealized and the beauty of love made with her king on their wedding night. What the commandment tells us negatively by way of "You shall not commit adultery"[13] this text teaches us positively by way of rapturous example. This is not only a remarkably positive view of life and sexuality, but it is also a text that soars in praise of both their beauty and ecstasy.

When the Lord tells us that sex belongs to marriage, it is because that is where it belongs. The Lord has placed it there for our blessing, but we are to use it in the way that it is intended and for the purposes that it was created. Only then does it find its beauty.

SEX AS SACRED, LIFE AS GOOD

The Song of Songs is a part of what we call *wisdom literature*. Along with books like Proverbs and Ecclesiastes, it speaks to us about how to live successfully in the midst of a real world. If it is saying to us that sex is sacred and filled with mystery, passion, and joy, then it is also necessarily speaking to us about our place in nature and creation.

The dramatic celebration of sex in this passage in the end is really saying that all of life, although fallen, is good. It is saying that getting our hands physically into all of life is sacred. Our work, like our relationships, may be backbreaking, especially when we find ourselves pulling weeds or driving out the foxes. Life is about planting vineyards, reaping fruit, providing for families, and going to wedding feasts in which young men and women are overcome with the delights of their love. For this reason, Christians understand why we are given the resurrection of the body. We are body and soul, and both are being redeemed in God's new creation.

Of course, this can slip easily into a materialism where what we do and have becomes the end in itself. We know this is happening to us when we begin to take our identity and our security from how well we are doing or not doing, rather than who we are in Christ. When we are more excited about getting than giving, we have been taken captive. Then not

---

13. Exodus 20:14.

just our work, but also our relationships, begin to collapse because we have begun to make our possessions the source of our happiness rather than an expression of the blessings God has given us.

Instead:

> The answer of Song of Songs is that all of life is a love song. Every subatomic particle, from the Big Bang to the senility of the sun, is a note in this incredibly complex symphony. Every event, everything that has ever happened, the fall of every hair and of every sparrow, is a theme in the surpassingly perfect melody of this song. But we who are in it do not hear or know it unless we are told by the Singer, who is outside it and who alone can know the meaning of the whole.[14]

REFLECTION

Yet, this song ends not as we might expect with a great and grand celebration of sensual pleasure but with love and affirmation.

> All beautiful you are, my darling;
> there is no flaw in you.

No one has been truly loved until they have heard those words of considered appreciation, rapturous affirmation, and unconditional acceptance.

How can God say that to us? Because he takes away the sins of his people and nails them to the cross of his Son and then clothes his people and transforms them in the beauty of Christ. The larger text into which this book is bound ends with God saying to us in Christ, "You are so beautiful, there is no flaw in you."

> Let us rejoice and be glad and give him glory! For the wedding of the Lamb has come, and his bride has made herself ready. Fine linen, bright and clean, was given her to wear." (Fine linen stands for the righteous acts of the saints.) Then the angel said to me, "Write: 'Blessed are those who are invited to the wedding supper of the Lamb!'" And he added, "These are the true words of God" (Rev 19:7–9).

In the end, it is of God we say in regard to his love, his acceptance, his plans, and his blessings, "You are so beautiful, there is no flaw in you."

---

14. Kreeft, *Song*, 105.

Life lived out of gratitude, and to the glory of God, is likewise filled with passion and joy.

Meditation

God Is Awesome. Our Lives Are Lived for His Glory out of Gratitude for His Love

> Give thanks to the LORD, for he is good;
> his love endures forever. . . .
> Whoever is wise, let him heed these things
> and consider the great love of the LORD (Ps 107:1, 43).

> A man can do nothing better than to eat and drink and find satisfaction in his work. This too, I see, is from the hand of God, for without him, who can eat or find enjoyment? To the man who pleases him, God gives wisdom, knowledge and happiness . . . (Eccl 2:24–26).

> So whether you eat or drink or whatever you do, do it all for the glory of God (1 Cor 10:31).

> Rejoice in the Lord always. I will say it again: Rejoice! . . . Finally, brothers, whatever is true, whatever is noble, whatever is right, whatever is pure, whatever is lovely, whatever is admirable—if anything is excellent or praiseworthy—think about such things. Whatever you have learned or received or heard from me, or seen in me-put it into practice. And the God of peace will be with you (Phil 4:4, 8–9).

PRAYER

Lord, thank you for making all of life good and to be enjoyed. I am grateful for your life that has made it our love song.

Forgive me for thinking that it is mine to use as I please.

Instead, this day help me to play every note to your glory, and may the sounds that are heard bring comfort, joy, beauty, harmony, and healing. Amen.

Day 28

Poem 12 (4:8–9) A

Disclosure: "Come with me"

Man
A. Come with me from Lebanon, my bride,
   come with me from Lebanon.
Descend from the crest of Amana,
   from the top of Senir, the summit of Hermon,
From the lion's dens
   and the mountain haunts of the leopards.
B. You have stolen my heart, my sister, my bride;
   you have stolen my heart
with one glance of your eyes,
   with one jewel of your necklace.

COME WITH ME

We are still at the wedding feast—or at least on the way to the honeymoon. For a brief moment, the passion subsides and we are allowed to take a deep breath and reflect on what is going on. Our poem on the surface is an invitation for the bride to come to her lover. On a deeper level, it is an exploration of what it means for a man and a woman to come together as one in body and soul.

> Come with me from Lebanon, my bride,
>   come with me from Lebanon.
> Descend from the crest of Amana,
>   from the top of Senir, the summit of Hermon,
> from the lion's dens
>   and the mountain haunts of the leopards.

When two human beings meet, it is as if we are coming together from far distant places. When we are in love, those places may seem lofty and exotic, but they remain at the same time equally remote and even dangerous. In either case, there is a distance that must be bridged and an intimacy that must be forged.

For our lover, it is as if his bride comes from these strange, exotic, and even inaccessible[15] places. Moses longed to see the "good land beyond the Jordan—that fine hill country and Lebanon," but he never made it there. The people of God regarded such places to be the exotic northern boundaries that marked the very outer limits of their land.[16] The rocky slopes of Lebanon's peaks were said to be covered with snow,[17] and for the Psalmist the heights of Hermon sang for joy unto the Lord.[18] It was also a wilderness of sorts, the mountain haunts of leopards and the place where lions dwelled in their dens. There is an element of danger and uncertainly in such places.[19]

For the lover, his bride is all these things; she is awesome but also in a sense inaccessible.[20] When we get to know another human being, where we are coming from is at once remote, inaccessible, and exotic. Love must accept the invitation to come and meet, to reveal yourself and tell who you are and where you come from. Who are the people and what are the places that mark the dark and the dangerous, as well as the lofty and exotic experiences that make up who we are? Unless there is that disclosure, says the man, you will remain loftily removed and largely inaccessible to me. His desire is that she be close to him.[21]

YOU HAVE STOLEN MY HEART

Once again, we are given insight into this thing called sex and why it is at once so sacred, mysterious, and sensual. In fact, the poem is about to break out yet another time in a rash of passion. The groom exclaims:

> You have stolen my heart, my sister, my bride;
> you have stolen my heart

15. Murphy, *Song*, 160.
16. Deuteronomy 3:25; 11:24; Joshua 1:4.
17. Jeremiah 18:14.
18. Psalm 42:6; 89:12; 133:3.
19. Gledhill, *Song*, 160.
20. Ibid.
21. Longman, *Song*, 150.

> with one glance of your eyes,
> with one jewel of your necklace.

Our translation here is tame to say the least. The phrase "stolen my heart" actually carries with it a sense of being ravished and aroused. One commentator has gone so far as to say that its meaning "can be missed only by dint of studious evasion."[22] At least two otherwise sober scholars suggest the translation, "You drive me crazy!" indicating that "she affects his heart so that it no longer functions normally."[23]

It is a phrase that is highly emotional, intensifying, and erotic.[24] It incorporates both ravishment and arousal, while at the same time conveying a sense of being "heartened, encouraged, emboldened."[25]

REFLECTION

There is here an anticipation of the man and woman coming together as one flesh, a union of the body and the soul, but it is a union that is at the same time a result of the deepest self-disclosure of the soul and the person. It is nothing less than the giving away of our self to another person.

It is that which gives sex its mystery, its sanctity, and its ecstasy, and which makes sex outside of marriage a promiscuity that necessarily prostitutes who we are as a human being. It is for this reason that the Scripture says, "Flee from sexual immorality. All other sins a man commits are outside his body, but he who sins sexually sins against his own body" (1 Cor 6:18). What Paul seems to have at least partly in mind here is that it eats away at our very person and self, not to mention our union with Christ and his body.[26]

The excitement, joy, and passion of the text come from the lover's anticipation of discovery, "Come with me." As someone has suggested, "Love elopes, God calls us, as he called Abraham, away from the security we knew, out of our old, familiar, little room, down the ladder of faith

---

22. Pope, *Song*, 480.
23. See also Longman, *Song*, 151; Keel, *Song*, 162.
24. Ibid.
25. Bloch and Bloch, *Song*, 175.
26. See the discussion in Morris, 1 *Corinthians*, 103.

and into his arms. Jesus called his disciples that way—just as a lover elopes with his beloved."[27]

MEDITATION

The Lord Shows Us Who He Is, and We Find Joy in His Presence

> The king is enthralled by your beauty;
> honor him, for he is your lord (Ps 45:11).

> Why spend money on what is not bread,
> and your labor on what does not satisfy?
> Listen, listen to me, and eat what is good,
> and your soul will delight in the richest of fare.
> Give ear and come to me;
> hear me, that your soul may live (Isa 55:2–3).

> For everything God created is good, and nothing is to be rejected if it is received with thanksgiving, because it is consecrated by the word of God and prayer (1 Tim 4:4–5).

PRAYER

Father, you have not hidden yourself from me. You have shown me who you are in your world, in your word, and even in this song.

Forgive me for trying to keep my life private from you. I have been afraid to share my life with you in the event that you might not like what you see. But of course, I have it all wrong. You have shared yourself with me in Christ, and you have revealed yourself in your word. You have caused your Spirit to show me everything about you.

Help me this day to share my life with others that in the transparency of grace they may find friendship, comfort, and strength. Amen.

---

27. Keel, *Song*, 126.

Day 29

Poem 12 (4:8–9) B

Friendship: "My sister, my bride"

Man
A. Come with me from Lebanon, my bride,
  come with me from Lebanon.
Descend from the crest of Amana,
  from the top of Senir, the summit of Hermon,
From the lion's dens
  and the mountain haunts of the leopards.

B. You have stolen my heart, my sister, my bride;
  you have stolen my heart
with one glance of your eyes,
  with one jewel of your necklace.

MY SISTER, MY BRIDE

Now comes my favorite phrase in all of the Song. Beginning in 4:12, it appears four times, culminating a few verses later in 5:1. To the shepherd she is "my sister, my bride."[28]

> How delightful is your love, my sister, my bride!
>   How much more pleasing is your love than wine,
>   and the fragrance of your perfume than any spice!

Two great things come together in this little phrase that always awaken the heart. To say that she is "my sister" is about a relationship that simply is. There is a closeness, permanence, and familiarity[29] that is as if it has always been there. To say that she is "my sister" means that she

---

28. Song of Songs 4:9, 10, 12; 5:1.
29. Carr, *Song*, 121.

understands everything about me. They have come to understand each other so closely that nothing is or can be hidden from each other. It is about a sharing of one's life with another to such an extent that even to strangers they "look" like each other. It is to begin to feel as if you have shared every moment of your life together.

We know that we have achieved this sense of being brother and sister when we are comfortable in public with each other. Near the end of the book, she will say, "If only you were to me like a brother, who was nursed at my mother's breasts! Then, if I found you outside, I would kiss you, and no one would despise me" (Song 8:1).

To say that she is "my bride" is about a relationship that has been chosen. At its core "my sister, my bride" is about belonging to another in a tender relatedness and togetherness.[30] It is not merely about present intimacy and future relationship but also closeness of relationship.[31] When he says "my sister," he indicates the closeness that he feels. When he says "my bride," he suggests the treasure that has been given to him.

There is an excitement here that goes back to the Garden of Eden, when God says that it is not good for the man to be alone. The woman is created and brought over to Adam, and he exclaims, "Wow!" Then in what is virtually a precursor to "my sister, my bride," he exults, "This is bone of my bone and flesh of my flesh."[32]

The nature and security of the relationship is such that it generates an ecstasy that is not lost upon the lovers. It is, according to the shepherd, delightful, more pleasing than wine, and more fragrant than any spice, no matter how exotic it may be.

It is about "current intimacy and future relationship."[33] And the wonderful insight here is that a passionate relationship over the long run is all about an enduring friendship that is close and committed, and summed up in the phrase, "My sister, my bride."

FRIENDSHIP

One Sunday morning, we were privileged to have a visiting head of state in attendance at our worship. He addressed the congregation briefly.

---

30. Keel, *Song*, 164.
31. Fox, *Love Songs*, 136.
32. Genesis 2:23. See Keel, *Song*, 163.
33. Fox, *Love Songs*, 136.

With secret service agents at the doors, we thought he might begin, "Good morning. It is good to be with you today." Instead he began, "Brothers and sisters in Christ." Right then and there, all barriers were broken down in the face of who we are in Christ and what *is*.

Friendships are about being brothers and sisters. It is about a relationship that simply *is*. We come down from the mountains of pride and share our lives with one another. We don't pretend to be what we are not, because brothers and sisters are made of the same flesh and blood and know each other's history. The same spiritual genes run through all of us. We share the same father, who is God, and the same mother, who the ancient fathers taught us is the church.[34] In the security of that relationship of being brothers and sisters in Christ, unconditional love and accountability begin to thrive and we can be open, honest, real, and there for one another.

REFLECTION

Once again, we have to say that what is true of human love is true of God's love because one takes its capacity from the other. It is here that we are reminded that Jesus is bone of our bone and flesh of our flesh. The gospels make a point of telling us that even when Christ revealed his glory to us, he did not stay up on the mountain, transcendent and unapproachable, but came down and lived among us.[35] The apostle Paul would put it this way:

> Who, being in very nature God,
>   did not consider equality with God something to be grasped,
> but made himself nothing,
>   taking the very nature of a servant,
>   being made in human likeness.
> And being found in appearance as a man,
>   he humbled himself
>   and became obedient to death—even death on a cross!
> (Phil 2:6-11).

The word became flesh. He knows all about us, he shares our lives, and he lays down his life for his brothers and sisters. Here is how the writer to the Hebrews put it:

---

34. First attributed to Cyprian, this thought is repeated in the Reformers such as John Calvin in *Institutes of the Christian Religion*, 1011.

35. Luke 9:28-37; John 1:14.

Both the one who makes men holy and those who are made holy are of the same family. So Jesus is not ashamed to call them brothers. He says,

> "I will declare your name to my brothers;
> in the presence of the congregation I will sing your praises."

And again,

> "I will put my trust in him."

And again he says,

> "Here am I, and the children God has given me."

Since the children have flesh and blood, he too shared in their humanity so that by his death he might destroy him who holds the power of death—that is, the devil—and free those who all their lives were held in slavery by their fear of death. For surely it is not angels he helps, but Abraham's descendants. For this reason he had to be made like his brothers in every way, in order that he might become a merciful and faithful high priest in service to God, and that he might make atonement for the sins of the people (Heb 2:11–17).

And he is not only our brother but he has also made us his bride. In the end, it is he who can truly say to us, "My sister, my bride." Nothing and no one can take that from us once we have known his redemption. It is a relationship that simply *is,* and it is a commitment sworn to us in his covenant. It is not surprising therefore that Christians have often used the proverb to describe their relationship to the Lord:

> A man of many companions may come to ruin,
> but there is a friend who sticks closer than a brother
> (Prov 18:24).

Meditation

Christ Is My Brother. He Has Brought Me into His Family. Nothing Can Change That.

> I will declare your name to my brothers;
> in the congregation I will praise you.
> You who fear the LORD, praise him!
> All you descendants of Jacob, honor him!
> Revere him, all you descendants of Israel!

> For he has not despised or disdained
>> the suffering of the afflicted one;
> he has not hidden his face from him
>> but has listened to his cry for help.
> From you comes the theme of my praise in the great assembly;
>> before those who fear you will I fulfill my vows
>
> (Ps 22:22–25).

And Jonathan made a covenant with David because he loved him as himself. Jonathan took off the robe he was wearing and gave it to David, along with his tunic, and even his sword, his bow and his belt (1 Sam 18:3–4).

Near the cross of Jesus stood his mother, his mother's sister, Mary the wife of Clopas, and Mary Magdalene. When Jesus saw his mother there, and the disciple whom he loved standing nearby, he said to his mother, "Dear woman, here is your son," and to the disciple, "Here is your mother" (John 19:25–27).

Both the one who makes men holy and those who are made holy are of the same family. So Jesus is not ashamed to call them brothers. He says,
> "I will declare your name to my brothers;
>> in the presence of the congregation I will sing your praises"
>
> (Heb 2:11–12).

PRAYER

Father, thank you for giving me Jesus as my brother. I am comforted by the fact that it is a relationship that simply is and that can never be changed. Thank you that you know all about me and yet you have chosen me for yourself.

Forgive me for thinking that we are worlds apart, when in fact you have drawn so close to me.

Teach me this day what it means to be a friend and a brother to others. Draw me into the family of Christ, that there the whole world may see the wonders of your love displayed. Amen.

Day 30

Poem 13 (4:10—5:1) A

Consummation: "Let my lover come"

Man
How delightful is your love, my sister, my bride!
　How much more pleasing is your love than wine,
　and the fragrance of your perfume than any spice!
Your lips drop sweetness as the honeycomb, my bride;
　milk and honey are under your tongue.
　The fragrance of your garments is like that of Lebanon.

You are a garden locked up, my sister, my bride;
　you are a spring enclosed, a sealed fountain.
Your plants are an orchard of pomegranates
　with choice fruits,
　with henna and nard,
　nard and saffron,
　calamus and cinnamon,
　with every kind of incense tree,
　with myrrh and aloes
　and all the finest spices.
You are a garden fountain,
　a well of flowing water
　streaming down from Lebanon.

Woman
Awake, north wind,
　and come, south wind!
Blow on my garden,
　that its fragrance may spread abroad.
Let my lover come into his garden.
　and taste its choice fruits.

Man
I have come into my garden, my sister, my bride;
   I have gathered my myrrh with my spice.
I have eaten my honeycomb and my honey;
   I have drunk my wine and my milk.

Chorus
Eat, O friends, and drink;
   drink your fill, O lovers.

After a brief interlude (4:8–9) we are back at the wedding feast. Once again, the newlyweds continue their *wasf*, the game that they play in front of "everyone here present," in which each tells what it is that they so like about the other. It is still the man who is speaking.

How delightful is your love, my sister, my bride!
   How much more pleasing is your love than wine,
   and the fragrance of your perfume than any spice!
Your lips drop sweetness as the honeycomb, my bride;
   milk and honey are under your tongue.
   The fragrance of your garments is like that of Lebanon.

THE GARDEN

As the man's imagination runs away with him, he is off to the honeymoon. What immediately strikes us is the sense of anticipation that overcomes the man and of entering places where he has never been before. As far as he is concerned, he is about to enter paradise! It is as if he has come to the very Garden of Eden, a place, as the name suggests, of great delights, joy, and rapture.[36]

Gardens have always been places of great delight. Genesis makes reference, even after the Fall, to the place called the garden of the Lord. The character cast as Solomon in Ecclesiastes would boast of his great gardens filled with every kind of fruit tree. Most treasured of all in the Ancient Near East was what we might call the secret garden. We know from both Jeremiah and Nehemiah that a royal garden existed in the courts of Jerusalem. The Psalmist would describe the righteous prospering like an olive tree flourishing in the house of the Lord.[37]

---

36. See Carr, *Song*, 56. The garden theme is most helpfully explored in Keel, *Song*, 169–73.

37. Genesis 13:10; Ecclesiastes 2:5; Jeremiah 39:4; Nehemiah 3:15; Psalm 52:8.

In the Ancient Near East, to have a private garden in the midst of a city, surrounded by a wall and with its own water supply, was something that only kings and princes could afford. As our young man anticipates entering his garden, his passion has taken him over the top. It is, he says, a garden filled with saffron, calamus, cinnamon, the incense tree, myrrh, aloes, and spices.

No garden could have all of these plants because they are not even all to be found in Israel. They are plants that come from far-flung, exotic places.[38] That is exactly his point. If previously he had lovingly made his way over her eyes and hair, lips and cheeks, and soon become enraptured elsewhere, now he lovingly continues his journey onward.[39] As far as he is concerned, she is a garden filled with the delights of famous, faraway places that only the most privileged know anything about. Cool winds blow and spread their scents of joy and rapture over the garden. He is filled with anticipation.

> You are a garden locked up, my sister, my bride;
>   you are a spring enclosed, a sealed fountain.
> Your plants are an orchard of pomegranates
>   with choice fruits,
>   with henna and nard,
>   nard and saffron,
>   calamus and cinnamon,
>   with every kind of incense tree,
>   with myrrh and aloes
>   and all the finest spices.
> You are a garden fountain,
>   a well of flowing water
>   streaming down from Lebanon.

Then anticipation gives way to invitation.[40] This is, after all, his wedding, and she is his bride. The woman exclaims:

> Awake, north wind,
>   and come, south wind!

---

38. Murphy, *Song*, 160–61, Fox, *Love Songs*, 138.

39. Longman, in *Song*, 152, indicates, "The metaphor is that of a garden, which ... is not only the place of lovemaking but a metaphor of the woman's most private and intimate part. The same is true of the fountain imagery. . . . He enters the garden and partakes of its pleasures, while the chorus celebrates their union."

40. The description of the movement from anticipation through invitation, to consummation and affirmation is from Gledhill, *Song*, 164–67.

> Blow on my garden,
>> that its fragrance may spread abroad.
> Let my lover come into his garden.
>> and taste its choice fruits.

As we might expect, invitation gives ways to consummation.

> I have come into my garden, my sister, my bride;
>> I have gathered my myrrh with my spice.
> I have eaten my honeycomb and my honey;
>> I have drunk my wine and my milk.

And finally, consummation gives way to the affirmation of the chorus.

> Eat, O friends, and drink;
>> drink your fill, O lovers.

BEAUTY

Clearly, there is an erotic passion that is present everywhere here. This is not unique imagery. There are parallels to be found in the poetry of the Ancient Near East, especially in the use of the garden, that are very explicit.[41]

We are not wrong to take a look at how this imagery was used in its Ancient Near Eastern context. As Christians, we are not afraid of passion. However, if we read the Song only through this lens, we will miss the point.

As one commentator has suggested, the book retains "innocent delight . . . since it relies on metaphor rather than explicit statement, the language of the Song is restrained and delicate even where it is most sensuous. And because the lovers seem new to love, tender and proud and full of discovery, their words have a kind of purity . . ."[42]

So it is not just that "as any poet knows, allusion and innuendo stimulate the imagination more than graphic images."[43] It is that here we are at the very climax of this book, at its emotional peak,[44] and we discover that the passion, and it is real passion, has been transformed in the Song of Songs by what we can only call beauty. There is a delicacy

---

41. "In Arabic *shalch* can mean 'vagina.' The Sumerian and Egyptian poems quoted previously associate 'garden,' 'canal,' 'womb,' and 'vagina.' Even legal texts (Lev 12:7; 20:18) use 'fountain' or 'spring' as a metaphor for the female genitalia." Keel, *Song*, 176.

42. Bloch and Bloch, *Song*, 4.

43. Exum, *Song*, 177.

44. Carr, *Song*, 127, Gledhill, *Song*, 164.

and sensibility that accompany the description of the erotic. This is an exquisite poem because it is unmatched in achieving its combination of purity, passion, fragrance, and beauty. It is as if we have returned to the Garden of Eden with all its delights and our lovers find themselves naked and unashamed.

We do well to remember that this passionate text begins with the line, "How delightful is your love, my sister, my bride!" There is a purity here that is lost on those who will not take the time to believe that it is possible. When true friendship and covenant commitment come together, they result in a purity of passion.

That truth is not lost on the community of friends, repeatedly described as the "daughters of Jerusalem."[45] They represent the community of faith that finds its expression as nowhere else in the ancient world in Jerusalem. More than that, they function as an invitation to the reader.[46] It is they who erupt in an excited affirmation.[47]

> Eat, O friends, and drink;
> drink your fill, O lovers.

REFLECTION

As this song illustrates, there are four things that a great life cannot be lived without. They are purity, passion, community, and beauty. Purity is about the integrity of faithfulness, passion is about strength of purpose, community is about life lived in relationship to others, and beauty is what happens when these all come together in a life lived in proper harmony with God, the world, our neighbors, and ourselves. All are integral parts of the love of God and then of our neighbors as ourselves.[48]

MEDITATION

The Lord Is Pure and Trustworthy, Bringing Joy to His People

> All your robes are fragrant with myrrh and aloes and cassia;
> from palaces adorned with ivory
> the music of the strings makes you glad. . . .

---

45. See Song of Songs 1:5; 2:7; 3:5, 10; 5:8, 16; 8:4.
46. Exum, *Song*, 7.
47. Gledhill, *Song*, 167.
48. Matthew 22:37–39.

All glorious is the princess within her chamber;
> her gown is interwoven with gold.
In embroidered garments she is led to the king;
> her virgin companions follow her
> and are brought to you.
They are led in with joy and gladness;
> they enter the palace of the king (Ps 45:8, 13–15).

Drink water from your own cistern,
> running water from your own well. . . .
May your fountain be blessed,
> and may you rejoice in the wife of your youth.
A loving doe, a graceful deer—
> may her breasts satisfy you always,
> may you ever be captivated by her love (Prov 5:15, 18–19).

To the pure, all things are pure, but to those who are corrupted and do not believe, nothing is pure. In fact, both their minds and consciences are corrupted (Titus 1:15).

The Spirit and the bride say, "Come!" And let him who hears say, "Come!" Whoever is thirsty, let him come; and whoever wishes, let him take the free gift of the water of life (Rev 22:17).

PRAYER

Father, I praise you for already bringing us back into the garden even if weeds and woes still grow there. I am so glad that already you are filling my life with inexplicable joy and passion.

Forgive me for ever doubting that you have begun your new creation in Jesus Christ. When I have done so, it has been because I have wanted to live in the old way. I am sorry.

Teach me this day to live my life with purity, passion, beauty, and in community. Allow my life to be a blessing to others as it is lived in the strength of purpose, in the integrity of faithfulness, and in harmony with you. Amen.

Day 31

Poem 13 (4:10—5:1) B

Realization: "I have come into my garden"

Man
How delightful is your love, my sister, my bride!
  How much more pleasing is your love than wine,
  and the fragrance of your perfume than any spice!
Your lips drop sweetness as the honeycomb, my bride;
  milk and honey are under your tongue.
  The fragrance of your garments is like that of Lebanon.

You are a garden locked up, my sister, my bride;
  you are a spring enclosed, a sealed fountain.
Your plants are an orchard of pomegranates
  with choice fruits,
  with henna and nard,
  nard and saffron,
  calamus and cinnamon,
  with every kind of incense tree,
  with myrrh and aloes
  and all the finest spices.
You are a garden fountain,
  a well of flowing water
  streaming down from Lebanon.

Woman
Awake, north wind,
  and come, south wind!
Blow on my garden,
  that its fragrance may spread abroad.
Let my lover come into his garden.
  and taste its choice fruits.

Man
I have come into my garden, my sister, my bride;
  I have gathered my myrrh with my spice.
I have eaten my honeycomb and my honey;
  I have drunk my wine and my milk.

Chorus
Eat, O friends, and drink;
  drink your fill, O lovers.

DISCOVERY

We have seen our lovers swept away by the expectation of their coming together as man and woman. It is the anticipation of discovery. We have heard the refrain before, "Do not awaken love until it so desires."[49] Well, now the time has come.

The woman has been a locked garden and a sealed fountain, signs of a previously inaccessible virginity.[50] Now, long anticipation and exclusive participation gives way, as it always does, to an excited invitation and fulfilled consummation.

This is their wedding night, and it is good. Our lover is like a king entering and enjoying the delights of the royal garden. This is not about so-called lovemaking that is hidden away from sight in dark places. It follows their public declaration of love and covenant that has taken place in their marriage.

FRIENDS AND LOVERS

We have previously met the remarkable little phrase, "my sister, my bride," but now it is repeated three times over in the context of this passionate exchange.[51] The point surely is that this is not so much a celebration of sex, although it is that as well, as it is a celebration of *their* intimacy, friendship, and passionate closeness of relationship.[52]

---

49. Song of Songs 2:7; 3:5.
50. Longman, *Song*, 155.
51. Song of Songs 4:9, 10, 12; 5:1.
52. Fox, *Love Songs*, 136.

She has already shared so much about her past, the abuse that she has experienced, and the anxiety and insecurity that followed.[53] There is more to come, but already they are like brother and sister, and the closeness and the intimacy is matched with the commitment and covenant. The result is a delightful friendship and passion of "my sister, my bride."

Indeed, the whole literary character of the Song that functions by way of dialogue emphasizes the importance of mutual respect and reciprocity. "The poem is in dialogue form, bride and groom singing to each other antiphonally, because love is essentially dialogue, and the form of a perfect poem manifests the content; the medium manifests the message."[54]

MUTUAL EXCHANGE

Not surprisingly, the poem is characterized by a mutual exchange of anticipation and participation. What sort of passion can we have if it is not mutual? In fact, a man finds his greatest pleasure in seeing the delight of the woman, so true passion is an excited celebration of one another. Sex may take place where one animal takes advantage of another, but real passion is a mutual exploration of love, commitment, and covenant.

The poem knows nothing of the idea that men and women are qualitatively different in their sexuality. To the contrary, the delights of this moment are no less real for the woman than for the man. This garden is hers to share with her lover, and she can't wait to do so. Their exchange leaves no doubt that it is good.

> Woman
> Awake, north wind,
>   and come, south wind!
> Blow on my garden,
>   that its fragrance may spread abroad.
> Let my lover come into his garden.
>   and taste its choice fruits.
>
> Man
> I have come into my garden, my sister, my bride;
>   I have gathered my myrrh with my spice.

---

53. See Song of Songs 1:5–7; 3:1–4.
54. Kreeft, *Three Philosophies*, 105.

> I have eaten my honeycomb and my honey;
> I have drunk my wine and my milk.

REFLECTION

Once again, we must note that this is about a healthy, positive, and passionate view of life that is celebrated by their religious community of friends. The "daughters of Jerusalem" exclaim:

> Eat, O friends, and drink;
> drink your fill, O lovers.

Put in contemporary terms, the people of God wish to say that in the midst of broken relationships and prevalent divorce, there is another way. It is discovered in the place where friendship and love meet in mutual delight and in an exclusive abandonment one for the other. "Love is perpetually reinforcing: the more we love, the more we are loved, and the more we are loved, the more we love. There is no necessary limit to this process. . . . When love wears down that is due to external friction. . . . love itself has no tendency to wear down, only to increase."[55]

We discover this no less in our relationship with the Lord. This is what God has given us, and it is good.

MEDITATION

The Lord Brings Us into His Garden and Gives Us New Life

> But I am like an olive tree
>   flourishing in the house of God;
> I trust in God's unfailing love
>   for ever and ever.
> I will praise you forever for what you have done;
>   in your name I will hope, for your name is good.
>
> I will praise you in the presence of your saints (Ps 52:8–9).

> Build houses and settle down; plant gardens and eat what they produce. Marry and have sons and daughters; find wives for your sons and give your daughters in marriage, so that they too may

---

55. Ibid., 106.

have sons and daughters. Increase in number there; do not decrease. Also, seek the peace and prosperity of the city to which I have carried you into exile. Pray to the LORD for it, because if it prospers, you too will prosper (Jer 29:5–7).

But seek first his kingdom and his righteousness, and all these things will be given to you as well (Matt 6:33).

For from him and through him and to him are all things. To him be the glory forever! Amen (Rom 11:36).

PRAYER

Father, I praise you for bringing us back into the garden and for the relationship that we have with you there. Thank you for teaching us to praise you so that we can have a mutual interchange and I am not always "taking" from you.

Forgive me, Lord, when my relationship with you has been all about me. That happens far more than it should, and it always leaves me anxious and exhausted.

Teach me to enjoy you this day and to always be in conversation with you. Help me to change my one-way relationships so that I will learn both to give and to receive. Amen.

Day 32

Poem 13 (4:10—5:1) B

Contrast: "Broken down walls"

Man
How delightful is your love, my sister, my bride!
   How much more pleasing is your love than wine,
   and the fragrance of your perfume than any spice!
Your lips drop sweetness as the honeycomb, my bride;
   milk and honey are under your tongue.
   The fragrance of your garments is like that of Lebanon.

You are a garden locked up, my sister, my bride;
   you are a spring enclosed, a sealed fountain.
Your plants are an orchard of pomegranates
   with choice fruits,
   with henna and nard,
   nard and saffron,
   calamus and cinnamon,
   with every kind of incense tree,
   with myrrh and aloes
   and all the finest spices.
You are a garden fountain,
   a well of flowing water
   streaming down from Lebanon.

Woman
Awake, north wind,
   and come, south wind!
Blow on my garden,
   that its fragrance may spread abroad.
Let my lover come into his garden.
   and taste its choice fruits.

Man
I have come into my garden, my sister, my bride;
  I have gathered my myrrh with my spice.
I have eaten my honeycomb and my honey;
  I have drunk my wine and my milk.

Chorus
Eat, O friends, and drink;
  drink your fill, O lovers.

A WORD FOR THE WISE

We are now at the end of our part 2, and we need to take a break for a moment. It is entirely possible that the beauty of our lovers' garden has left us with a deep sense of loss in regard to our own. What do we do about it?

It has often been noted[56] that there is a parallel passage to our song found in Proverbs (5:1–23). In fact, it is all but impossible to talk about our text without reference to it because Proverbs also explores the image of the garden and even makes reference to honey under the tongue! What is striking, however, is that it does so by way of contrast and opposite example.

> For the lips of an adulteress drip honey,
>   and her speech is smoother than oil;
> but in the end she is bitter as gall,
>   sharp as a double-edged sword.
> Her feet go down to death;
>   her steps lead straight to the grave.
> She gives no thought to the way of life;
>   her paths are crooked, but she knows it not (Prov 5:3–6).

It is not that Proverbs explores our theme only by way of warning. It knows the same positive example of the Song. It contains the insight implicit in our Song, that the best way to disarm addiction and to take the sting out of the forbidden is to develop positive, respectful, and passionate relationships, both in terms of the Lord and the one with whom we share our life and love.

---

56. For example, Fox, *Love Songs*, 137; Gledhill, *Song*, 165; Longman, *Song*, 155; Murphy, *Song*, 161.

> Drink water from your own cistern,
>   running water from your own well.
> Should your springs overflow in the streets,
>   your streams of water in the public squares?
> Let them be yours alone,
>   never to be shared with strangers.
> May your fountain be blessed,
>   and may you rejoice in the wife of your youth.
> A loving doe, a graceful deer—
>   may her breasts satisfy you always,
>   may you ever be captivated by her love.
> Why be captivated, my son, by an adulteress?
>   Why embrace the bosom of another man's wife?
> For a man's ways are in full view of the LORD,
>   and he examines all his paths (Prov 5:15–21).

Yet, even here we must say that this passage is not about a shallow moralism that says, "Don't do this, do that, and all will be well." Set in its context of the library of the Scriptures, it is written for the people of God who have been redeemed out of slavery in Egypt and who go up to the temple to have the blood of the sacrifice sprinkled upon them. It answers the same question as the Song. "When we are numbered among the people of God and have been redeemed out of slavery; how do we live in a world gone wrong?"

BROKEN DOWN WALLS

The more pressing question that might come to mind in light of the beauty of our Song is, "What do I do if the walls have already been broken down, the foxes have ruined the vineyard, and the garden is trampled down and overgrown?"

We should begin again with Proverbs, and with taking responsibility for ourselves and our actions. It is called repentance. Scripture is quite blunt.

> At the end of your life you will groan,
>   when your flesh and body are spent.
> You will say, "How I hated discipline!
>   How my heart spurned correction!
> I would not obey my teachers
>   or listen to my instructors.
> I have come to the brink of utter ruin
>   in the midst of the whole assembly" (Prov 5:11–14).

However, having said that, we realize that the Scriptures are never taken by surprise. The Lord understood Israel to be his bride, and if there is any one thing that must be noted of Israel as the bride, it is the history of her unfaithfulness. In the most explicit and shocking of terms, Ezekiel will tell of the Lord's providing for the orphan Israel, taking her to be his bride, and treating her royally, only to see her trust in her beauty and use her fame to become a prostitute.[57] The whole story of the book of Hosea is a similar allegory.

The Psalmist, while not denying that the broken-down walls are entirely of Israel's own doing, also sees them as somehow being of God's doing. He understands that through them we come to long for salvation and yearn for grace. More than that, he teaches us to long for a Savior who will be the Christ.

> Why have you broken down its walls
>   so that all who pass by pick its grapes?
> Boars from the forest ravage it
>   and the creatures of the field feed on it.
> Return to us, O God Almighty!
>   Look down from heaven and see!
> Watch over this vine,
>   the root your right hand has planted,
>   the son you have raised up for yourself.
>
> Your vine is cut down, it is burned with fire;
>   at your rebuke your people perish.
> Let your hand rest on the man at your right hand,
>   the son of man you have raised up for yourself.
> Then we will not turn away from you;
>   revive us, and we will call on your name.
> Restore us, O LORD God Almighty;
>   make your face shine upon us,
>   that we may be saved (Ps 80:12–19).

REFLECTION

The great thing about a garden is that when weeded, tended, and nourished, it has a remarkable way of springing back up again! Spiritual and emotional renewal come from being one with Christ, as the branch is

---

57. Ezekiel 16.

in the tree. The Lord is the source both of new life and refreshment and renewal.

As we have seen in the Song, "There is no upper limit, no wall to love. And there is no drag, no gravity built into love. When love wears down it is due to external friction, not internal friction: love itself has no tendency to wear down, only to increase."[58] This is the renewing power of God's love and of his relationship with us.

At the same time, these Scriptures also help us to understand that the Lord is not a pathetic lover, but someone who always wins back his love and never loses any who belong to him.[59] The prophet Hosea would go through the gut-wrenching unfaithfulness and promiscuity of his wife, but in so doing, he would come to understand the Lord's love, discipline, care for, and restoration of his bride.

In the end, we understand that it is the Lord who comes knocking on the door, weeding out the vines, building up the walls, and restoring the beauty of the garden. He knows what he is doing, and he always wins. Grace says that; faith grasps it.

MEDITATION

The Lord Is at Work in My Life, and He Knows What He Is Doing

> Sing to the LORD, you saints of his;
>   praise his holy name.
> For his anger lasts only a moment,
>   but his favor lasts a lifetime;
> weeping may remain for a night,
>   but rejoicing comes in the morning (Ps 30:4–5).

> "Do not be afraid; you will not suffer shame.
>   Do not fear disgrace; you will not be humiliated.
> You will forget the shame of your youth
>   and remember no more the reproach of your widowhood.
> For your Maker is your husband—
>   the LORD Almighty is his name—

---

58. Kreeft, *Three Philosophies*, 106.

59. Jesus pointedly said, "And this is the will of him who sent me, that I shall lose none of all that he has given me, but raise them up at the last day. For my Father's will is that everyone who looks to the Son and believes in him shall have eternal life, and I will raise him up at the last day" (John 6:39–40).

> the Holy One of Israel is your Redeemer;
>   he is called the God of all the earth.
> The LORD will call you back
>   as if you were a wife deserted and distressed in spirit—
> a wife who married young,
>   only to be rejected," says your God.
> "For a brief moment I abandoned you,
>   but with deep compassion I will bring you back."
> (Isa 54:4–7).

> If anyone does not remain in me, he is like a branch that is thrown away and withers; such branches are picked up, thrown into the fire and burned. If you remain in me and my words remain in you, ask whatever you wish, and it will be given you. This is to my Father's glory, that you bear much fruit, showing yourselves to be my disciples (John 15:6–8).

> Since we have now been justified by his blood, how much more shall we be saved from God's wrath through him! For if, when we were God's enemies, we were reconciled to him through the death of his Son, how much more, having been reconciled, shall we be saved through his life! Not only is this so, but we also rejoice in God through our Lord Jesus Christ, through whom we have now received reconciliation (Rom 5:9–11).

PRAYER

Lord, I praise you for making all things new, that you are never taken by surprise, and that you are always at work to accomplish your purposes in our lives.

Forgive me for breaking your laws, acting as your enemy, and being a perfect fool.

Fill me with confidence that you are at work in my life and that your desire is that I should be a garden once broken down but now resplendent with the fruits of your own planting. Amen.

Part 3

Lost and Found 5:2—8:14

> Where has your lover gone,
>   most beautiful of women?
> Which way did your lover turn,
>   that we may look for him with you? 6:1

Section 6

Fear and Joy, 5:2—8:4

Day 33

Poem 14 (5:2–8) A

Abuse: "They bruised me"

Woman
I slept but my heart was awake.
  Listen! My lover is knocking:
"Open to me, my sister, my darling,
  my dove, my flawless one.
My head is drenched with dew,
  my hair with the dampness of the night."
I have taken off my robe—
  must I put it on again?
I have washed my feet—
  must I soil them again?
My lover thrust his hand through the latch-opening;
  my heart began to pound for him.
I arose to open for my lover,
  and my hands dripped with myrrh,
my fingers with flowing myrrh,
  on the handles of the lock.
I opened for my lover,
  but my lover had left; he was gone.
  My heart sank at his departure.
I looked for him but did not find him.
  I called him but he did not answer.
The watchmen found me
  as they made their rounds in the city.
They beat me, they bruised me;
  they took away my cloak,
  those watchmen of the walls!

> O daughters of Jerusalem, I charge you—
> if you find my lover,
> what will you tell him?
> > Tell him I am faint with love.

A NEW SECTION

With this poem we have entered part 3 of the Song, which we have called "Lost and Found."[1] We have emerged from the calm of part 2, which was the eye of the storm. As one commentator has suggested, "We have left our lovers enjoying the bliss of the marriage bed, and it seems a pity to have to wrench ourselves away from contemplating their joy. But they cannot stay in bed forever, and a new scenario presents itself to us in the next cycle of Songs."[2]

Now as we emerge out of the central section of the Song, we are immediately thrust back into the swirling passions that surround the center. We remember that the book had begun with a stunning outburst of passion on the part of the woman, "Let him kiss me . . ." We saw the lovers locked in praise of one another, but we also observed as they were torn apart by insecurity. As they went off to the shepherd's hut, we noted that praise and affirmation brought healing, security, and self-confidence. We heard them declare that the winter is past, the season of singing has come, and that the blossoming vines are everywhere spreading their fragrance. Then we heard of the foxes digging away at the roots of the vine. We saw the woman descend into the long, dark night of the soul, restlessly turning on her bed, seeking her lover, and being accosted by the watchmen of the night. We noted that she again found the one her heart loves, and we all but blushed at the ecstasy of the couple as they entered into their secret garden to become one flesh and to share their bodies and their souls.

As we emerge from out of the wedding sequence, we find ourselves caught up once again in the storm that is love and passion, in this thing that we call relationships. What is it that we find?

---

1. This designation comes from Carr, *Song*, 130.
2. Gledhill, *Song*, 175.

A LOVER REBUFFED

In a sense, the "story" that we enter now is simple enough. As has happened before, the woman is lying on her bed in the middle of the night. It is not quite clear if she is dreaming. She appears to be asleep but somehow awake at the same time. The scene is almost surreal,[3] even Freudian with its dream-like sequences. This is as it is should be, because this is poetry. What we can discern to be going on literally is not as important as what is said to be happening.

The lover is at the door and is knocking, but she is slow to get up. She complains that she has taken off her robe for the night, washed her feet, and gone to bed. No sooner does she say this than her lover puts his hand through the latch of the door and she finds herself awakened and aroused. As she goes to open the door, her hands are dripping as it were with myrrh, but her lover has gone.

There is a great deal of sexual tension here.[4] Once again, we have to be careful not to get into such detailed explanation that we destroy the beauty, the poetry, and the intentional ambiguity of the moment. Then what is really being said to us is all but lost.[5]

At the same time, we do not shrink from the expression of their sexuality. We are even willing to admit that to a large extent Freud was right when he suggested that sexuality permeates the development of ourselves as human beings. We have no fear in saying that because Genesis tells us that we are created male and female. We remember that when the first man and woman came together as one flesh, God said that it was good, and Adam exclaimed:

> This is now bone of my bones
> and flesh of my flesh.[6]

More fundamentally, what this indicates is that we are created in God's image, capable of desiring and needing this thing called love and

---

3. Longman, *Song*, 165.

4. Longman suggests that "*feet* are a well-known euphemism for genitalia both male (Exod 4:25; Judg 3:24;1 Sam 24:4 [English 24:3]; Ruth 3:4,7) and female (Deut 28:57; Ezek 16:15), in the Old Testament. . . . We might add that the noun *hand*, said to be thrust through the hole itself, is used occasionally in Hebrew for the male penis (Isa 57:8–10)." Ibid., 166–67. Pope is even more explicit in *Song*, 519.

5. Murphy believes that "there is not sufficient reason to see here a reference to sexual activity." *Song*, 171.

6. Genesis 2:23.

relationships. In the one God there exists a perfect union and communion of Father, Son, and Holy Spirit. Relationships are, therefore, at the core of who we are as human beings. In the end, this text is not about sex but about relational tension, as it is signified to us most powerfully in the passion, arousal, and disappointment of the lovers.

IN SEARCH OF LOVE

Her heart sinks at his departure, and once again, she goes in search of him. As has happened before,[7] she is met by the watchmen. This time they are not only unable or unwilling to help her, but they also do more than that. They beat her, bruise her, and treat her like a woman of the night. They tear off her clothes and leave her naked and exposed. As has happened before, the absence or the departure of the significant man in her life and the presence of abusive males in her surrounding culture come home to haunt and hurt her.

Everything has gone wrong. The tender approach of the lover has given way to the unexpected apathy of the woman.[8] The joyful and intimate union of the previous poem has been replaced by isolation and alienation.[9]

MY HEART SANK

Relationships are like this. They can be dreadfully confusing. Sometimes we are not quite sure if we are awake or asleep or just what is going on in them. On the one hand, relationships can seem to encroach upon us too much. There are times when we want to be alone with our inner selves. On the other hand, the moment we push others away, we find ourselves longing for them with a passion. There is an irrationality to love. The tension between presence and absence becomes excruciating. We want our space but are soon afraid of the loss, and we become overcome with anxiety.[10]

This tension between space and intimacy and between presence and absence awakens powerful passions fed by anxiety, desire, longing, and fear. In our search for the recovery of intimacy and the power of

---

7. Song of Songs 3:1–5.
8. Carr, *Song*, 130.
9. Longman, *Song*, 160.
10. See the discussion in Gledhill, *Song*, 180–81.

presence, there are few who understand, and many who not only don't help, but actually hurt. In the end, we find ourselves beaten up, bruised, naked, exposed, and above all, deeply confused.

THE LOVER AS POET

That is what the text "says." It is about the poetry of life, love, and relationships, and in a sense, we simply need to leave it right there. It is enough to live as poets, because when we discover this ability as human beings to feel and to sense, to know and to understand, and to express and to articulate, we have already weathered the worst of the storm. Love is not a science; it is a passion. Relationships are not learned in a lab; they are discovered in the storm.

This is not about what we do; it is about who we are. Until we understand the hurt, the anxiety, the alienation, the loss, the "bruised-ness," and the nakedness of relationships gone wrong, we will never know what it means to be a lover. The whole point of love is that lovers know and understand, and it is enough to have one who knows and understands.

REFLECTION

It is precisely at this point that we may begin to enter into the heart of God to discover what it is that he feels when his bride pulls away, only to come rushing back passionately to him. It is here that we begin to understand what the Scriptures mean when they say that "the Word became flesh and made his dwelling among us" (John 1:14).

Our eyes are opened, and we begin to discern what it means to say that we can have one with us who has been there before us, knows all about us, and goes through it all with us. We discover the depths of his love as he agonized in the garden, considering what it would mean to be "separated" from his Father in the passion of the cross. He knew what it would entail to bear our sins, and yet he desired above all else to do the will of his Father in heaven.[11] We begin to realize what the prophet means when he tells us that "he was wounded for our transgressions, he was bruised for our iniquities" (Isa 53:5 KJV).

No sooner have we turned him away than we go in search of his love once again. In gratitude for that love on the cross, which turned

---

11. Luke 22:39–44.

aside God's displeasure from us, we find our passion, our love, and our life. We cannot live without him.

MEDITATION

The Lord Knows the Depths of Our Innermost Feelings and Resolves Them in His Love

> Listen to my prayer, O God,
>   do not ignore my plea;
>   hear me and answer me.
> My thoughts trouble me and I am distraught . . .
>   I said, "Oh, that I had the wings of a dove!
>   I would fly away and be at rest—
> I would flee far away
>   and stay in the desert;
> I would hurry to my place of shelter,
>   far from the tempest and storm." . . .
> Evening, morning and noon
>   I cry out in distress,
>   and he hears my voice.
> He ransoms me unharmed
>   from the battle waged against me,
>   even though many oppose me. . . .
>
> Cast your cares on the LORD
>   and he will sustain you;
>   he will never let the righteous fall
> (Ps 55:1–2, 6–8, 17–18, 22).

> But he was pierced for our transgressions,
>   he was crushed for our iniquities;
> the punishment that brought us peace was upon him,
>   and by his wounds we are healed (Isa 53:5).

> Jesus wept (John 11:35).

> Such a high priest meets our need . . . The point of what we are saying is this: We do have such a high priest, who sat down at the right hand of the throne of the Majesty in heaven, and who serves in the sanctuary, the true tabernacle set up by the Lord, not by man (Heb 7:26, 8:1–2).

PRAYER

Father, I thank you that you know and understand all about me, and that when I am confused, you are not!

Forgive me for all the times when I have tried to turn you away.

This day, help me to live as one who knows and understands what others are going through. Out of the knowledge of your care and love, allow me to be a part of the transforming power of your presence in the world. Amen.

Day 34

Poem 14 (5:2–8) B

Understanding: "What will you tell him?"

Woman
I slept but my heart was awake.
   Listen! My lover is knocking:
"Open to me, my sister, my darling,
   my dove, my flawless one.
My head is drenched with dew,
   my hair with the dampness of the night."
I have taken off my robe—
   must I put it on again?
I have washed my feet—
   must I soil them again?
My lover thrust his hand through the latch-opening;
   my heart began to pound for him.
I arose to open for my lover,
   and my hands dripped with myrrh,
my fingers with flowing myrrh,
   on the handles of the lock.
I opened for my lover,
   but my lover had left; he was gone.
   My heart sank at his departure.
I looked for him but did not find him.
   I called him but he did not answer.
The watchmen found me
   as they made their rounds in the city.
They beat me, they bruised me;

> they took away my cloak,
> those watchmen of the walls!
>
> O daughters of Jerusalem, I charge you—
> if you find my lover,
> what will you tell him?
> Tell him I am faint with love.

We have felt with the Shulammite the sheer pain of loss and anxiety and experienced the hurt, the alienation, the loss, the "bruised-ness," and the nakedness of relationships gone wrong. We understand that it is part and parcel of what it means to love and be loved. In the lines of the poet, we have found reflected our very own lives and experiences.

We are also willing to admit that as human beings we are not only poets, but we are also Philistines,[12] and we will not go away entirely happy if we have not been given ten things to do to "fix it." Still, we must insist that love is a matter of the heart, and giving ourselves ten things to do to "be successful" is more often than not the pride of self-will rather than the heart of the humble that finds true love. Having said that, we should begin to talk about the practical aspects of love that we discover in our song.

WHAT WENT WRONG?

So, what do we make of the man's knocking on the door, coming in presumably from tending the sheep all night long, and ready, it seems, for love?

Our culture tells us, "Men are like that. They only have one thing on their minds." Wiser commentators of our culture will say that men and women approach sexuality in different ways. Because men knock down the door and thrust their hands into the latch while women approach more slowly, tenderly, and sensitively, it does not mean that men and women are qualitatively different in their sexuality.

After all, this is the woman's song. In the culture of this book, the woman initiates love more often than the man. This is "her book."[13] She is filled with passion. "Most of the lines are hers, including the first work in the poem—'Kiss me'—and the last. As a rule she is the more forceful

---

12. These were enemies of the people of God, like Goliath (1 Sam 17). They were harsh, pragmatic, and unfeeling.

13. Carr, *Song*, 130.

of the two . . ."[14] Truth be told, as the man knocks on the door, he approaches her with sensitivity and love, describing her as "my sister, my darling, my dove, my flawless one."

So what has happened? A number of commentators suggest that our episode is nothing more than a lover's tease gone wrong,[15] "a coy pretense intended to tease the eager male."[16] Or perhaps it is the woman's hesitancy that has led to the man's changing his mind. Equally, it could be that the man is impetuous and impatient and the lovers have lost the opportune moment, succumbing to a cycle of "when he wants to, she does not; when she wants to, he does not (any longer)."[17]

In any event, the poem is not about determining guilt. We do the emotional complexity of the lovers' parting a disservice if we try to apportion responsibility.[18] It is seldom as simple as that. We may even agree that the woman shows a certain "petulant unwillingness,"[19] but even that should be understood as a symptom of the fact that the lovers have fallen out of sync, and misunderstanding and petty alienation are the result. The real point is that the lovers have lost their way for a moment, and that is what it is like in relationships.

I, MY, ME

Yet having said that, from a literary point of view, we cannot help but notice that in the previous poem (4:1—5:1), the words *you* and *your* appear some twenty-six times in seventeen verses. It was all about "your eyes," "your hair," "your teeth," "your lips," "your temples," "your neck," "your breasts." Even if we grant that this poem is a first-person narrative, which it is, we are nevertheless struck by the fact that "I," "me," and "my" appear thirty-five times in seven verses. They go off like shots in the night, appearing ten times in the first verse alone. "I, my, my, me, my, my, my, my, my, my."

---

14. Bloch and Bloch, *Song*, 4.
15. For example, Murphy, *Song*, 170.
16. Pope, *Song*, 515.
17. Keel, *Song*, 194, 186.
18. See the discussion of ibid., 194.
19. Carr, *Song*, 133.

The mutual playfulness and frolicking in the fields have been lost. It is now the dark of night, and there appears to be a self-absorption here that has let the air out of their relationship. Everything has gone flat.

When we consult with the teaching of the apostle Paul on marriage, mutual respect is present everywhere. In Ephesians 5, the whole topic is introduced with the line, "Submit to one another out of reverence for Christ." Only then are we are told, "Wives, submit to your husbands as to the Lord. . . . Husbands, love your wives just as Christ loved the church and gave himself up for her . . ." (Eph 5:21, 22, 25).

When the apostle teaches about sex, he breaks not only the cultural taboos of his time but also the prejudices of our own with its inherent put down of both men and women in regard to their different sexual needs. Whatever may be the culturally different approaches of men and women to sex, at least in our imaginations, the apostle Paul treats their needs in exactly the same way. The opening line turns everything upside down for starters.

> The husband should fulfill his marital duty to his wife, and likewise the wife to her husband. The wife's body does not belong to her alone but also to her husband. In the same way, the husband's body does not belong to him alone but also to his wife. Do not deprive each other except by mutual consent and for a time, so that you may devote yourselves to prayer. Then come together again . . . (1 Cor 7:2–5).

Mutuality is a fundamental biblical principle that begins with each giving to the other. Or as Jesus puts it, "It is more blessed to give than to receive" (Acts 20:35). "For whoever wants to save his life will lose it, but whoever loses his life for me will find it" (Matt 16:25). Or again, "The greatest among you will be your servant" (Matt 23:11). It is in the giving of ourselves to one another that we receive.

It is this that we suggest has caused the lovers to lose their timing and to fall painfully out of sync with one another. When mutual love, playfulness, service, and thoughtfulness for one another is lost, the dance is always out of step, and the music will be entirely off key. We are always tempted to assign blame, but it takes two to dance.

REALITY

The tensions in our marriages or in our relationships are not strange or unique to us, nor do they prove that we are dysfunctional. They are entirely "normal" in a world in which our sin and selfishness have turned us inward.

We all like to believe that we will live happily ever after, but the truth is that relationships are never smooth sailing. Just when we think we have worked it out, we are disappointed to find ourselves out of step and back into a storm that is at once filled equally with passion as well as with the capacity to be torn apart and left in shreds.

We have seen these lows before in the Song. Back then, she sought and found him. Now, once again she intends to seek and find him. She turns to her friends in the community of faith that surrounds her and says:

> O daughters of Jerusalem, I charge you—
> If you find my lover,
> What will you tell him?
> Tell him I am faint with love.

There is a time to seek help. She will find him, and love will overcome because love never gives up.[20] She goes out, seeks, and finds. Or perhaps as it is better put in matters of love and grace, she is found. In fact, as the story suggests, the lover was absent, but he never really was lost to her.[21]

REFLECTION

What we especially appreciate about this poem is that there is a remarkable transparency in the text. The lover comes right out and says, "I messed up. I was only thinking about me, myself, and I. Look at me. I have this wonderful lover and here I am beaten up, bruised, confused, and naked."

This is where grace comes from. It comes from transparency, honesty, and authenticity. There is none of this sitting in church, all dressed up, and pretending to be such a fine couple. Nor is there the arrogance of singing our songs of praise among a people who are so in love with

---

20. First Corinthians 13:8.
21. Murphy, *Song*, 173.

themselves and their spirituality that they never seem to ever feel the need to stop and share in the confession of sin.

More properly, we practice this every week when we follow Jesus's instruction in the Lord's Prayer and publicly confess our sins, and frankly say to the Lord, "Since last time we met in this place, 'I, me, myself, and I' have messed up big time." That's where grace and help come from. We disarm pride and open up our hearts to healing and to help. We find our sisters and our brothers, and we share our hurts and learn from one another.

MEDITATION

God Delights to Meet the Needs of Those Who Know They Need His Grace

> I cried out to God for help;
>   I cried out to God to hear me.
> When I was in distress, I sought the Lord;
>   at night I stretched out untiring hands
>   and my soul refused to be comforted.
>
> I remembered you, O God, and I groaned;
>   I mused, and my spirit grew faint. . . .
> I remembered my songs in the night.
>   My heart mused and my spirit inquired:
>
> "Will the Lord reject forever?
>   Will he never show his favor again?. . ."
>
> Then I thought, "To this I will appeal:
>   the years of the right hand of the Most High."
> I will remember the deeds of the LORD;
>   yes, I will remember your miracles of long ago.
> I will meditate on all your works
>   and consider all your mighty deeds.
>
> Your ways, O God, are holy.
>   What god is so great as our God?
> (Ps 77:1–3, 6–7, 10–13).

> "For I know the plans I have for you," declares the LORD, "plans to prosper you and not to harm you, plans to give you hope and a future. Then you will call upon me and come and pray to me, and I will listen to you. You will seek me and find me when you seek me

with all your heart. I will be found by you," declares the LORD, "and will bring you back from captivity" (Jer 29:11–14).

"The man who enters by the gate is the shepherd of his sheep. The watchman opens the gate for him, and the sheep listen to his voice. He calls his own sheep by name and leads them out. When he has brought out all his own, he goes on ahead of them, and his sheep follow him because they know his voice. But they will never follow a stranger; in fact, they will run away from him because they do not recognize a stranger's voice" (John 10:2–5).

So I say, live by the Spirit, and you will not gratify the desires of the sinful nature. For the sinful nature desires what is contrary to the Spirit, and the Spirit what is contrary to the sinful nature. They are in conflict with each other, so that you do not do what you want. But if you are led by the Spirit, you are not under law (Gal 5:16–18).

PRAYER

Lord, I praise you for your love, for knocking on the door of my heart in such a way as to wake me up and get me out of my slumber. Thank you for being there for me in the dark nights of the soul.

Please forgive me for my selfishness, for self-centeredness, and for thinking that my life is all about me.

This day, teach me to walk in harmony in with you, and in the presence of others to be real about who I am and what you have done for me. Amen.

Day 35

Poem 14 (5:9—6:3) A

Strength: "My lover is radiant and ruddy"

Friends
A. How is your beloved better than others,
  most beautiful of women?
How is your beloved better than others,
  that you charge us so?

Woman
My lover is radiant and ruddy,
  outstanding among ten thousand.
His head is purest gold;
  his hair is wavy
  and black as a raven.
His eyes are like doves
  by the water streams,
washed in milk,
  mounted like jewels.
His cheeks are like beds of spice
  yielding perfume.
His lips are like lilies
  dripping with myrrh.
His arms are rods of gold
  set with chrysolite.
His body is like polished ivory
  decorated with sapphires.
His legs are pillars of marble
  set on bases of pure gold.
His appearance is like Lebanon,
  choice as its cedars.
His mouth is sweetness itself;
  he is altogether lovely.

> This is my lover, this my friend,
>   O daughters of Jerusalem.
>
> Friends
> Where has your lover gone,
>   most beautiful of women?
> Which way did your lover turn,
>   that we may look for him with you?
>
> Woman
> My lover has gone down to his garden,
>   to the beds of spices,
> to browse in the gardens
>   and to gather lilies.
> I am my lover's and my lover is mine;
>   he browses among the lilies.

RECOVERY

For the sake of convenience and because of its length, we have broken off this text (5:9—6:3) from our last section (5:2-8). They clearly are a part of a single song because both sections join around the woman's charge and the questioning response of the chorus of friends. "What will you tell him?" holds hand with, "How is your lover better than others?

Our last section simply cannot remain as it stands because we were left holding the tension of loss and the anxiety of misunderstanding. Whether it was the result of a lover's tease gone wrong or selfishness become rampant, the lovers had fallen out of step with each other.

We understand that this happens to the best of relationships, so we are not surprised that the last section ended with the plaintive note,

> O daughters of Jerusalem, I charge you—
>   if you find my lover,
> what will you tell him?
>   Tell him I am faint with love.

The chorus of friends opens our new section. From a literary point of view, they function to link the two sections together and to draw us into the action that is taking place. They also point to the way ahead, as the remark to the woman makes plain.[22]

> How is your beloved better than others,
>   most beautiful of women?
> How is your beloved better than others,
>   that you charge us so?

MY LOVER, THE KING

Their question is all the provocation the woman needs to launch into yet another paean of praise![23] What happens next is that we are treated to an extravagant description of what it is that the woman finds to be so wonderful about her lover. She speaks of him in terms reminiscent of the way in which the Bible describes the early kings of Israel.[24] Saul, the first king of Israel, we are told, was "an impressive young man without equal among the Israelites—a head taller than any of the others" (1 Sam 9:2). More importantly, it was King David who was described as being "ruddy, with a fine appearance and handsome features."[25] Of him the women in Israel sang, "Saul has slain his thousands, and David his tens of thousands" (1 Sam 18:7). It is this same language that the woman picks up as she exclaims,

> My lover is radiant and ruddy,
>   outstanding among ten thousand.

As far as she is concerned, her lover stands head and shoulders above all the rest. He is a king among men. As such, he is distinguished, splendid, and almost divine in his qualities.

> His head is pure gold;
>   his hair is wavy
>   and black as a raven.

---

22. Murphy, *Song*, 171.
23. Exum, *Song*, 202.
24. Gledhill, *Song*, 184.
25. First Samuel 16:12. Bloch and Bloch also point us to Genesis 49:11–12 and Joel 3:18 in *Song*, 185. Both of these are messianic prophecies.

There is a vivacity about him and a liveliness that sparkles.[26]

> His eyes are like doves
>   by the water streams,
> washed in milk,
>   mounted like jewels.
> His cheeks are like beds of spice
>   yielding perfume.

When all is said and done, no one can compare to him. He stands tall, erect, magnificent, and strong. Like one of the gods among mere mortals, he exudes a sensual fragrance of great value and worth.[27]

> His lips are like lilies
>   dripping with myrrh.
> His arms are rods of gold
>   set with chrysolite.
> His body is like polished ivory
>   decorated with sapphires.
> His legs are pillars of marble
>   set on bases of pure gold.
> His appearance is like Lebanon,
>   choice as its cedars.

To top it off, she exclaims passionately:

> His mouth is sweetness itself;
> he is altogether lovely.

CHARACTER

It may be true that our bodies are no match for the man in our poem, but that would be to miss the point. Great heroes often look more like Winston Churchill and Martin Luther in their larger-than-life humanity than Zeus and Adonis in their mythological splendor. This poem is not about the vigor of youth or the body of a shepherd who has been hard at work on the hills of Israel, although we would be foolish to deny that for the young lovers that is also in play here.

Poetically what is being suggested to us here is strength of character and relationship. Buried within the song is that combination that makes

---

26. Keel, *Song*, 198.
27. Ibid., 204.

an everyday shepherd into a hero with arms that are rods of gold, a body that appears polished like ivory, and legs that are pillars of marble set on bases of pure gold. The imagery and poetry of the song is about those qualities that are to characterize a lover.

"MY FRIEND"

First, she comes up with a concluding description of him that matches his own "my sister, my bride." Of him she says proudly to her companions:

> This is my lover, this my friend,
> O daughters of Jerusalem.

He may appear like a divine king in her eyes, but it is his friendship and love that seal their relationship and make him to be such in her eyes. Her description of him is tender and affectionate, but more than that, it is supremely human. In the end, the beauty of this passage lies in the fact that this man who is her lover is in fact her friend.

As we have noted before, there may be sex without love, but it will destroy us by the inherent power of its nature. There is no love without friendship and commitment. It is the friendship of this divine king of a man who has taken her as his bride, and is now her lover, that is essential to the passionate nature of a lasting relationship.

Respect, praise, admiration, commitment, friendship, and passion meet to form the perfect storm. It is who this man is to her and how he relates to her as lover and friend that ignites the passion. He is "my lover, my friend."

At the same time, given the object of the poem and the rapture of the woman, it is not too much to suggest that this is particularly about what it means to be manly:[28] a man who is numbered among the people of God.

REFLECTION

There are other descriptions of men of stature in the Old Testament that are close to this one.[29] There is, for example, Daniel's description of a statue representative of Nebuchadnezzar, his kingdom, and the fate that awaited it with its feet of clay.

---

28. Carr suggests that the etymology of "ruddy" suggests "manly" in *Song*, 140.
29. See Longman, *Song*, 171.

> You looked, O king, and there before you stood a large statue—an enormous, dazzling statue, awesome in appearance. The head of the statue was made of pure gold, its chest and arms of silver, its belly and thighs of bronze, its legs of iron, its feet partly of iron and partly of baked clay (Dan 2:31-32).

It is quite a picture of kingly strength, but its fatal flaw lies in what has now become a proverbial phrase, its "feet of clay." In contrast, Daniel would describe the coming of one that he calls the Son of Man.

> In my vision at night I looked, and there before me was one like a son of man, coming with the clouds of heaven. He approached the Ancient of Days and was led into his presence. He was given authority, glory and sovereign power; all peoples, nations and men of every language worshiped him. His dominion is an everlasting dominion that will not pass away, and his kingdom is one that will never be destroyed (Dan 7:13-14).

In case we have any doubt about who this really is, we have only to hear the words of Jesus.

> The high priest said to him, "I charge you under oath by the living God: Tell us if you are the Christ, the Son of God. . . .
>
> "Yes, it is as you say," Jesus replied. "But I say to all of you: In the future you will see the Son of Man sitting at the right hand of the Mighty One and coming on the clouds of heaven" (Matt 26:63-64).

This is not "gentle Jesus, meek and mild." He is the One who stands tall, strong, faithful, and true, King Jesus. What Jesus taught us was that the strength of his love and the fragrance of his friendship came not from pretending to be big, strong, tall, and handsome, but in laying aside his glory. He had no feet of clay. Instead, he wrapped himself in a towel and washed the feet of his disciples and went to the cross for his bride. He never leaves her and he never forsakes her, and like our lover, he comes back for her.

There is a movement in our poem from magnificence of body to strength of character and confidence in relationship. These are divine qualities that characterize the man in our song and that are to be understood as essential to the relationship between husband and wife.

MEDITATION

The Lord Is Strong and Gentle, and Both at the Same Time

My heart is stirred by a noble theme
  as I recite my verses for the king;
  my tongue is the pen of a skillful writer.

You are the most excellent of men
  and your lips have been anointed with grace,
  since God has blessed you forever (Ps 45:1–2).

He who loves a pure heart and whose speech is gracious
  will have the king for his friend (Prov 22:11).

"When the Son of Man comes in his glory, and all the angels with him, he will sit on his throne in heavenly glory. All the nations will be gathered before him, and he will separate the people one from another as a shepherd separates the sheep from the goats. He will put the sheep on his right and the goats on his left.
  "Then the King will say to those on his right, 'Come, you who are blessed by my Father; take your inheritance, the kingdom prepared for you since the creation of the world . . .'" (Matt 25:31–34).

Your attitude should be the same as that of Christ Jesus:
Who, being in very nature God,
  did not consider equality with God something to be grasped,
but made himself nothing,
  taking the very nature of a servant,
  being made in human likeness.
And being found in appearance as a man,
  he humbled himself
  and became obedient to death—even death on a cross!
Therefore God exalted him to the highest place
  and gave him the name that is above every name,
that at the name of Jesus every knee should bow,
  in heaven and on earth and under the earth,
and every tongue confess that Jesus Christ is Lord,
  to the glory of God the Father (Phil 2:5–11).

PRAYER

Father, we worship you. You are King of kings and Lord of lords. There is no one like you. You are strong, tall, and magnificent in your righteousness, justice, and mercy. We thank you that you have every intention of both showing yourself once more in all of your glory and in coming again to complete what you have begun in your new creation.

Forgive us for thinking of you as weak and ineffective, a friend not worth having.

Help me to live this day in the knowledge of your presence and power, your friendship and love. Teach me to live as one who knows that you know what you are doing and that you will complete what you have begun. Amen.

Day 36

Poem 14 (5:9—6:3) B

Confidence: "My lover is mine"

Friends
How is your beloved better than others,
  most beautiful of women?
How is your beloved better than others,
  that you charge us so?

Woman
My lover is radiant and ruddy,
  outstanding among ten thousand.
His head is purest gold;
  his hair is wavy
  and black as a raven.
His eyes are like doves
  by the water streams,
washed in milk,
  mounted like jewels.
His cheeks are like beds of spice
  yielding perfume.
His lips are like lilies
  dripping with myrrh.
His arms are rods of gold
  set with chrysolite.
His body is like polished ivory
  decorated with sapphires.
His legs are pillars of marble
  set on bases of pure gold.
His appearance is like Lebanon,
  choice as its cedars.
His mouth is sweetness itself;
  he is altogether lovely.

> This is my lover, this my friend,
> > O daughters of Jerusalem.
>
> Friends
> B. Where has your lover gone,
> > most beautiful of women?
> Which way did your lover turn,
> > that we may look for him with you?
>
> Woman
> My lover has gone down to his garden,
> > to the beds of spices,
> to browse in the gardens
> > and to gather lilies.
> I am my lover's and my lover is mine;
> > he browses among the lilies.

BACK IN STEP

No sooner has the section of this song (5:2–8) ended with the woman's praises of the man then it becomes clear that they have fallen back into step with one another. The friends ask:

> Where has your lover gone,
> > most beautiful of women?
> Which way did your lover turn,
> > that we may look for him with you?

It is as if nothing had ever happened to intrude into their relationship. The woman answers with complete confidence:

> My lover has gone down to his garden,
> > to the beds of spices,
> to browse in the gardens
> > and to gather lilies.
> I am my lover's and my lover is mine;
> > he browses among the lilies.

As one commentator has put it, "the whole painful episode of missed opportunity and frantic searching in 5:2–8 seem a mere misunderstanding. . . . it becomes a fleeting cloud that only briefly overshadows the couple's love."[30] She knows that her lover is going nowhere but to

---

30. Keel, *Song*, 209.

her. Misunderstanding has given way to a confidence apart from which no love can flourish.

CONFIDENCE

What comes next reinforces that point. She now knows and understands that he is there for her. He is strong and stands tall, faithful, and dependable. And after their recent misunderstanding where they fell out of step with each other, the chorus in this poem again makes the point for us by asking her:

> Where has your lover gone,
>   most beautiful of women?
> Which way did your lover turn,
>   that we may look for him with you?

Without missing a beat, she replies:

> My lover has gone down to his garden,
>   to the beds of spices,
> to browse in the gardens
>   and to gather lilies.
> I am my lover's and my lover is mine;
>   he browses among the lilies.

She replies with a complete confidence, "I am my lover's and my lover is mine." She "is secure in the knowledge that they still totally belong to one another. A temporary set-back would never lead to an inseparable break. They have made their vows to one another for life."[31]

Not only is there confidence in his commitment to her, but beyond that, there is a sense of self that now radiates out from her. Gone is the girl who once had said:

> Do not stare at me because I am dark,
>   because I am darkened by the sun.
> My mother's sons were angry with me
>   and made me take care of the vineyards;
>   my own vineyard I have neglected.

Now comes a woman confident in her lover and in herself. In delicate language, but in terms that leave no doubt about what she has in

---

31. Balchin, "The Song of Songs," 625.

mind,[32] she speaks of her sexual charms and her confidence that her lover is already on his way home to enjoy them.

> My lover has gone down to his garden,
>   to the beds of spices,
> to browse in the gardens
>   and to gather lilies.

That sense of confidence belongs to the bride for whom faithfulness and friendship, commitment and confidence have met, kissed, and inseparably embraced. Character and confidence grasp hands to create heroic lovers.

> I am my lover's and my lover is mine;
>   he browses among the lilies.

COMMON-UNION

This is also the second of three occasions in which we encounter this line with its covenant associations, "I am my lover's and my lover is mine."[33] It is filled with a deep understanding that lovers can so give themselves to each other that "'the two become one' without ceasing to be two," and that in such a way that "the unity between lover and beloved is closer than the unity between the lover and himself. He is more one with his beloved; he finds his oneness, his unique selfhood, his identity, more in her than in himself; he 'identifies' more with her than with himself."[34]

Yes, this poem is a description of her lover, but it ends up being a song in praise of their union, their "common-union." It is celebration of the confidence and joy that belongs to covenant relationships even, and perhaps especially, in the midst of crisis. "I am my lover's, and my lover is mine."

In the broader sense, the blessings of character, faithfulness, friendship, and covenant relationships also may be legitimately applied to parents and children, to neighbors and friends, and even to those with

---

32. Gledhill, in *Song*, 141, suggests, "It seems probable that to browse among the lilies is a metaphor to represent some very close intimate behavior such as kissing or fondling some tender part of each other's body." Longman, in *Song*, 175, points out, "The *garden*, for instance, is a symbol both for the woman herself as well as for the place where love is made (4:12, 15; 5:1)." Pope suggests the same, and more in *Song*, 405–07.

33. See the comments on Song of Songs 2:16 (day 19) and 7:10.

34. Kreeft, *Three Philosophies*, 129.

whom we work and play. It belongs equally to kings and shepherds, to husbands and fathers, to lovers and friends.

REFLECTION

There is also here a transparency on the part of the woman that leads to the discovery of grace. The woman asks her friends to help her find her lover and tell him if they find him that she is sick with love.

Coming out into the light and sharing our need for help are essential to breaking the cycle of being beaten up in the dark. There will remain brooding moments in the Song, but the dark nights now appear largely to be broken as she emerges fully into the confidence of his love and the splendor of his commitment and abiding presence.

This is the mystery of grace. As the poem ends, we realize that she is already found by him. He is tending his garden and is discovered grazing among the lilies, a sure reference to her delights and that of their relationship.

MEDITATION

The Lord Is Strong, Faithful, Kind, and Gracious

A man of many companions may come to ruin,
  but there is a friend who sticks closer than a brother
(Prov 18:24).

"I revealed myself to those who did not ask for me;
  I was found by those who did not seek me.
To a nation that did not call on my name,
  I said, 'Here am I, here am I'" (Isa 65:1).

The Word became flesh and made his dwelling among us. We have seen his glory, the glory of the One and Only, who came from the Father, full of grace and truth (John 1:14).

For it is by grace you have been saved, through faith—and this not from yourselves, it is the gift of God—not by works, so that no one can boast (Eph 2:8).

PRAYER

Lord, I thank you for your character, that you are ever faithful, absolutely reliable, and unchanging in your love, mercy, compassion, and strength. I am grateful to you for always being there, and most of all, for finding me.

Forgive me for the times when I have thought that you were missing.

Teach me this day to be reliable and faithful and to just be there for others. Amen.

Day 37

Poem 15 (6:4–9)

Admiration: "You are beautiful"

Man
You are beautiful, my darling, as Tirzah,
  lovely as Jerusalem,
  majestic as troops with banners.
Turn your eyes from me;
  they overwhelm me.
Your hair is like a flock of goats
  descending from Gilead.
Your teeth are like a flock of sheep
  coming up from the washing.
Each has its twin,
  not one of them is alone.
Your temples behind your veil
  are like the halves of a pomegranate.
Sixty queens there may be,
  and eighty concubines,
  and virgins beyond number;
but my dove, my perfect one, is unique,
  the only daughter of her mother,
  the favorite of the one who bore her.
The maidens saw her and called her blessed;
  the queens and concubines praised her.

We are now well into the Song, and we find ourselves locked into what we could almost describe as a holding pattern of praise. It would have become tedious by now were it not so fascinating, not to mention passionate. No sooner has the woman finished her sizzling poem of praise than the man comes right back at her with one of his own. "He finds her captivatingly beautiful, desirable, and awe-inspiring (6:4–5, 10). He has said all this before (4:1–9), but lovers never tire of saying, or of hearing, familiar words of affection and adoration."[35]

DESCRIPTION

Much of the poetry may still seem strange to us even after having made our way through most of the book, but we have begun to catch its rhythm and fall into its patterns. We learn to begin to think as an artist. "Greek statues, impressionist paintings, Hebrew poetry, all are creating their own special ambience which invites us to taste and see through the eyes of the artist."[36]

If parts of the poetry still seem odd to us, we need only remember that the references are to objects of beauty and awe in their own time and place. One only has to think of the effect upon a shepherd or a young peasant girl first going up to Jerusalem or to some other famous city like Tirzah,[37] not to mention the first time the young shepherd saw Solomon's armies arrayed in all their splendor. We can understand why he would exclaim:

> You are as beautiful, my darling, as Tirzah,
>   lovely as Jerusalem,
>   majestic as troops with banners.

Our translation "majestic" is not so strong as it might be. The emphasis here is on the awe that she inspires.[38] "The beauty of the woman is so overpowering that it arouses fear as well as joy."[39]

And then in a classic line that has been used many times at least after our Song, he begs his lover to turn her eyes away from him. He can hardly bear being driven crazy anymore!

> Turn your eyes from me;
>   they overwhelm me.

Some of his lines we have met before[40] as once again he uses imagery drawn from the shepherd's life. Flocks of goats descending from

---

35. Exum, *Song*, 215.
36. Gledhill, *Song*, 183.
37. First Kings 14:17; 16:17–18, 23. See Keel, *Song*, 213.
38. Keel, in *Song*, 211, calls this "Tremendum et fascinosum II," drawing attention to the awe she inspires.
39. Longman, *Song*, 180.
40. Song of Songs 4:1–3.

a mountain would have a shimmering effect not unlike her dark, curly hair, and the festive moments of sheep shearing and washing excite him, as do her teeth and mouth.

> Your hair is like a flock of goats
>   descending from Gilead.
> Your teeth are like a flock of sheep
>   coming up from the washing.
> Each has its twin,
>   not one of them is alone.

Some lines we just cannot ignore even though we live in a time when kings no longer surround themselves with multiple queens, concubines, and attending virgins. Here is a truly splendid stanza, especially when put on the lips of a shepherd who is imagining that even if he were a king who could have as many women as he would want, he would have none of it.

> Sixty queens there may be,
>   and eighty concubines,
>   and virgins beyond number;
> but my dove, my perfect one, is unique,
>   the only daughter of her mother,
>   the favorite of the one who bore her.

What he is saying is that she is lacking in nothing that any other woman could bring. She is unique, as anyone who has known her in every moment from her birth will be able to attest.

This is wisdom literature, and in case we are missing it, the "exclusivity of the monogamous relationship enjoyed by the woman but not by the queens" is also in view here.[41] There is a populist sentiment here as the shepherd points out that peasant girls can know greater joys than the queens and consorts of kings. The real point is once again that faithfulness is what makes a relationship special. The praise of the woman on the lips of the man is that she is more than deserving of it.

In the event that we are still neglecting to notice or be impressed by what it is that makes a lover effective and a relationship delightful, the poet points it out to us. It is of course the ability to give praise and affirm others. Here the lover puts it not on his own lips but out of the mouth of other women, whose observation makes it doubly impressive.

---

41. Keel, *Song*, 218.

Her praise is magnified in his assertion that even they must concede her unique excellence.[42]

> The maidens saw her and called her blessed;
> the queens and concubines praised her.

COMMENT

Once again, this is what we might describe as a *praise song*.[43] It would be difficult to find anywhere in all of human literature a more sustained litany of praise, affirmation, and affection than this.

There are great love poems filled with extravagant praise and admiration, but more often than not they turn out to be the product of a giddy naiveté or a compulsive obsession, not to mention lovers pining over a lost object of affection. They end up being one more example of unrequited love or misplaced affection. Here, there is a perfect harmony of praise, affirmation, and affection that is joyfully and passionately exchanged between the two lovers. They virtually compete to outdo one another in their praise of each other.

This is all the more impressive because no longer is this the gleeful expression of first love. They have known what it is to experience insecurity and misunderstanding. Fear of loss has intruded into their relationship, and the music has faltered. Misunderstanding has brought separation, and the woman has been beaten up and bruised on the streets looking for her lover. Here they are back together, and their love and their lives are being bathed in this sustained exchange of praise, appreciation, and admiration.

REFLECTION

Our lives and how we relate to others is going to be characterized either by guilt or grace. Guilt motivates through condemnation. Grace produces praise. Depending on which we have chosen as the defining characteristic of our lives, we will either drive others away or else draw others to us. We will either tend to beat them down or build them up, to discourage or encourage.

---

42. Longman, *Song*, 182.
43. Fox, *Love Songs*, 150.

One of the great examples of this is the apostle Paul. He is writing to the Corinthians, one of the most difficult of his churches, a congregation that he will even be briefly afraid to visit in case he should be unwelcome. Before speaking the truth in love to them, he looks for that which is praiseworthy in their lives, and he catalogs the evidences of God's grace at work in their lives. One might even say that his opening words to them have something of the feel of the Song of Songs.

> I always thank God for you because of his grace given you in Christ Jesus. For in him you have been enriched in every way—in all your speaking and in all your knowledge—because our testimony about Christ was confirmed in you. Therefore you do not lack any spiritual gift as you eagerly wait for our Lord Jesus Christ to be revealed. He will keep you strong to the end, so that you will be blameless on the day of our Lord Jesus Christ. God, who has called you into fellowship with his Son Jesus Christ our Lord, is faithful (1 Cor 1:4–9).

Paul's own ministry is described for us in this way: "When the uproar had ended, Paul sent for the disciples and, after encouraging them, said good-by and set out for Macedonia. He traveled through that area, speaking many words of encouragement to the people, and finally arrived in Greece . . ." (Acts 20:1–2).[44]

We are almost at the end of the Song of Songs, and we have to be sure that we are "getting it." This is what the book is all about. It is not that we are naïve about the difficult nature of relationships—it is that it belongs to the very nature of love to praise, encourage, comfort, and console. When we learn to speak the truth with grace, the music of the Song of Songs prevails, and lovers dance to the litany of praise. This is the way it has to be because we were made to discover the joy of the worship of God and the exhilaration of his grace.

MEDITATION

In the Praise of God Our Hearts Discover Joy and Freedom

> Great is the LORD, and most worthy of praise,
>   in the city of our God, his holy mountain.
> It is beautiful in its loftiness,
>   the joy of the whole earth.
> Like the utmost heights of Zaphon is Mount Zion,
>   the city of the Great King.

---

44. Cf. Acts 15:30–41.

> God is in her citadels;
>> he has shown himself to be her fortress. . . .
>
> As we have heard,
>> so have we seen
> in the city of the LORD Almighty,
>> in the city of our God:
> God makes her secure forever (Ps 48:1–3, 8).

> The LORD their God will save them on that day
>> as the flock of his people.
> They will sparkle in his land
>> like jewels in a crown.
>
> How attractive and beautiful they will be!
>> Grain will make the young men thrive,
>> and new wine the young women (Zech 9:16–17).

The men were sent off and went down to Antioch, where they gathered the church together and delivered the letter. The people read it and were glad for its encouraging message. Judas and Silas, who themselves were prophets, said much to encourage and strengthen the brothers. After spending some time there, they were sent off by the brothers with the blessing of peace to return to those who had sent them (Acts 15:30–33).

PRAYER

Lord, you are awesome, beautiful, and majestic. The "city" where you dwell with your people is splendid and magnificent. You have given your beauty to your bride, and we worship you.

Forgive me for all the times that my prayers have been about me and not about you.

This day, help me to live my life in praise of you, and may the music of my life draw attention to you and what you have done. Amen.

Day 38

Poem 16 (6:10–12)

Transcendence: "Who is this that appears"

Friends
Who is this that appears like the dawn,
   fair as the moon, bright as the sun,
   majestic as the stars in procession?

Woman
I went down to the grove of nut trees
   to look at the new growth in the valley,
to see if the vines had budded
   or the pomegranates were in bloom.
Before I realized it,
   my desire set me among the royal chariots of my people.

THE CHORUS

Once again, it is the chorus of friends that makes the transition for us from one poem to another. They bring us back into the action and point us to the way ahead. After the stunning litany of praise from the woman and the shepherd's reply, the friends now take everything to a new level. What they do is point out a special quality that belongs to the woman and locate her once again in the midst of the beauties of nature and especially of the garden.

> Who is this that appears like the dawn,
>   fair as the moon, bright as the sun,
>   majestic as the stars in procession?

In a sense, this song is simply saying that her beauty is "out of this world." Other poets have done this, evoking at the same time the ethereal nature of beauty and love.[45] Byron for example:

> She walks in beauty, like the night
>   Of cloudless climes and starry skies;
> And all that's best of dark and bright
>   Meet in her aspect and her eyes:
> Thus mellow'd to that tender light
> Which heaven to gaudy day denies.[46]

There is more going on here than even that. In the Ancient Near East the dawn (*Shahar*) was regarded as a deity. The word translated in our text as *appears* is used of the Lord in the Bible, and the moon is used to speak both of God's rule over Jerusalem and the future work of redemption.[47] A sense of the divine is breaking through, and we see its radiance everywhere. Her appearance is like the stars in all the splendor of their procession. We are left holding our breath in wonder and awe.

In other words, her beauty is striking, almost ethereal; that is, it belongs to another world and realm. It is the stuff that legends are made of, and it is a beauty that would be entirely at home in the realm of mythology.

It is not just that the friends think that her beauty is "out of this world"; it is that this is "her epiphany,"[48] used almost in a religious sense of that word of a divine appearing. What we have here is the language of love and the poets, pointing to a transcendent quality that belongs to the nature of beauty and love and that leaves us with a sense of awe. Commentators use translations such as "awe-inspiring as visions" and "splendid as the heavenly phenomena."[49] They remind us that "awe-inspiring" is used of theophanies when God shows up and makes an appearance.[50]

What is happening here is that we are being caught up into the awe. In fact, without ever having to say so, the Song has been suggesting to us all along that there is a transcendent quality to beauty that always speaks

---

45. Gledhill, *Song*, 198.
46. Lord Byron, "She Walks in Beauty," quoted by Gledhill, *Song*, 198.
47. Longman, *Song*, 183. See Isaiah 24:23; 30:26.
48. Gledhill, *Song*, 197.
49. See the discussion in Longman where he quotes Murphy and Snaith, *Song*, 180.
50. Murphy, *Song*, 175. See Genesis 15:12.

to more than that which lies on the surface, or that which at first appears in our culture as the strange details of the imagery.

PASSION

All this is reinforced in the next lines as we find her wandering down into the garden among the nut trees, the pomegranates, and the blossoming vines. As we would expect, it is the spring, and she portrays herself as "going down" to see if the vines have budded, or if the pomegranates are in bloom. Again, we lose the beauty of the moment if we try to take apart the imagery and the specific erotic connotations that can be attached to each,[51] but they are there to be sure, because this is a moment of passion, not indifference.

> I went down to the grove of nut trees
>   to look at the new growth in the valley,
> to see if the vines had budded
>   or the pomegranates were in bloom.

It is spring, and as nature awakes, the mind of the ancient world would turn not only to the cycles of nature and love, but also to the fact the divine one is alive and at work.[52]

FANTASY

Once again, the dreamlike sequence is emphasized for us.

> Before I realized it,
>   my desire set me among the royal chariots of my people.

Yes, she is in love and she is swept away in the romantic world of fantasy. Transformed by the power of love, this is a royal fantasy.[53] Before she knows it, she finds herself dreaming of being alongside her lover as she is whisked away in his royal chariot to the acclamation of imaginary crowds.[54] She is "overwhelmed with excitement. It was as if he had

---

51. Longman, in *Song*, 184–485 follows Pope in suggesting that the whole nut and the open nut represent male and female genitalia. Keel, in *Song*, 223, points to the parallels between breasts and clusters of grapes, and ends up suggesting that, "The lack of breasts symbolizes immaturity (cf.8:8); their appearance, along with the growth of pubic hair, announces that the time for love has arrived (Ezek 16:7–8)."

52. Ibid.

53. Exum, *Song*, 223.

54. Gledhill, *Song*, 200.

placed her, a young commoner, in a chariot with a nobleman, for such is he to her."⁵⁵

REFLECTION

There is a transcendent quality to beauty and to love. Indeed, we might go back to speaking of Beauty with a capital "B." We can hardly miss it, precisely because of the sheer grandeur of what is going on here. The transcendent quality of both love and the dawn reminds us that we are created in the image of God and in reflection of God's own beauty and who he is.

The poets of Israel understood this perfectly well. It is we who in our secular banality have lost sight of the awe and wonder of life, of living, of loving, and of God.

> The heavens declare the glory of God;
>   the skies proclaim the work of his hands.
> Day after day they pour forth speech;
>   night after night they display knowledge.
> There is no speech or language
>   where their voice is not heard (Ps 19:1–3).

The sheer beauty of this literature, drawing as it does upon the splendor of creation, is a sure reminder to us of how priceless it is to have relationships that are in harmony with God's own intentions. It reflects the nature of God's own person in the perfect union of Father, Son, and Holy Spirit. In love we drink of the beauty of God.

For this reason, people of faith come into God's presence each week to be caught up in the beauty of his holiness and to be transformed by his love. God is perfect in his goodness, fearful in his absolute holiness, and awesome in his perfect righteousness. We would find that not only fearsome but absolutely terrifying were it not for the fact that we are in the presence of those who, like us, have seen the appearance of God's love in the Lamb. Then we begin to learn what it means to live our lives each day, characterized by the joyful notes of praise.

As we are caught up in the beauty of the Song, we understand how it is that we are to live our lives. The radiance of the woman and the splendors of love so rapturously described in our text all become a part of how we learn to live our lives as people who have known the Exodus,

---

55. Fox, *Love Songs*, 156.

seen God's glory on the mountain, followed his cloud in the wilderness, and beheld the glory of his presence among his people.

That having taken place, we become caught up in the transcendent quality of life. Love, poetry, drama, art, film, nature, architecture, and music begin to lift our hearts in praise or else in engaging our minds and emotions in asking what is going on and what we need to do about it. Life lived in pursuit of the merely material and an obsession with that which is only entertaining is a life that is lost.

The beauty of the Song has an inherent quality that calls us to disengage from the ugliness of our culture—not in the sense of disengaging from our world, but of rejoicing with those who rejoice and weeping with those who weep.[56] As Jesus pointed out, there is a transcendent quality to love and mercy. When we share our lives with the hungry and help clothe the naked, it ends up being done as unto him. It takes on a quality all its own.[57]

MEDITATION

The Lord Shines above All, Transforming Our View of the World in Which We Live

> Praise the LORD.
>
> Praise the LORD from the heavens,
>   praise him in the heights above.
> Praise him, all his angels,
>   praise him, all his heavenly hosts.
> Praise him, sun and moon,
>   praise him, all you shining stars.
> Praise him, you highest heavens
>   and you waters above the skies.
> Let them praise the name of the LORD,
>   for he commanded and they were created (Ps 148:1–5).
>
> The moon will be abashed, the sun ashamed;
>   for the LORD Almighty will reign
> on Mount Zion and in Jerusalem,
>   and before its elders, gloriously (Isa 24:23).

---

56. Romans 12:15.
57. Matthew 25:37–40.

> The moon will shine like the sun, and the sunlight will be seven times brighter, like the light of seven full days, when the LORD binds up the bruises of his people and heals the wounds he inflicted (Isa 30:26).

> Immediately after the distress of those days
>   "the sun will be darkened,
>   and the moon will not give its light;
>   the stars will fall from the sky,
>   and the heavenly bodies will be shaken."
>
> At that time the sign of the Son of Man will appear in the sky, and all the nations of the earth will mourn. They will see the Son of Man coming on the clouds of the sky, with power and great glory. And he will send his angels with a loud trumpet call, and they will gather his elect from the four winds, from one end of the heavens to the other (Matt 24:29–31).

> I did not see a temple in the city, because the Lord God Almighty and the Lamb are its temple. The city does not need the sun or the moon to shine on it, for the glory of God gives it light, and the Lamb is its lamp. The nations will walk by its light, and the kings of the earth will bring their splendor into it. On no day will its gates ever be shut, for there will be no night there. The glory and honor of the nations will be brought into it (Rev 21:22–26).

PRAYER

Lord you are perfect in your goodness, fearful in your holiness, and awesome in your righteousness. We are in awe of you.

    Forgive us, Lord, when we have lived our lives without beauty and awe and become consumed with the ordinariness of life lived without you.

    Fill me with praise today, and cause me to live in the light of your extraordinary presence. Allow that others may see your beauty in me. Amen.

Day 39

Poem 17 (6:13—7:10) A

Dance: "That we may gaze on you!"

Friends
A. Come back, come back, O Shulammite;
   come back, come back, that we may gaze on you!

Woman
Why would you gaze on the Shulammite
   as on the dance of Mahanaim?

Man
How beautiful your sandaled feet,
   O prince's daughter!
Your graceful legs are like jewels,
   the work of a craftsman's hands.
Your navel is a rounded goblet
   that never lacks blended wine.
Your waist is a mound of wheat
   encircled by lilies.
Your breasts are like two fawns,
   twins of a gazelle.
Your neck is like an ivory tower.
Your eyes are the pools of Heshbon
   by the gate of Bath Rabbim.
Your nose is like the tower of Lebanon
   looking toward Damascus.
Your head crowns you like Mount Carmel.
   Your hair is like royal tapestry;
   the king is held captive by its tresses.
How beautiful you are and how pleasing,
   O love, with your delights!
Your stature is like that of the palm,
   and your breasts like clusters of fruit.

> I said, "I will climb the palm tree;
>   I will take hold of its fruit."
> May your breasts be like the clusters of the vine,
>   the fragrance of your breath like apples,
>   and your mouth like the best wine.
>
> Woman
> May the wine go straight to my lover,
>   flowing gently over lips and teeth.
> I belong to my lover
>   and his desire is for me.

We have come to the last of the great ecstatic poems of praise that characterize the Song. Before we can read and enjoy it, there are a couple of things that we need to look at in terms of understanding what is going on.

THE SHULAMMITE

This is the first and only time in the book that the woman is described as "the Shulammite." We really don't know what the name means or refers to. With some slight changes to the word, we can get it to read either as the name of an Ancient Near Eastern goddess, the village from which the beautiful Abishag came, or the female form of Solomon. This last suggestion is the most attractive, since its root meaning suggests peace or wholeness.[58]

Later in 8:10, the root of the word will be used when she says, "I have become in his eyes like one bringing contentment." In its form as an adjective, we get "perfect" or "unblemished."[59] So in 4:7 we read, "All beautiful you are, my darling; there is no flaw in you." If peace and perfection are at the root of the name, it would certainly contain an appropriate poetic suggestion. In fact, we are reminded of the superlative in the title given in the very first verse, "Solomon's Song of Songs." This, after all, has been all about the perfection of love and beauty, desire and intimacy, and peace and wholeness.

---

58. See for example, Longman, *Song*, 192–93.
59. See Fox, *Love Songs*, 157–58.

THE MAHANAIM

To complicate matters, we have a second unknown word in verse 1 where we read,

> Why would you gaze on the Shulammite
> as on the dance of Mahanaim?

Our text takes Mahanaim to be a place, which it certainly can be. The name appears some thirteen other times in the Old Testament. If it is referring to a particular city, then we have no idea of what the reference to the "dance of Mahanaim" would mean. Most commentators read the word in its literal meaning, which is "two camps." The suggestion would then be of a dance performed by two groups, circles, or rows of dancers, or something to that effect![60]

THE DANCE

Once again, we begin with the chorus of friends. Poetically, they function to call the Shulammite back to reality, her having just been lost in a romantic swoon that had her being whisked away by her lover in a royal chariot. Then they invite us to take yet another look at the woman to see what it is about her beauty and perfection that brings such joy and contentment to her lover.

The text begins probably with the woman designating herself as "the Shulammite" and warning the audience not to watch her, as if this is some sort of dance in which she is the object of erotic entertainment.[61] That would be insulting to the dignity of both her and her lover. In fact, there is no direct evidence that she actually dances. More likely what is happening here is that comparisons are being made to the dance of the Mahanaim.[62]

Sensual her "dance" may be, but to take it as a form of voyeurism is to miss what her dance is all about. Indeed, it is to miss everything that the book is about.[63] The dance is about the joy that they find in each other. It is about the pleasure of intimacy and the beauty and harmony of their union.

---

60. Bloch and Bloch, *Song*, 199.
61. Gledhill, *Song*, 201.
62. Exum, *Song*, 229.
63. Gledhill, *Song*, 203–4.

THE DESCRIPTION

This description of her dance is not as before, when the man had moved from the head downward.[64] Because it is a dance, this song begins with her feet and moves with rhythm and grace upward over her body.

Her sandaled feet are like a prince's daughter in their delicateness and beauty. Her legs are like a piece of exquisite jewelry that has been lovingly sculpted by craftsman. As he moves upward, her navel (and probably the reference is even more explicit than that,[65] since the word is literally "valley") is a place of delight where one finds the most exotic of wines. Her waist and belly are honey colored like wheat, but more to the point, he is enamored with her graceful curves and the way everything forms together, especially her thigh and belly. Her neck is long and graceful, her eyes are delightful, and her nose is straight and elegant, proudly facing outward.[66] Her head is majestic, crowning her with splendor. Her hair, curly and long, is captivating. Its tight curls are woven like a royal tapestry holding even kings captive to her charms. Like a palm tree, she is "tall, slender, and graceful." Her breasts are its fruit, and these he will gently caress and handle.[67] Her mouth, like the finest of wine, he will linger over and savor.

The whole description is filled with form and beauty, movement and dance, and elegance and grace. As the passion mounts, especially in the second half of the song, the whole description from lilies to mouth is a subtle but tasteful allusion to the intimacies of sex and oneness.[68]

INTIMACY

As we near the end of the Song, we must take one last opportunity to remind ourselves that the way in which sex is crudely portrayed in our culture bears little resemblance either to this song or what it is meant to be. True passion is not to be confused with pornography, in which intimacy is absent and true abandonment is impossible in the context

---

64. See Song of Songs 4:1–7.

65. Carr, *Song*, 157; Gledhill, *Song*, 206; Longman, *Song*, 194–95 all follow Pope and others in seeing this as a euphemism for the female genitals. See the discussion of Keel, *Song*, 234, and Murray, *Song*, 182.

66. Bloch and Bloch, *Song*, 203. Keel, *Song*, 236.

67. Balchin, *Song*, 626.

68. See Longman, *Song*, 195.

of a lack of covenantal union. The passions of the Song swirl around the great center of the book, which, of course, was the royal marriage sequence.[69]

In our culture, sex is an addictive drug that promises much but ends up fulfilling little. In the Song, it is a joyful dance of exquisite pleasure that belongs to a man and a woman whose lives are inextricably intertwined and that swirls around their commitment and their covenant with each other. The Song is a type of wisdom literature written to tell us that properly understood, these joys can be the possession of any man and woman who delight in the ways of God.

> How beautiful you are and how pleasing,
>   O love, with your delights!
> Your stature is like that of the palm,
>   and your breasts like clusters of fruit.
> I said, "I will climb the palm tree;
>   I will take hold of its fruit."
> May your breasts be like the clusters of the vine,
>   the fragrance of your breath like apples,
>   and your mouth like the best wine.

The dance is about the intoxicating joy they find in each other. It is about intimacy and union.

SELF-EXPRESSION

Even more than that, it is about being filled with the self-confidence that comes from being loved, affirmed, praised, encouraged, valued, and built up. As the Shulammite dances, we understand that she "is enjoying the exhilaration of physical self-expression."[70]

The Shulammite has come a long way from being the timid and abused young woman who complained of the treatment she received from the hands of her mother's sons. Gone is the self-deprecation that comes from neglecting one's own appearance and well-being.

Most importantly, for the first time we are given her name, or more significantly, she gives it to us. She has come into her own, and at last we can name her. And in the confidence of being named, she will not allow the indignity of being seen as an object to be possessed.

---

69. Song of Songs 3:6–11.
70. Gledhill, *Song*, 204.

> Why would you gaze on the Shulammite
> as on the dance of Mahanaim?

All of this comes from confidence born of love, of affirmation, and of being valued. It is born of knowing that the person who has given this to you is in fact yours, and that you belong to that person alone, that at last you have come into your own, and that finally you are free to give yourself away to another.

> May the wine go straight to my lover,
> flowing gently over lips and teeth.
> I belong to my lover,
> and his desire is for me.

REFLECTION

Even more fundamentally, our identity comes from God and who he says we are. We may need the praise of others and feel distraught when we are not sure of our acceptance. This is especially true of us in our adolescence when we are just beginning to separate our identity from our parents and work out who we are. Receiving our "name" and our identity from God is of first importance, because all other praise and acceptance is made relative by the transcendent One.

All of us as human beings are created in the image of God and therefore are of incalculable worth and dignity. All other premises upon which so called "human rights" are built are shifting sands and utterly unreliable in the face of the extreme political and religious currents that characterize our various human cultures.

As Christians, we understand that God says that we are his sons, with the word *son* being used in its original biblical context to refer to the one who inherited the family fortune and name. Even more than that, we understand that we take our identity from Christ, who is our righteousness. We take his name as Christ-ians. All that to which he is heir is ours. It is shown to be ours in the wedding ring of faith[71] that he has given to us.

---

71. "By the wedding ring of faith he shares in the sins, death, and pains of hell which are his bride's. As a matter of fact, he makes them his own and acts as if they were his own . . . Thus the believing soul by means of the pledge of its faith is free in Christ, its bridegroom, free from all sins, secure against death and hell, and is endowed with the eternal righteousness, life, and salvation of Christ its bridegroom." Luther, "The Freedom of a Christian," 604.

Once we truly grasp this, then fear and failure have a way of falling away. When we are still grasping for our sense of identity, promiscuity, addictions, and craving begin to hold us prisoner, and we fail to grasp what it means to dance for joy.

MEDITATION

Christ Gives Us Our True Name, and We Dance for Joy

Let Israel rejoice in their Maker;
   let the people of Zion be glad in their King.
Let them praise his name with dancing
   and make music to him with tambourine and harp.

For the LORD takes delight in his people;
   he crowns the humble with salvation.
Let the saints rejoice in this honor
   and sing for joy on their beds (Ps 149:2–5).

I will build you up again
   and you will be rebuilt, O Virgin Israel.
Again you will take up your tambourines
   and go out to dance with the joyful . . .
For the LORD will ransom Jacob
   and redeem them from the hand of those stronger than they.
They will come and shout for joy on the heights of Zion;
   they will rejoice in the bounty of the LORD—
the grain, the new wine and the oil,
   the young of the flocks and herds.
They will be like a well-watered garden,
   and they will sorrow no more.
Then maidens will dance and be glad,
   young men and old as well.
I will turn their mourning into gladness;
   I will give them comfort and joy instead of sorrow
(Jer 31:4, 11–13).

"But the father said to his servants, 'Quick! Bring the best robe and put it on him. Put a ring on his finger and sandals on his feet. Bring the fattened calf and kill it. Let's have a feast and celebrate. For this son of mine was dead and is alive again; he was lost and is found.' So they began to celebrate.

"Meanwhile, the older son was in the field. When he came near the house, he heard music and dancing" (Luke 15:22–25).

For this reason I kneel before the Father, from whom his whole family in heaven and on earth derives its name. I pray that out of his glorious riches he may strengthen you with power through his Spirit in your inner being, so that Christ may dwell in your hearts through faith. And I pray that you, being rooted and established in love, may have power, together with all the saints, to grasp how wide and long and high and deep is the love of Christ, and to know this love that surpasses knowledge—that you may be filled to the measure of all the fullness of God (Eph 3:14–19).

PRAYER

Father, thank you for giving me your name, making me beautiful in your sight, creating me in your image, and clothing me in the righteousness of Christ. Thank you for taking away my sins and giving me an elegance that could only come from you.

Forgive me, Lord, for doubting that you love your bride and for failing to dance.

This day help me to walk in the confidence and joy of one who is loved and to share that love with others. Amen.

Day 40

Poem 17 (6:13—7:10) B

Dignity: "His desire is for me"

Friends
A. Come back, come back, O Shulammite;
   come back, come back, that we may gaze on you!

Woman
Why would you gaze on the Shulammite
   as on the dance of Mahanaim?

Man
How beautiful your sandaled feet,
   O prince's daughter!
Your graceful legs are like jewels,
   the work of a craftsman's hands.
Your navel is a rounded goblet
   that never lacks blended wine.
Your waist is a mound of wheat
   encircled by lilies.
Your breasts are like two fawns,
   twins of a gazelle.
Your neck is like an ivory tower.
Your eyes are the pools of Heshbon
   by the gate of Bath Rabbim.
Your nose is like the tower of Lebanon
   looking toward Damascus.
Your head crowns you like Mount Carmel.
   Your hair is like royal tapestry;
   the king is held captive by its tresses.
How beautiful you are and how pleasing,
   O love, with your delights!
Your stature is like that of the palm,
   and your breasts like clusters of fruit.

> I said, "I will climb the palm tree;
>   I will take hold of its fruit."
> May your breasts be like the clusters of the vine,
>   the fragrance of your breath like apples,
>   and your mouth like the best wine.
>
> Woman
> B. May the wine go straight to my lover,
>   flowing gently over lips and teeth.
> I belong to my lover,
>   and his desire is for me.

For the first time since the beginning of our poem (6:13), the Shulammite has given us her name. She is confident in herself, her love, and her ability to give it away to another. She will no longer allow herself to be abused. Filled with the self-confidence that comes from being loved, affirmed, praised, encouraged, valued, and built up, the Shulammite dances. In this confidence, she concludes the song:

> I belong to my lover,
>   and his desire is for me.

DESIRE

It is worth taking note of the word *desire*, not least of all because it appears in only two other places in the Bible, and in both cases, it is given to us in a negative context. Both are in Genesis, and the first is in the Garden. There it comes to us as a part of the curse. The Lord explains to Eve that as the result of sin coming into the world, "Your desire will be for your husband and he will rule over you" (Gen 3:16).

The second is when Eve's son Cain is told by the Lord, "Sin is crouching at your door; it desires to have you, but you must master it" (Gen 4:7). Cain neglects the advice and murders his brother. In both cases the "desire" is oppressive, dangerous, and destructive.[72]

As we trace the history of the "city of man," we soon come to a descendant of Cain, whose name is Lamech. He has already perverted the original intention of the Lord that a man and a woman should come together as a single joining of "one flesh," and he is filled with a chauvinistic arrogance in regard to his wives, to whom he boasts of his violence, lack of self-restraint, and disdain for justice.

---

72. See the discussion of Longman, *Song*, 198–99.

> "Addah and Zillah, listen to me;
>   wives of Lamech, hear my words.
> I have killed a man for wounding me,
>   a young man for injuring me.
> If Cain is avenged seven times,
>   then Lamech seventy-seven times" (Gen 4:23–24).

In other words, sin plays out in the taking and exploitation of women and in heavy-handed violence and oppressive dominance. Such is the consequence of the woman's "desire" for her husband and his rule over her.

In addition to all of this, the curse should probably also be understood as a frustration of the woman's desire for the original intimacy and closeness of the garden. The husband's attention is now both diminished and diverted by the fall.[73]

Some say that a woman wishes to be at the center of her husband's life, not a compartment along with his job, family, and home.[74] It is sometimes said, "For man love is a thing apart; for woman it is her very heart." In western cultures, that may be in large part a result of the industrial revolution, in which the family no longer worked together on the farm or in the cottage industry, but rather the man went off to work, first in the factory and then in the office. That tendency has of course expanded with the woman's also going off to work in the factory and office. At the very least, it represents a frustration that intrudes into the once-intimate relationship between the man and the woman in their work and in their lives shared together in the Garden.

In this regard, the following "feminist" observation on our text is particularly instructive on the concept of "desire" and the way in which our text reverses it.

> In Eden, the yearning of the woman for harmony with her man continued after the disobedience. Yet the man did not reciprocate: Instead, he ruled over her to destroy unity and pervert sexuality. Her desire became his dominion. But in the Song male power vanishes. His desire becomes her delight. Another consequence of disobedience is thus redeemed through the recovery of mutuality

---

73. See the excellent discussion in Carr, *Song*, 164.
74. Gledhill, *Song*, 228.

in the garden of eroticism. Appropriately, the woman sings the lyrics of this grace: "I am my lover's and for me is his desire."[75]

Perhaps the phrase "the garden of eroticism" is not the best, since it could be understood to be precisely the pagan opposite of what we have seen "the garden" to truly represent in the Song. Nor does "male power" disappear in the Song. The man is strong.[76] But the point is well-taken. Where the curse implied friction and the woman's desire for the man would lead to his taking advantage of her, now love reverses the curse. His desire is for her. In this sense, it is a "return to paradise."[77] Not only is her desire reciprocated, but instead of her being diminished by the man, she is being built up and finds herself free to give herself away.

In the place of domination and control, we find a mutual giving of love, one to the other. Instead of the woman cowering in fear and wilting like a flower cut down, she is alive with passion. Instead of being put down as Lamech did to Addah and Zillah, the man praises, encourages, nurtures, and affirms the woman so that she blossoms like the spring and dances like the Shulammite.

UNION

It is worth noting that this is the third time the phrase, or its equivalent, "I belong to my lover and his desire is for me" is used.[78] This line, with its covenant associations, suggests that, "The lover sees the beloved not as one among many but as the center of the universe; . . . standing at the same place as himself, his own center, his own uniquely individual I."[79] Such a union precludes the exploitation of the other. "Love does not adulterate itself. . . . true love is naturally true. Love wants to be faithful. It wants to give all of itself to one, not to disperse and divide itself upon many."[80]

Paradoxically, it is out of this union and sense of oneness that freedom comes. What the Song teaches is us that "lovers do not talk about freedom; they are free already. They do not desire to be free; they desire

---

75. Phyllis Trible, quoted in Murphy, *Song*, 187.
76. Cf. Song of Songs 5:10–16.
77. See Keel, *Song*, 252.
78. Also Song of Songs 2:16, 6:3.
79. Kreeft, *Three Philosophies*, 124.
80. Ibid., 133.

to be bound forever to their beloved." From this we understand, "To be free from love, free from God, is precisely Hell."[81]

REFLECTION

Frustration between the sexes is written into the very DNA of the relationship between the sexes. For that reason, love is a whole new way of a man and a woman relating to each other. This is especially true of men's attitudes to women, as our song so powerfully illustrates. Despite the veneer of feminism and political correctness, love's turning of everything upside down, especially for the man, is as necessary as ever in our culture.

We may be sure of this. There can be no intimacy, initiative, passion, or delight where one or the other, the man or the woman, exhibits a domineering spirit and is bent on exercising a suffocating control. As the apostle Paul insists:

> Love is patient, love is kind. It does not envy, it does not boast, it is not proud. It is not rude, it is not self-seeking, it is not easily angered, it keeps no record of wrongs. Love does not delight in evil but rejoices with the truth. It always protects, always trusts, always hopes, always perseveres. Love never fails" (1 Cor 13:4–8).

It is the love of Christ that teaches this to us. He humbled himself and became a servant, pitching his tent among us, loving and serving us by giving his life upon a cross. Amazingly, his desire is for us!

MEDITATION

Christ Has Given Himself for Us. Love Gives Itself to Others

> Jacob was in love with Rachel and said, "I'll work for you seven years in return for your younger daughter Rachel."
> Laban said, "It's better that I give her to you than to some other man. Stay here with me." So Jacob served seven years to get Rachel, but they seemed like only a few days to him because of his love for her (Gen 29:18–20).

> The king is enthralled by your beauty;
> honor him, for he is your lord (Ps 45:11).

---

81. Ibid., 117.

Jesus called them together and said, "You know that the rulers of the Gentiles lord it over them, and their high officials exercise authority over them. Not so with you. Instead, whoever wants to become great among you must be your servant, and whoever wants to be first must be your slave—just as the Son of Man did not come to be served, but to serve, and to give his life as a ransom for many" (Matt 20:25-28).

Submit to one another out of reverence for Christ.
    Wives, submit to your husbands as to the Lord. For the husband is the head of the wife as Christ is the head of the church, his body, of which he is the Savior. Now as the church submits to Christ, so also wives should submit to their husbands in everything.
    Husbands, love your wives, just as Christ loved the church and gave himself up for her to make her holy, cleansing her by the washing with water through the word, and to present her to himself as a radiant church, without stain or wrinkle or any other blemish, but holy and blameless. In this same way, husbands ought to love their wives as their own bodies. He who loves his wife loves himself. After all, no one ever hated his own body, but he feeds and cares for it, just as Christ does the church—for we are members of his body. "For this reason a man will leave his father and mother and be united to his wife, and the two will become one flesh." This is a profound mystery—but I am talking about Christ and the church. However, each one of you also must love his wife as he loves himself, and the wife must respect her husband (Eph 5:21-33).

PRAYER

Lord, your love is more than we can understand! You laid aside your glory that you might become one with us in our humanity, dying for our sins, being raised on the third day, making us a part of your new creation. That your desire should be for us is more than we can ever fully comprehend. Thank you!
    Forgive me for all the times when I have wanted to dominate and control rather than love and serve.
    Teach me to be strong so that in giving myself to others this day I may be a part of bringing your grace to a hurting world. Amen.

Day 41

Poem 18 (7:11–13)

Invitation: "Let us go early"

Woman
Come, my lover, let us go to the countryside,
   let us spend the night in the villages.
Let us go early to the vineyards
   to see if the vines have budded,
if their blossoms have opened,
    and if the pomegranates are in bloom—
   there I will give you my love.
The mandrakes send out their fragrance,
   and at our door is every delicacy,
both new and old,
   that I have stored up for you, my lover.

THE RETURNS OF LOVE

Once again, the lovers come right back at each other in the mutual expression of their love and desire. The man has just spoken his remarkable "Praise Song," and now the woman immediately responds with her "Admiration Dialogue."[82] Her caresses and promises of love (verse 12) correspond to his (verses 8–9), and even the plant metaphors and vines are to be found in each.[83] The reciprocal nature of love is everywhere present, and as we should have by now grown accustomed, the passion is building in this lover's tit for tat. As on the two previous occasions of the man giving a "long speech" (4:1—5:1 and 6:4—7:9), this one also leads to an erotic crescendo.[84]

82. Fox, *Love Songs*, 162.
83. Keel, *Song*, 253.
84. Exum, *Song*, 240.

Praise expressed is irresistible. Love returned is irrepressible. Invitation is everywhere present. Love, when joyfully given and liberally expressed, can never be stopped. "Love never fails" (1 Cor 13:8).

THE BUDDING OF SPRING

We also should not be surprised that it is out to the garden and into the vineyards that the Shulammite takes the man, intending to give him her love. Her invitation to escape into the countryside reads more literally in the Hebrew, "Out into the fields and among the henna bushes."[85]

As we have seen before (cf. 2:11–13; 6:11), it is springtime in our text, and love and passion are budding and bursting forth. By the end of our poem, they are in full bloom. By now we understand, "Love in the spring time is a common literary motif. It seems to suggest that powers and urges that have long lain dormant can now burst forth unhindered and without restraint. The imagery seems to indicate that there is a time and a season for everything. There were times when restraint was necessary, but now it is a time to embrace."[86]

It is possible, of course, that the repetition of the love-in-the spring theme, now for the third time, might all have taken place in a single season. This is poetry before it is history. So much has happened between the three springtime references. There have been so many ups and downs that the repetition suggests if not the passing of time, then at least the continued renewal and revival of love. Love is forever springing up and being renewed in their relationship to each other.

The point the poet is making is that love surely does not have to become tired out and worn down, much less characterized by a wintery chill. Winter never appears in the Song, and whatever chills may occur in their relationships, it is always spring and not winter of which the Song speaks.

The faithful in Israel would surely understand the poetry of that to which our author speaks. After all, they sang the Psalms:

> Weeping may remain for a night,
>   but rejoicing comes in the morning. . . .
> He who goes out weeping,
>   carrying seed to sow,

---

85. Gledhill, *Song*, 211.
86. Ibid., 212.

will return with songs of joy,
   carrying sheaves with him (Ps 30:5; 126:6).

Love is being renewed and revived in our text. Indeed, it breaks forth with such passion that our lovers have forgotten that it can be anything but spring. "The whole of nature seems to be sprouting and blossoming, and the two lovers want to be part of that. Their love has blossomed and become fragrant, they are ripe for love."[87]

What is more, the lovers are not only aware that it is spring, but it is also out in the midst of the fields and the vineyards that they want to give their love to each other. What is in view here is the wild and uninhibited playfulness of the lovers. As in the story of Rachel and Leah,[88] inhabitants of ancient Israel understood mandrakes to be an aphrodisiac, and the lovers are exploring new ways of pleasing each other. As always, the Shulammite is suggestive and seductive and never stops taking the initiative. She is confident in her ability to satisfy him, and her advanced planning for the "weekend" is driving the man wild with frenzied anticipation.[89]

THE WELL-KEPT GARDEN

As many have pointed out, the garden poetically represents and is in fact symbolic of the Shulammite.[90] The woman herself is the garden where these exotic plants grow.[91] It is herself that she gives as she repeatedly states her desire to give him her love.

> Come, my lover, let us go to the countryside,
>   let us spend the night in the villages.
> Let us go early to the vineyards
>   to see if the vines have budded,
> if their blossoms have opened,
>   and if the pomegranates are in bloom—
>   there I will give you my love.

This passion is both secure and sustained because the notes of the previous song are left ringing in her ears.

87. Ibid., 211–12.
88. Genesis 30:14–16.
89. Gledhill, *Song*, 213.
90. Longman, *Song*, 199.
91. Murphy, *Song*, 187.

> I belong to my lover,
>> and his desire is for me.

Repeatedly she exclaims, "There I will give you my love" (verse 12), and with confidence she exclaims:

> and at our door is every delicacy,
> both new and old,
>> that I have stored up for you, my lover.

The security of the relationship does not lead to a wilting of the passion. To the contrary, it breaks out in fresh and surprising ways. The text in verse 13 may be translated, "My caresses are saved up for you."[92] What this indicates is that "she has stored up or *treasured* . . . everything that is near and dear to her," and she intends to give him everything.[93] Even more than that, it indicates that she is not beyond suggesting that she intends to teach him a thing or two![94]

A TIME FOR EVERYTHING

It is not simply that spring is poetically the time of love and lovemaking and that the countryside is a fantasy place for lovemaking and romance.[95] She suggests that she wants them to explore the progress of spring and observe the beauty of the vegetation as it begins to grow and blossom and flourish. Lovers are always cultivating, exploring, and delighting in what is taking place between them. If in the past she has said that love is not to be awakened before its time, now she is suggesting that the time is right for love as nature itself indicates. "The fruits of love are ripe for eating."[96]

Again, the passion and initiative that is written everywhere over this text is not the frenzied promiscuity of modern culture, where women and men are desperately and anxiously seeking love in all the wrong places and not finding it. Her passion is not born of an anxiety that wants to know that she is found desirable, "Please love me, please." It is a passion that comes from being his bride and knowing beyond a

---

92. Fox, *Love Songs*, 165.
93. Longman, *Song*, 202.
94. Gledhill, *Song*, 213.
95. Longman, *Song*, 199, 201.
96. Fox, *Love Songs*, 165.

shadow of a doubt that she not only belongs to him, but also that he desires for her to belong to him.

Nor can we miss that there is a confidence behind her passion born of the fact that the music of praise, encouragement, and affirmation has not failed to miss a single beat for many moons now. The woman is filled with confidence so that she is not only able to dance but also to take delight in love and to be filled with passion and initiative. Her love, as she says, is hers to give, and she has stored it up for him alone.

TIME SPENT TOGETHER

This is also about time spent together. If the city has been the place of alienation, the countryside is the location of intimacy.[97] It is clear that they cannot spend too much time together; but more than that, it is not planned, forced, or mechanical. It is at its heart adventurous, romantic, and less mechanical[98] than is often the case in even the best of relationships. It is spontaneous in its suggestion, relational in its implementation, and almost irrational in the times and places where it finds its expression.

REFLECTION

There is everywhere present in our song the theme of our being a part of creation and of our "unashamed delight in participating in the natural order of things."[99] Like the first couple before the fall, the lovers are, as it were, "naked and unashamed"[100] as they "splash around in creation." All of the senses take part in the experience of love in the midst of nature and creation. The external realm is poetically in complete harmony with the internal world of the lovers who are still, once again and always, in the spring of their lives and their love.[101]

The whole Song is thoroughly sensual, not just because of their passion for each other, but also in terms of the totality of the pleasures that the lovers derive from both nature and love. They are frolicking in the fields and finding love.

97. Longman, *Song*, 200.
98. Gledhill, *Song*, 213.
99. Ibid., 212.
100. Genesis 2:25.
101. Fox, *Love Songs*, 162.

> This is my Father's world,
>   And to my list'ning ears
> All nature sings, and round me rings
>   The music of the spheres.
> This is my Father's world,
>   I rest me in the thought,
> Of rock and trees, of skies and seas—
>   His hand the wonders wrought.[102]

In the great order of things, it is not only human beings who long for love. The creation of which we are a part, as every environmentalist knows, also longs for its redemption, the return of its harmony, and the full expression of its splendor. In the meantime, the budding of the flowers and the lovers in the garden remind us that all is not lost. The pleasures of love and the beginning harmony of relationships shout the pleasures of God and the redemption begun already in the midst of Christ's new creation.

The Song turns out to be not just about love but also about life and its questions. "The answer of Song of Songs is that all of life is a love song. Every subatomic particle, from the Big Bang to the senility of the sun, is a note in this incredibly complex symphony.... But we who are in it do not hear or know it unless we are told by the Singer, who is outside it and who alone can know the point of the whole."[103]

MEDITATION

As in His Creation, God Is Always Renewing Our Hearts and Our Lives

> The earth is the LORD's, and everything in it,
>   the world, and all who live in it;
> for he founded it upon the seas
>   and established it upon the waters (Ps 24:1–2).

> He will also send you rain for the seed you sow in the ground, and the food that comes from the land will be rich and plentiful. In that day your cattle will graze in broad meadows (Isa 30:23).

---

102. Babcock, "This Is My Father's World."
103. Kreeft, *Three Philosophies*, 105.

> Give, and it will be given to you. A good measure, pressed down, shaken together and running over, will be poured into your lap. For with the measure you use, it will be measured to you (Luke 6:38).

> Land that drinks in the rain often falling on it and that produces a crop useful to those for whom it is farmed receives the blessing of God (Heb 6:7).

PRAYER

Father, thank you for the magnificence of your creation and the splendor of your purposes for it. I praise you for the new life that is everywhere bursting out in it and for the renewal given to us in your love.

Forgive me for thinking that my efforts make anything new.

Please renew me by your grace and the strength of your Spirit so that, fed by your love, I may bring joy and blessing to others this day. Amen.

Day 42

Poem 19 (8:1–4)

Yearning: "If only you were"

Woman
If only you were to me like a brother,
   who was nursed at my mother's breasts!
Then, if I found you outside,
   I would kiss you,
and no one would despise me.
   I would lead you
and bring you to my mother's house—
   she who has taught me.
I would give you spiced wine to drink,
   the nectar of my pomegranates.
His left arm is under my head
   and his right arm embraces me.

Daughters of Jerusalem, I charge you:
   Do not arouse or awaken love
   until it so desires.

INTIMACY

Many have suggested that in our song the Shulammite is wishing that she and her lover "had the freedom of public expression of their love. What was not in good taste even for husband and wife was perfectly permissible between brother and sister."[104] Hence, the Shulammite's longing, "If only you were to me like a brother..."

---

104. For example, Carr, *Song*, 166. Longman suggests that we cannot be so sure in *Song*, 204.

The story of Isaac and Rebekah and Jacob and Rachel suggest otherwise.[105] Besides, the passionate woman who opened the Song of Songs by turning to her friends and saying, "Let him kiss me with the kisses of his mouth," strikes us as likely not to be too worried about social conventions in this regard.

Whatever the delicate cultural mores that may or may not be going on here, the suggestion that the Shulammite displays here a "charming lack of logic"[106] is very appealing. Love has its own way of expressing its confused emotions and passionate longings. She desires for her lover to be as close to her as a brother, and we might add, she wants him to be the type of brother she never had—one who was truly a brother that nursed at her mother's breasts, not just in fact but in a spiritual and emotional reality.

This is also about an intense desire for intimacy and privacy.[107] It is a longing to have someone who is so close to her and knows so much about her that no room is left for embarrassment, public or otherwise.

> Then if I found you outside,
>   I would kiss you,
>   and no one would despise me.

It is as if she is convinced that nothing can stop the longing for intimacy that exists in our text. So close, intimate, mutual, and affectionate is their love that the Shualammite is always looking for a time and a place where they can be outside of the gaze of the public and where there is no need to be self-conscious about their desire for each other.

Clearly, as at least one scholar suggests, she wants to have her lover for herself and to enjoy the security of having him without leaving her familiar surroundings. Perhaps she thinks that this might help her avoid the risk that comes with love.[108]

The whole affair is heightened by her fantasy of taking him to her mother's house, giving him spiced wine to drink, and sharing herself with him.

> I would lead you
>   and bring you to my mother's house—

---

105. Genesis 26:8; 29:11.
106. Rudolph, quoted by Murphy, *Song*, 188.
107. Murphy is particularly helpful here. Ibid.
108. Keel, *Song*, 261.

> she who has taught me.
> I would give you spiced wine to drink,
>   the nectar of my pomegranates.

Spiced wine is suggestive of an erotic intoxication that has been super charged, the picture of wine having already been used of the kisses of the mouth (1:2, 7:9). The pomegranates return again but this time it is she who is the aphrodisiac.

RESOLUTION

We have come full circle back to her mother and to a yearning for an enduring resolution of the tensions that first arose when her mother's sons abused her and forced her to work in the vineyards, the result of which was that she had neglected her own (1:6).

If her shepherd and king had been a real brother, none of this would ever have happened, nor would it have been a part of their history together. He would have nursed at her mother's own breasts, which in its own way suggests both the intimate and erotic nature of their relationship.[109] This is about "intimate familiarity from the very beginning."[110] Where once he called her "my sister, my bride," now she exclaims:

> If only you were to me like a brother,
>   who was nursed at my mother's breasts!

ACCEPTANCE

In the end, we have to say that this is also about public expectations and private intentions and the way that they often collide. The public figures mentioned in our Song "act as a brake on the amorous activities of the young lovers, so that they are in constant tension. They want to be free of the restraint, yet they want to possess that public recognition of their love."[111] Perhaps it is a tension that is not without its value, as the refrain seems to suggest:

> Daughters of Jerusalem, I charge you:
>   Do not arouse or awaken love
>   until it so desires.

---

109. Longman, *Song*, 204.
110. Keel, *Song*, 261.
111. Gledhill, *Song*, 217.

In fact, the Shulammite "wishes for the public acceptance of her right to love and to be united with the one she has chosen."[112] For all the modern pretense that love is what matters and that marriage is not important, this text shows us that there is a fundamental human yearning for love to be properly and publicly acknowledged, and it is only in that setting of commitment and security that love truly is able to lie down both in passion and in rest.

Some have even suggested that in this song the lovers are not yet married.[113] That may be true in as much as it would explain something of the yearning that permeates the text, but in a real sense, it is beside the point. We have already pointed out that the individual songs swirl around the central theme of the wedding in 3:6—5:1 and that we do not have a clear timeline represented in our text.[114] The Song is a collage of poems that are arranged around the central image of the wedding. Their meaning is not to be found in a pedestrian chronology of the events but in their swirling relationship to the center. Only then do the individual songs, emotions, and scenarios revolve, come to life, and find their meaning. That is precisely what is happening in our text in terms of the yearning that is being expressed. We are beginning in this and the following songs to come full circle as we revisit the characters and issues that populate the Song.

There remains in our text a note of unfulfilled yearning, but at the same time we have to say that this whole section (5:2—8:4), which began with some sense of unresolved distance and yearning, now ends, at least in the imagination, with the lovers once again (cf. 2:6) in each other's arms.[115]

> His left arm is under my head
> and his right arm embraces me.

---

112. Fox, *Love Songs*, 166.

113. Ibid.

114. Longman, in *Song*, 204, asserts of verse 1, "This verse is a nearly insuperable problem for those who want to read the Song as a logical plot from courtship to wedding and then early marriage. Here the relationship is best understood as a secret one; at least it is highly unlikely that they are married at this time."

115. Carr, *Song*, 168.

REFLECTION

There is a deep, almost primordial, human yearning for a love that is so extraordinary as to be described as being of the same flesh. It is the "bone of my bones and flesh of my flesh" impulse of the first man.[116]

There are many great loves illustrated in the Bible. David and Jonathan come readily to mind, and even there, we find this longing for a brother. In his lament for his friend Jonathan, who had been killed in battle, David would say:

> I grieve for you, Jonathan my brother.
>   you were very dear to me.
> Your love for me was wonderful,
>   more wonderful than that of women (2 Sam 1:26).

We have seen that this human yearning for an extraordinary love is suggested in one of the most famous of the ancient proverbs of Israel.

> A man of many companions may come to ruin,
>   but there is a friend who sticks closer than a brother (Prov 18:24).

The Christian witness is that the "Word became flesh and made his dwelling among us" (John 1:14). It is the extraordinary love of a brother that, when apprehended, becomes the fulfillment of human yearning. "Very rarely will anyone die for a righteous man, though for a good man someone might possibly dare to die. But God demonstrates his own love for us in this: While we were still sinners, Christ died for us" (Rom 5:7).

MEDITATION

Christ Is Our Brother. He Is Always Close to Us.

> O LORD, you have searched me
>   and you know me.
> You know when I sit and when I rise;
>   you perceive my thoughts from afar. . . .
> For you created my inmost being;
>   you knit me together in my mother's womb.
> I praise you because I am fearfully and wonderfully made;
>   your works are wonderful,
>   I know that full well (Ps 139:1–2, 13–14).

---

116. Genesis 2:23.

A friend loves at all times,
    and a brother is born for adversity (Prov 17:17).

"Say of your brothers, 'My people,' and
    of your sisters, 'My loved one'" (Hos 2:1).

One of them, the disciple whom Jesus loved, was reclining next to him (John 13:23).

For this reason he [Jesus] had to be made like his brothers in every way, in order that he might become a merciful and faithful high priest in service to God, and that he might make atonement for the sins of the people. Because he himself suffered when he was tempted, he is able to help those who are being tempted (Heb 2:17–18).

PRAYER

Thank you, Lord, for being my brother, sharing my flesh and blood, and knowing and understanding all about me.

Forgive me for acting as if you could never understand. You have been tempted and tried and suffered more than I even can or will be.

Teach me now to be so much a part of your family that I will be there for others even as you are present for me. Amen.

Section 7

Desire and Confidence, 8:5–14

Day 43

Poem 20 (8:5–7) A

Continuity: "Under the apple tree"

Friends
A. Who is this coming up from the desert
  leaning on her lover?

Woman
Under the apple tree I roused you;
  there your mother conceived you,
  there she who was in labor gave you birth.

B. Place me like a seal over your heart,
  like a seal on your arm;
for love is as strong as death,
  its jealousy unyielding as the grave.
It burns like blazing fire,
  like a mighty flame.
Many waters cannot quench love;
  rivers cannot wash it away.
If one were to give
  all the wealth of his house for love,
  it would be utterly scorned.

We have now come to the final cycle of songs. This is the last section of the Song, and we move in part 3, "Lost and Found" (5:2—8:14), from what we have called "Fear and Joy" (5:2—8:4) to "Desire and Confidence" (8:5–14). This section forms a type of curtain call in which all the characters who have appeared in the Song will make a final appearance before bringing the book to an end.[1]

---

1. See Gledhill, *Song*, 219.

Before we get into the heart of this final movement, we need to be aware of the friends and what they say to us. We should also notice that the tensions that emerged in the last song will soon continue to reappear in the final cycle of songs.

COMING UP FROM THE WILDERNESS

As the friends introduce us to a new song, it is to the Shulammite that they point our attention. We have seen this opening line before in 3:6, where it also functioned to introduce us to a new unit of the Song.[2] As on that occasion, the object of attention is coming up from the wilderness.

> Who is this coming up from the desert
> leaning on her lover:

On a previous occasion when she was invited to come from the wilderness (4:8), she appeared as a woman emerging from the mountain heights: wild, perhaps untamed, and certainly inaccessible. In a second such incident when the friends pointed to a chariot coming up out of the wilderness (3:6–8), the incident was surrounded by a sense of mystery and distance.[3] Here, as in the rest of the Song, the countryside has become associated with privacy and intimacy. It is the place where their togetherness can blossom, fostered as it is by being a retreat for the lovers.[4]

As she comes up from the wilderness leaning on her lover, it is not so much that she has become tame and complaisant, as some suggest,[5] nor weary and dependent, as it is that what the poem suggests is closeness and intimacy.[6] Her leaning on her lover is not intended to suggest dependency in the narrow sense of the word but of her finding him trustworthy and true. It conveys a sense of, "This is one whom I can trust!" It denotes intimacy and mutual dependence[7] and reflects a strong and comfortable companionship that we have seen grow out of their

---

2. Murphy, *Song*, 195.
3. Keel, *Song*, 265.
4. Longman, *Song*, 208.
5. Ibid.
6. Carr, *Song*, 168–69.
7. Longman, *Song*, 208.

union one with the other. Perhaps we can even say that she is "proudly displaying her beloved on her arm."[8]

HER MOTHER

We are now well into our Song, and it is her mother who once again becomes a part of the "story." It is not surprising that she appears yet again, given the tensions present in our last song (8:1–4) related to disapproval. As we might expect, the brothers will soon make an entrance of their own. The defining moments in our childhood that have shaped our identity and our insecurities (as in 1:6) never entirely leave us. These experiences trigger fears of disapproval that have been reinforced by incidents in which the "watchmen" have failed to help us or else done us harm (3:3; 5:6–7).

This text is about becoming an adult, with all the tensions of standing on our own while reflecting upon and honoring the one who has raised us. It is about what the Scriptures call "leaving mother and father and becoming one flesh" (Eph 5:31).

HER SELF

Now she is coming up out of the wilderness, confident in the companionship of the one who has loved and honored her and who in the last such incident (3:6–11) had been to her as a king. He had lavishly and lovingly spared no expense to provide for her security and to display her as the jewel in his crown. Everything in the Song has revolved around that moment when he took her to be his bride.

She is confident in their love. In the strength of this moment, she is able not only to overcome the past, but she is also ready to look to the future. She takes her lover to the place where his mother had conceived him.

> Under the apple tree I roused you;
>   there your mother conceived you,
>   there she who was in labor gave you birth.

Returning to the place where one has been conceived is apparently a reference to the popular superstition that the place of one's conception

---

8. Gledhill, *Song*, 219.

affected the nature of the offspring.⁹ In other words, as she begins to think about their having children together, she wants to make sure that her child is as fragrant, strong, shady, fruitful, and delightful as her lover who has all the characteristics of the apple tree.¹⁰

THEIR CHILDREN

So far in the Song, sex has been about mutual self-giving, pleasure, passion, and bonding. We need to underline that this is as it should be. It is entirely in keeping with God's purposes, exemplified in our much-repeated refrain on Adam's delight when the woman was first given to him in the garden.¹¹

Although this goes against some Christian tradition, we should not shrink from being able to say, "The procreation aspect of the act is only a by-product of its primary recreational function." The first pair of lovers delights in one another and on their own terms. Children are understood as a blessing given only after the creation of the sexual pair.¹² This in part explains what would otherwise be the surprising lack of reference to a yearning for children as the lovers' ultimate expression of their coming together.

If we do not insist on the priority of sex as the ecstatic union of a man and a woman, then we will begin to define both the purpose of marriage and the function of women as primarily for the bearing of children. We will forfeit the joy of marriage, which will become impersonal, and we will lose what has always been the radical, counter-cultural, Christian assertion that the woman is not only created with the man in the image of God, but also that women are "heirs with you of the gracious gift of life" (1 Pet 3:7). For the apostle Peter who made that statement, this is about respect. The genius of the Song is precisely this. Passionate sex and joyful marriage are about companionship, "mutual self-giving and bonding."¹³

The implication of the passage that is before us is that the woman now comes up out of the countryside where she has spent time together

---

9. See Gledhill, *Song*, 224; Fox, *Love Songs*, 169; Genesis 30:31–43.
10. Cf. Song of Songs 2:3–5.
11. Genesis 2:23.
12. See the discussion in Gledhill, *Song*, 225.
13. Ibid.

with her lover, and she is exhibiting all the signs and fruits of what we have called "confident companionship." We will see that she is coming to terms with the past and with the significant people in her in life. She is ready for the first time to think about the blessing of children and to celebrate the fact that she will soon be keeper of the family tree.[14]

> Under the apple tree I roused you;
> there your mother conceived you,
> there she who was in labor gave you birth.

The apple tree is an erotic symbol of fertility, but more than that, it is a reference to generations who have shared the same escapades and experiences.[15] She appears to be indicating that sex and love are an eternal bond conceived in faithfulness. "We have made love; now our bond is eternal."[16] Love "forges the link between the generations with the same tenacity that death employs in its attempt to destroy them."[17] In this context of love and sexual union, life continues.[18]

Not only is this continuity portrayed in the common location, but the tree also depicts the biblical notion of the unbroken continuity of the whole human race,[19] and especially of the people of God.

> They are re-enacting the conception and travail of their mothers. It looks backwards through their mothers to generations gone by. The future is made secure by their own participation in this act of union. They are expressing solidarity with the generations past and the generations yet to come. They see themselves participating in the flow of history . . . a history which is so importantly catalogued in the endless genealogies of the Old Testament.[20]

WHO WE ARE

This is a wonderful moment. Love is bringing about the confidence, strength, and maturity that take place as we come to terms with the people and experiences that populate our past. She is becoming confident in

14. Keel, *Song*, 268–69.
15. Gledhill, *Song*, 224.
16. Fox, *Love Songs*, 167.
17. Keel, *Song*, 270.
18. Exum, *Song*, 250.
19. Keel, *Song*, 269.
20. Gledhill, *Song*, 223.

her own identity compared to her mother, his mother, her mother's sons, who will soon reappear, and the broader community represented by the daughters of Jerusalem, who are mentioned some seven times.[21]

Whether we like it or not, there is, as in this text, "the presence of an audience, onlookers who participate in the unfolding of the lovers' relationship."[22] The difference is that the poem now portrays the value of both tradition and the community. She can understand what it means to say without fear, "I am, because we are."[23]

REFLECTION

There is great insight here. As we have seen before, love is set in the midst of community. That certainly brings its tensions, but lovers who spend their time in splendid isolation apart from the community of faith have their roots dangling in the air, not firmly planted in the soil of grace that belongs to the people of God. They are destined for anxiety and prone to separation, and their relationship tends to shrivel and die. We are created in the image of God and made in the likeness of the Trinity, for union and communion.

The Song of Songs is a part of the great tradition and library that belongs to the people of God in every place and across all time. As such, the man and the woman in our Song are not merely keeping in touch with family and community; they are caught up in that great tree that is of God's own planting.[24] They live among "the daughters of Jerusalem"— the city of God. They are now firmly planted in the purposes of God and in what it is he is doing in the world. Apart from that, they would be nothing more than two desperate lovers caught up in passion for themselves, an interesting example of ancient love and lovemaking but no more than a speck of dust in the wind. They would have no meaning either in the past or for the future, and their story would never have been passed down to us.

---

21. Song of Songs 1:5; 2:7; 3:5; 5:8; 5:16; 6:4; 8:4.
22. Exum, *Song*, 248.
23. John Mbiti, quoted by Gledhill, *Song*, 223.
24. Ezekiel 17.

MEDITATION

God Makes Us a Part of His Continuing Purposes

Blessed are all who fear the LORD,
  who walk in his ways.
You will eat the fruit of your labor;
  blessings and prosperity will be yours.
Your wife will be like a fruitful vine
  within your house;
your sons will be like olive shoots
  around your table.
Thus is the man blessed
  who fears the LORD.

May the LORD bless you from Zion
  all the days of your life;
may you see the prosperity of Jerusalem,
  and may you live to see your children's children.

Peace be upon Israel (Ps 128).

A shoot will come up from the stump of Jesse;
  from his roots a Branch will bear fruit (Isa 11:1).

Again he said, "What shall we say the kingdom of God is like, or what parable shall we use to describe it? It is like a mustard seed, which is the smallest seed you plant in the ground. Yet when planted, it grows and becomes the largest of all garden plants, with such big branches that the birds of the air can perch in its shade" (Mark 4:30–32).

He who has an ear, let him hear what the Spirit says to the churches. To him who overcomes, I will give the right to eat from the tree of life, which is in the paradise of God. . . .
    "Blessed are those who wash their robes, that they may have the right to the tree of life and may go through the gates into the city" (Rev 2:7, 22:14).

PRAYER

Father, I praise you for the great tree of life and for making me a part of it and what you are doing in the world.

Lord, I confess that I have often acted on my own and not in union with you. Were it not for your mercy, you would have long broken me off as a dead branch.

I praise you for all those who have gone before me and passed on the story of your love to me.

Teach me to cultivate my relationships and apply the Song in such a way that I will be a part of you passing on your grace to yet another generation. Amen.

Day 44

Poem 21 (8:5–7) B

Identity: "Like a seal over your heart"

Friends
A. Who is this coming up from the desert
   leaning on her lover:

Woman
Under the apple tree I roused you;
   there your mother conceived you,
   there she who was in labor gave you birth.

B. Place me like a seal over your heart,
   like a seal on your arm;
for love is as strong as death,
   its jealousy unyielding as the grave.
It burns like blazing fire,
   like a mighty flame.
Many waters cannot quench love;
   rivers cannot wash it away.
If one were to give
   all the wealth of his house for love,
   it would be utterly scorned.

THE CLIMAX

We have come to the very climax of the book. This is the Song's crescendo if not its finale. In these remarkable lines, the woman asserts both the power and the value of love.[25]

---

25. Fox, *Love Songs*, 167.

Her concluding exclamation not only forms the high point of the book, but it also contains a number of metaphors with which our culture is still familiar, even if it does not know from where they came.

In a moment, she is going to tell us what love is, but first we must observe that her definition will be set in the context of longing and desire. Love, as we have said, is not a science—it is an art. It is not an animal that can be dissected or a set of rational propositions that can be reduced to a twelve-step program. It is about relationships and is driven by deep personal yearnings of which reason often can make little sense. Here love is personalized. It can have a will of its own.[26]

HER DESIRE

> Place me like a seal over your heart,
> like a seal on your arm; . . .

In the ancient world, the validity of a document would be proven by its seal. Generally, there were two forms, either as a stamp or as a cylinder that could be rolled out onto the document. In the biblical world, it could also be worn like a ring on the finger, or it might be tied around the neck[27] or even be found hanging on the arm.[28]

We can still understand the impulse behind all this. It is not uncommon to see a charm hanging around one's neck signifying the desire to have its protection. A woman might have a picture of her lover in a locket around her neck as her prized possession, or a man might have a large gold chain or amulet hanging from his neck as an assertion of confidence and vitality. Even the toughest of bikers will tattoo mom's name on his arm. All of these things are signified here,[29] and she wants to be all these things to him.

The Shulammite wants to be stamped over his heart as sure proof that she is his precious possession, the one with whom he has a special intimacy,[30] the person to whom he belongs and with whom he is both

---

26. See Song of Songs 8:4; 3:5; 2:7. Exum, *Song*, 249.

27. Jeremiah 22:24; Genesis 38:18, 25. See also Genesis 41:42; 1 Kings 21:8; Ester 8:8; Haggai 2:23.

28. Exum, *Song*, 250.

29. Keel, *Song*, 272.

30. Fox, *Love Songs*, 169.

identified and committed.³¹ She wants to be indelibly written onto his heart, the place that makes him tick and beat with life,³² because she wants to know that she is the one who makes him pound with life. She desires to be placed like a seal over his heart so that an inner loyalty may characterize their intimacy, and she wants to be placed like a seal over his arm as a public profession of their belonging to one another.³³ The whole world must know that whether together or apart, they belong to each other, come what may.

This is not, "I wish you would." It is, "You must!" She has grown strong and confident, as we shall see in our next poems. Their union is secure and indissoluble. This is about identity and about being as intimately bound up with him as his seal might be.³⁴

REFLECTION

The idea of being sealed, with all of its public assertion of identity and ownership, has a deep tradition in the Scriptures. When ancient kings entered into covenants with their subjects, a sign or seal would always accompany their stipulations. From the very earliest of times, the people of God understood that when God entered into his gracious covenant with them, they would be signed and sealed as belonging to the Lord.³⁵

This was not merely a mark of ownership for the people of God, but also included is a deep sense of pride of ownership. Once the Lord entered into covenant with his people, the two parties, God and his people, belonged to one another. It carried with it a sense of obligation, but it also brought an assurance and confidence that comes from being claimed by grace. The characteristic refrain of this relationship would be, "I will be your God, and you will be my people."³⁶ We have seen this echoed in the covenant relationship between our lovers, "My lover is mine, and I am his."³⁷

---

31. Longman, *Song*, 209.
32. Ibid., 210.
33. Gledhill, *Song*, 227.
34. Exum, *Song*, 250.
35. Genesis 17:10.
36. For example, Leviticus 26:9–12; 2 Corinthians 6:16.
37. Song of Songs 2:16.

In the contemporary church, much of this has been lost because we have turned the signs of God's covenants upside down. We have made them primarily professions of *our* faith rather than signs of *his* covenant of grace in the first place. In so doing, we lose the comfort and assurance that the Shulammite is reaching for in this text by asking that she be placed like a seal over her lover's heart.

The signs of God's grace—circumcision and Passover in the Old Covenant and baptism and the Lord's Supper in the New—are God's public sealing of us as his own. They are signs of our entering and belonging.[38] Technically, they are not things that we do so much as things that God gives us and in which we participate.[39] As in a wedding, a ring is given to us as a sign and seal, and we wear it with pride, confidence, and joy.

Signs and sealing, as the Shulammite knows full well, are also representations of a deeper inner reality.[40] In God's case, they are about his choosing us and pouring out his grace upon us, giving us a new heart, sealing us with his Spirit,[41] owning us as his own, and numbering us among his people. It is about love, about finding and being found. It is about pride of ownership and the assurance, confidence, and joy that comes with being identified with, cared for, and loved.

MEDITATION

God Makes It Known That We Belong to Him

> "'On that day,' declares the LORD Almighty, 'I will take you, my servant Zerubbabel son of Shealtiel,' declares the LORD, 'and I will make you like my signet ring, for I have chosen you,' declares the LORD Almighty" (Hag 2:23).

> For no matter how many promises God has made, they are "Yes" in Christ. And so through him the "Amen" is spoken by us to the glory of God. Now it is God who makes both us and you stand

---

38. For example, Exodus 12:48; Acts 2:41; 1 Corinthians 12:13; 10:17.

39. Luke 22:19. Similarly, the refrain "be baptized" (Matt 3:13; Luke 3:12; Acts 2:38; 10:48) suggests not something that we do so much as it is something done to us in the name of another.

40. Colossians 2:9–14; 1 Corinthians 10:16.

41. Hebrews 8:10.

firm in Christ. He anointed us, set his seal of ownership on us, and put his Spirit in our hearts as a deposit, guaranteeing what is to come (2 Cor 1:20–21).

And you also were included in Christ when you heard the word of truth, the gospel of your salvation. Having believed, you were marked in him with a seal, the promised Holy Spirit, who is a deposit guaranteeing our inheritance until the redemption of those who are God's possession—to the praise of his glory (Eph 1:13–14).

PRAYER

Father, thank you for placing your love like a seal over my heart. I am glad that you are not afraid to do it in such a way that everyone can see that you love and own me as your own.

I confess yet again that I am always trying to prove that I am good enough for your love, and far too often I am trusting in my promises to you rather than your promise to me.

Lord, make me confident in your love today. Help me to wear the badge of your love proudly. By the grace of your Holy Spirit, cause what has been sealed and promised to me to come to fruition in my life so that others can also see your glory. Amen.

Day 45

Poem 20 (8:6–7) C

Love: "As strong as death"

Friends
A. Who is this coming up from the desert
   leaning on her lover?

Woman
Under the apple tree I roused you;
   there your mother conceived you,
   there she who was in labor gave you birth.

B. Place me like a seal over your heart,
   like a seal on your arm;
C. for love is as strong as death,
   its jealousy unyielding as the grave.
It burns like blazing fire,
   like a mighty flame.
Many waters cannot quench love;
   rivers cannot wash it away.
If one were to give
   all the wealth of his house for love,
   it would be utterly scorned.

CONFIDENCE

These are the most remarkable lines in the whole of our book. Here the Song reaches its crescendo because, "The Shulammite has discovered in herself the inexorable power of love and can now speak of it without seeming extravagant."[42] As someone else has said, "The teasing of her companions cannot affect her, nor will her brothers any longer hold her

---

42. Fox, *Love Songs*, 168.

under their control. She has already gone forth from her home to open spaces—literally and figuratively—to blossom with the land, even as her own "vineyard" has blossomed. She knows love, and she knows that none can stand up to the fierce power it bestows on its possessors."[43]

So far in the Song, love has been described to us by way of the interaction between the lovers. Here its grandeur is portrayed and its meaning probed in a way that is far more direct than before.[44] The Shulammite comes right out and gives us her remarkable conclusions in terms of how love is to be understood. This is a part of the confidence and maturity that has come to characterize her.

Her extraordinary conclusions are spoken with a force of poetry that is quite unforgettable. She will pile up image upon image to describe "the unconquerability of love in the face of all its foes."[45] To do so, she will go to powerful, almost mythological, images and metaphors familiar to the peoples of the Ancient Near East.

AS STRONG AS DEATH

The Shulammite's first assertion is that love is as strong as death. In other words, the "power of love's passion is just as unrelenting and elemental as death."[46] Once it makes its claim, it cannot be resisted.

The word "strong" is used in the Bible of an "irresistible assailant or an immovable defender."[47] The fact is that "love will not give up, but will pursue the loved one just as persistently as the great and fearful power of 'Death'"[48] Or as the apostle Paul put it, "It always protects, always trusts, always hopes, always perseveres. Love never fails" (1 Cor 13:7–8).

This is an astounding statement. Death robbed me of my father when I was fifteen, my mother when I was twenty-seven, and my wife of two of her brothers while still in their thirties. Sooner or later, we come to understand that death is an irresistible assailant and an immovable defender. But the assertion of Scripture is that so is love.

---

43. Ibid.
44. M. Sadgrove, quoted by Longman, *Song*, 209.
45. Gledhill, *Song*, 226
46. Keel, *Song*, 275.
47. Numbers 13:28; Judges 14:18. Carr, *Song*, 150.
48. Murray, *Song*, 197.

JEALOUSY

This is not the jealousy of the "green-eyed monster" that eats its victims alive or a silly stupidity that is born of insecurity. This jealousy is a positive virtue. It comes from being made in the image of God who said, "I, the LORD your God, am a jealous God" (Deut 9:5).

The Lord is described as a "devouring fire, a jealous god" who brooks no rivals.[49] He takes and protects what properly belongs to him,[50] not merely as a prized possession but as a covenanted responsibility. Like death, this jealousy will not give up what belongs to it. This is "the jealousy of love asserting its possession and right of property; the reaction of love against any diminution of its possession, against any reserve in its response, the 'self-vindication of angry love.'"[51]

There is, of course, a potential for danger in jealousy as in fire. Love will be threatened, and love must be handled with care.[52] Even as she says this, the Shulammite is warning off the wolves,[53] but she has learned enough to know that she will never let go of this love that belongs to her.

A BLAZING FIRE

Literally read, the text suggests that love is like an arrow of fire or like a bolt of lightning. The repetition of the poetry builds into a sense of its being a superlative. Like nothing else, it can strike and set on fire.

More particularly, buried in the original Hebrew text there appears to be a shortened form of the divine name that gives the fire its might. It is, if you will, a fire lit of God,[54] or a "God-fire." Just about every commentator ends up agreeing that the Hebrew suggests that love has its origins in a divine source.[55] In other words, love burns like a fire lit by God.

---

49. Ibid. Song of Songs 4:23-24; 5:9; 6:15; Exodus 20:5; 34:14. Exum, *Song*, 252.
50. Carr, *Song*, 170.
51. Delietzsch quoted in Fox, *Love Songs*, 170.
52. Longman, *Song*, 213.
53. Fox, *Love Songs*, 168.
54. Cf. Keel, *Song*, 275.
55. Murphy, *Song*, 191-92, 197-98.

MANY WATERS CANNOT QUENCH LOVE

Here her descriptions build to depict love as unquenchable even in the face of a mighty torrent. If the image of the "God-fire" speaks of is irresistible nature, here it is the unassailable force of love that is in view. Nothing can stop it or put it out. Like death, even in the face of great floods, nothing can stop this fire.

A number of scholars also point out that the Shulammite's words in their original context and time would be taken as alluding to primordial images of the gods fighting to bring order out of chaos.[56] There are similar biblical images also of the torrents that are pictured as swirling about in the underworld.[57] Not even these "gods" and demonic forces can quench love.[58]

MONEY CAN'T BUY LOVE

Now the Shulammite changes from images that have to do with the forces of nature to the equally strong and pervasive cultural forces that suggest that love should be compromised in the face of acquiring the comfort, glamour, and security of wealth. She finds contemptuous such "common sense" assumptions to do with a "good catch." Love is stronger than the passions of wealth and even the promise of security.

Even in a world of concubines and queens, the Shulammite has now grown strong and confident in love. Nothing can stop love; it can never be overcome. It refuses to be compromised.

REFLECTION

The Shulammite's words are breathtakingly beautiful. They sweep us up as in an epic romance. It is still possible, however, that the heady euphoria of the moment can quickly give way to the realities of life and the disappointments of love. If we have loved and lost, or seen the seal broken that we thought was placed over the heart, can we really say that love is as strong as death, its jealousy as unyielding as the grave, that it burns like a fire, and that many waters cannot quench love? Must common sense matters of financial security not win out in the end?

---

56. Longman, *Song*, 213–14.
57. For example, Ezekiel 31:15; Psalm 24:2; 76:3; 96:4; Isaiah 17:13; Job 1:16.
58. Longman, *Song*, 214.

Human disappointment, however, must never be allowed to be the arbiter of truth. Just about any mother who has ever held a baby to her breast knows that she would cling to that little one in the midst of a flood or brave the fires of a home to bring her child to safety. Only the utterly perverse would freely sell that child for money. At some level or another, we know that love is as strong as death and as unyielding as the grave. Our love can burn like a blazing fire and refuse to be quenched by the torrents of disappointment. Death has the ability to tear apart, but love has the ability to bind together.

God has given us this book to teach us how to love. It may be that we need to repent of our critical attitudes and learn to praise, or that we need to turn from a pathological need to control and dominate and learn to encourage and build up. We need to know that as we embark upon this thing called love or worry that we will fall victim to the disease called divorce. Love is an unquenchable fire lit by God.

As we have pointed out before, this is illustrated in the story of the biblical prophet Hosea—one of the most remarkable examples of human love that is to be found. His wife was unfaithful to him, but he would learn in the will of God to win her back with what today we would call "tough love."[59]

His story becomes an enactment of God's love for the unfaithful bride, Israel, even as Hosea would also describe love as being as strong as death.

> I will ransom them from the power of the grave;
> I will redeem them from death.
> Where, O death, are your plagues?
> Where, O grave, is your destruction? (Hos 13:14).

What is fascinating is that the apostle Paul would also pick up this verse and use it as a part of his explanation of the resurrection of Jesus Christ.[60] In other words, the truth of the Shulammite's assertions in regard to love are to be finally found in the love of God. "A perspective on human love is taken here that calls for theological evaluation,"[61] or as an

---

59. Hosea 1:2–3; 3:1–3.
60. First Corinthians 15:55.
61. Murphy, *Song*, 197.

ancient father of the church has said, love is as strong as death "because love slays guilt and sin and destroys the blows of death."[62]

Human love can be as blazing as a fire and as in the case of a Hosea, remain unquenched even in the face of the torrents of disappointment—but in the end it is but only a spark of the love that has been shown to us in Jesus Christ. He is the fire that has been lit of God, the one in whom the unassailable torrents of love and death have met. "Very rarely will anyone die for a righteous man, though for a good man someone might possibly dare to die. But God demonstrates his own love for us in this: While we were still sinners, Christ died for us" (Rom 5:7–8).

The prophets of ancient Israel, like the Shulammite, understood that nothing can stop love because God has made it to be so. God's love for his people would be won with a love unmatched in price, one that would place his people like a seal upon his heart that could not be broken. It was unassailable and unstoppable. As the Psalmist explains:

> No man can redeem the life of another
> or give to God a ransom for him—
> the ransom for a life is costly,
> no payment is ever enough—
> that he should live on forever
> and not see decay. . . .
>
> But God will redeem my life from the grave;
> he will surely take me to himself (Ps 49:7–9, 15).

The Shulammite's words form the crescendo of the book, and so it is with us. It is sealed on the cross. We know that because it is a fire lit in heaven that has been shot through our hearts. It is as strong as death, its demands for its right of possession as unyielding as the grave. Neither death nor the torrents of the underworld can overcome it. This is our Song's crescendo. It *is* "as good as it gets."

MEDITATION

The Love of God Is Unstoppable. Nothing Can Overcome It.

> The cords of death entangled me;
> the torrents of destruction overwhelmed me.

---

62. Ambrose, quoted by Pope, *Song*, 672.

> The cords of the grave coiled around me;
>   the snares of death confronted me.
> In my distress I called to the LORD;
>   I cried to my God for help.
> From his temple he heard my voice;
>   my cry came before him, into his ears. . . .
>
> He reached down from on high and took hold of me;
>   he drew me out of deep waters.
> He rescued me from my powerful enemy,
>   from my foes, who were too strong for me.
> They confronted me in the day of my disaster,
>   but the LORD was my support.
> He brought me out into a spacious place;
>   he rescued me because he delighted in me
> (Ps 18:4–6, 16–19).

> But now, this is what the LORD says—
>   he who created you, O Jacob,
>   he who formed you, O Israel:
> "Fear not, for I have redeemed you;
>   I have summoned you by name; you are mine.
> When you pass through the waters,
>   I will be with you;
> and when you pass through the rivers,
>   they will not sweep over you.
> When you walk through the fire,
>   you will not be burned;
>   the flames will not set you ablaze (Isa 43:1–2).

Who shall separate us from the love of Christ? Shall trouble or hardship or persecution or famine or nakedness or danger or sword? As it is written:

> "For your sake we face death all day long;
>   we are considered as sheep to be slaughtered."

No, in all these things we are more than conquerors through him who loved us. For I am convinced that neither death nor life, neither angels nor demons, neither the present nor the future, nor any powers, neither height nor depth, nor anything else in all creation, will be able to separate us from the love of God that is in Christ Jesus our Lord (Rom 8:35–39).

PRAYER

Thank you, Lord, for your love that is as strong as death. I praise you for your Son, Jesus Christ, who gave his life up in death so that we may be given new life in his resurrection. Thank you that your purposes and your love burn like a blazing fire and that neither death, hell, nor Satan can quench them.

Forgive me for even thinking that I can be lost to your love. Pardon me for acting as one who is striving for your love, insulting your grace, and failing to live as one who has been loved with a fire lit by you.

Lord, help me today not to sell out to things that are not worthy of your love, and teach me to give myself away even as you have given your Son to me. Amen.

Day 46

Poem 21 (8:8–10)

Self-Confidence: "My breasts are like towers"

Brothers
We have a young sister,
   and her breasts are not yet grown.
What shall we do for our sister
   for the day she is spoken for?
If she is a wall,
   we will build towers of silver on her.
If she is a door,
   we will enclose her with panels of cedar.

Woman
I am a wall,
   and my breasts are like towers.
Thus I have become in his eyes
   like one bringing contentment.

We have just finished in our last song the magnificent climax of our book. It is the striking crescendo that surely must be "as good as it gets."

Now we are even a little annoyed to have the brothers return. They form something of an anti-climax, but as we will discover, it is for a good reason. What is happening is that the volume is being turned back down to a more normal level, and as we have suggested, some characters we would rather forget make their appearance once again.

We are tempted to say that if this is the Song of Songs, the very best that there is in terms of love songs, then surely we might be allowed to expect that the concluding songs will end with a proud note of conquest, hope, and "success."

It is not that the Song will end with defeat and disappointment. To the contrary, the woman has grown confident in love and self-confident about her ability to love and be loved. But at the same time, we have to say that this is great literature and that as such, it speaks to the important and most meaningful issues of life that confront all of us as human beings. In other words, this is not a paperback romance novel written to leave us in an imaginary swoon that has nothing to do with real life. This is Scripture inspired by the Holy Spirit, and therefore, it is absolutely truthful in its reflections on the human condition, the meaning of love, the presence of hope, and above all, the need for healing, help, and reconciliation in our relationships.

WHAT'S GOING ON?

The first matter of frustration in our new song is that we have a last-minute appearance of a group of men we had met at the very beginning of the book. We have seen that the Shulammite's father, for whatever reason, has been nowhere present. Now we have to presume that those she had earlier called "my mother's sons" are the same group of characters that turn up once again to address her as their "young sister."

Most commentators suggest that they are simply carrying out their cultural duty and making sure that their younger sister is being well protected and taken care of in regard to the approaches of men and arrangements for marriage.[63]

> We have a young sister,
>   and her breasts are not yet grown.
> What shall we do for our sister
>   for the day she is spoken for?

It is even possible that the brothers may be offering reconciliation in light of their previous history and the tensions that it had caused.[64] If that is the case, they are not doing a very good job of it. Their words seem to undermine her sense of self, worth, and competence.

To be fair to them, their attitude, in fact, appears to be a mixed bag. It is possible that this is a playful tease on their part and that she even could be pleased with their approval.[65] But teasing and sibling banter can quickly go wrong, and it is rarely without some point that is to be made at the expense of the other.

---

63. Gledhill, *Song*, 236; Longman, *Song*, 215. Cf. Genesis 24:29–60; Judges 21:22.
64. Fox, *Love Songs*, 171.
65. Ibid., 172–73.

They appear to be suggesting that her sexual purity is very important for her marketability and they will do everything within their power to enhance her chances of a good marriage. Nice, I suppose?

> If she is a wall,
>   we will build towers of silver on her.
> If she is a door,
>   we will enclose her with panels of cedar.

Once again, the keepers of societal order are reluctant to believe that she is ready for love, and they wish to have the last word in saying when she is ready for marriage. Although headstrong younger sisters may need care and advice in regard to the attitudes of men, once again, this really is a put down.

Positively put, what they are saying is that if she is "a wall," that is, if she is sexually chaste, they will build a silver battlement for her that will further protect and enhance her wise decision. If she is "a door," that is, if she is "open" and not chaste, they will shut her away and wall her off with cedar panels.[66]

Just about everyone agrees that the Shulammite is a little testy in her reply.[67]

> I am a wall,
>   and my breasts are like towers.
> Thus I have become in his eyes
>   like one bringing contentment.

She is adamantly declaring her sexual purity, asserting her maturity, and pointing out that she is ready for love. Precisely because of her sexual maturity and exclusiveness, she is now fully ready for the type of intimate and satisfying relationship that will bring fulfillment, contentment, satisfaction, and wholeness.[68]

In the final line above, the word "contentment" or "peace" appears to be a play on the roots of her name, or even on Solomon's name. "There is a clear reference here to the 'Shulammite' as the 'completed one' of 6:13."[69] I take this verse of the song to mean therefore that she is saying,

---

66. Longman, *Song*, 216–17. See also Murphy, *Song*, 198–99.

67. See Fox, *Love Songs*, 172 for a helpful analysis of the various ways this text may be taken.

68. Longman, *Song*, 218.

69. Carr, *Song*, 173.

"You're putting me down. You think that I am young and unprepared for love. Listen, 'My breasts are towers.' They are strong, beautiful, and well formed. They have a power you know nothing about. Besides, I am the Shulammite. My name means 'peace.' I am like one who brings contentment. I already have the emotional maturity to complement and bring joy and contentment to the one whom I love."

Her confident reply makes it very clear that she is ready to leave her home and make life with another.

FLASHBACK

We have called this section the "curtain call" in which all the characters are coming out again to make a last appearance. This is a helpful image in that what they say will either suggest their growth in understanding and the development of their character or else it will serve to illustrate their lack of progress.

At the same time, it is not the most helpful of images because it implies that we are following a historical narrative in which one incident takes place after the other. As we have said, our Song is more creative than that. It is a collage of images clustered around the center, which is the wedding.

This song is best understood as a flashback—the reappearance of a topic that needs to be brought back up near the end of the video for the sake of resolution and understanding the progress, growth, and continuing issues of relationships.

THE POINT

The Shulammite, in her testy reply and play on her name of "contentment," is adamantly asserting that healthy relationships fulfill, round out, complement, and complete the other. Unlike her "brothers," love does not diminish, destroy, put down, or eat away at the sense of well-being of the one with whom we share our love. It encourages, builds up, restores, and brings healing to the other. This is what her experience has shown her to be true.

Relationships flourish where there is help, healing, and contentment. This may be especially true of lovers, but it is equally true of all relationships. Where there is genuine support and encouragement, joy and contentment follow, quite contrary to the tearing down that often characterizes siblings and colleagues.

At the same time, the reappearance of the brothers suggests that we are never entirely home free. They may have grown a little and their motives may not be entirely without virtue or even love, but something of the pestilence still hangs about in the air, and it has a way of coming back to hound and to hurt. As mature as the Shulammite has become, she remains sensitive to the challenges that her brothers represent.

We need to do them justice, however. Our supposedly well-meaning efforts to "protect" others can end up patronizing and putting them down, leaving them feeling demeaned and diminished. For example, the Scriptures point out how especially easy it is for fathers and husbands to fall into this trap.[70]

At the same time, we have to say that the Shulammite has grown strong and beautiful. Despite some justifiable testiness in her reply, she has gained an emotional maturity that proves her contention that she is ready for love. Where previously she would have said, "Do not stare at me, my mother's sons have ruined me by causing me to work out in the fields, my own vineyard I have neglected," now she is ready to deal with the situation. In contrast to what happened before, she now has been cultivating her garden with the love, praise, and affirmation of the one she always took out into the fields to be with her.

At the end of the video that we call the Song of Songs, we know that she is ready to leave home and set out with her love because she has learned to speak the truth in love. She has learned to say, "No, don't put me down. My breasts are towers, and I bring contentment and health to this relationship." She has gained a necessary maturity in terms of taking care of her own vineyard, in learning to dance, and in taking her love out into the fields, which were once the place of her hurt.

Her testiness is not a childish disobedience or an adolescent rebellion. It is a part of her maturity, which is evidenced by health and healing, as well as the praise of her friends, who have consistently told her, "What you have going is great. It is good, and to be praised."

---

70. Ephesians 6:4; 1 Peter 3:7.

REFLECTION

There is an incredible grace that permeates this passage, not in spite of the fact that the pestilence keeps coming back but precisely because it does return. The Shulammite has learned to handle it with confidence and strength. She has not grown weary but strong with what is an emotional and even sensual strength.

We all want to win the lottery, be "delivered," and never again have to face the stress that characterizes our daily lives. That is not the way it is in a fallen world. Grace is given to us to grow, and as hard as it is for us to understand, it is the very trials associated not least of all with relationships that help to form us into real human beings who are still standing at the end of the day. While we have been hard at work, we are surprised to discover that in fact it is grace that has been at work in our lives,[71] and that we have grown in strength, confidence, and even beauty.

MEDITATION

It Is in Our Trials that God Gives Us Confidence and Strength and We Grow Strong

> The LORD is my shepherd, I shall not be in want.
>   He makes me lie down in green pastures,
> he leads me beside quiet waters,
>   he restores my soul.
> He guides me in paths of righteousness
>   for his name's sake.
> Even though I walk
>   through the valley of the shadow of death,
> I will fear no evil,
>   for you are with me;
> your rod and your staff,
>   they comfort me.
>
> You prepare a table before me
>   in the presence of my enemies.
> You anoint my head with oil;
>   my cup overflows.
> Surely goodness and love will follow me
>   all the days of my life,

---

71. Philippians 2:12–13.

and I will dwell in the house of the LORD
  forever (Ps 23).

LORD, you establish peace for us;
  all that we have accomplished you have done for us.
O LORD, our God, other lords besides you have ruled over us,
  but your name alone do we honor (Isa 26:12–13).

"All this I have spoken while still with you. But the Counselor, the Holy Spirit, whom the Father will send in my name, will teach you all things and will remind you of everything I have said to you. Peace I leave with you; my peace I give you. I do not give to you as the world gives. Do not let your hearts be troubled and do not be afraid" (John 14:25–27).

His divine power has given us everything we need for life and godliness through our knowledge of him who called us by his own glory and goodness. Through these he has given us his very great and precious promises, so that through them you may participate in the divine nature and escape the corruption in the world caused by evil desires (2 Pet 1:3–4).

PRAYER

Father, thank you for leading me and helping me through all the trials I have encountered in my life. I praise you even for the difficult relationships that sometimes have plagued me. I am grateful that all along you have been at work in my life to use these things to make me more like Christ. Thank you for giving me grace and strength to grow and mature even when I thought I was getting nowhere.

Forgive me for complaining about the difficult things you have allowed and for thinking they had no purpose or that I could not endure.

Lord, now help me to make others strong with the same strength that you have given to me. Amen.

Day 47

Poem 22 (8:11–12)

Freedom: "Mine to give"

Woman
Solomon had a vineyard in Baal Hamon;
   he let out his vineyard to tenants.
Each was to bring for its fruit
   a thousand shekels of silver.
But my own vineyard is mine to give;
   the thousand shekels are for you, O Solomon,
   and two hundred are for those who tend its fruit.

THE SHULAMMITE'S LIBERATION

We are almost at the end of the Song of Songs, and we have come to what we may call the Shulammite's statement of liberation. It is a celebration of the freedom that she has found, an indication of her emotional maturity, and a proud, but proper, affirmation of her worth and dignity.

Even if we take our Song to be poetry and not a historical narrative, this text is quite shocking because her affirmation of freedom comes in the face of the most powerful, influential, and now most oppressive man in the land.[72] It is a brazen, almost revolutionary reference to the king, an act for which women have lost their necks for less.

We don't know where these vineyards of Solomon existed, although no one doubts that he owned many vineyards. We are supposed to understand this as a "guest appearance" by the great man himself. The ap-

---

72. Solomon's grand building projects became a harsh burden on his people. It eventually led to the division of his kingdom when his son refused to "lighten the yoke" around their necks (2 Chr 10:3–11).

pearance of Solomon is a literary device,[73] and as we are about to see, he is clearly not the hero of these songs. The best option is probably to take the name of the vineyards as also being a poetic allusion. Literally, the name Baal Hamon means, "owner of wealth" or "owner of a crowd."[74]

Solomon is an owner of many vineyards and a keeper of a crowd of women[75] acquired by his great wealth and power. He possessed one of the legendary harems of the world. This is in stark contrast to the ideal couple, who have only each other[76] and want only one another.

The Shulammite, who, of course, is a peasant girl with a great deal of spunk and not without a good sense of humor,[77] is basically saying, "Solomon, you can keep your thousands that you make off your vineyards and pay your tenants and laborers a few hundred. You can buy all the women and vineyards you want, but you can't buy love, and you could never buy me. My love is mine to give. I have tended my vineyard, and I have saved my love and only I can give it, and only my lover will receive it." This is a joyful, exuberant statement of a sense of self and worth.

Notice that she who had previously neglected her vineyard is now cultivating it. There is a confident assertion that as fertile as Solomon's vineyards may be, they are not to be compared with her garden. Unlike Solomon, who has to have other people cultivate his vineyards, she takes care of her own and now freely gives it to her lover for his keeping.[78]

There is a populist polemic here that once again asserts that shepherds and Shulammites who give their love exclusively to one another find greater wealth than kings with all of their possessions at hand. What is argued against is polygamy and promiscuity[79] but also a fascination with celebrity as "if only I were like" Solomon I would be happy. In fact, what Solomon is not in real life, she is.

It has been pointed out that here the woman is certainly understood as the sexual other, but she speaks of herself as the beloved ("my own vineyard is mine to give"). She does not understand herself to be a

---

73. Gledhill, *Song*, 238.
74. Ibid., 239.
75. First Kings 11:3. Cf. Ecclesiastes 2:4.
76. Longman, *Song*, 219.
77. Bloch and Bloch, *Song*, 218.
78. Fox, *Love Songs*, 174. However, Fox believes it is the man who is speaking here.
79. Longman, *Song*, 220.

sexual object to be protected by others and kept waiting for the owner to arrive. "The poem advocates the one-to-one I-thou relationship and rejects the debasement of sexuality inherent in treating others as sexual objects or property.[80]

REFLECTION

We may well argue that this song seems to fly in the face of the opening line of the Song of Songs, which reads, "Solomon's Song of Songs." We have already discussed how this should be understood,[81] but our present song does not preclude the fact that Solomon could have come to appreciate the wisdom of this song. In another great work that also wears Solomon's mantle, at least at its beginning, we are brought to the same conclusion.

> I undertook great projects: I built houses for myself and planted vineyards. I made gardens and parks and planted all kinds of fruit trees in them. I made reservoirs to water groves of flourishing trees. I bought male and female slaves and had other slaves who were born in my house. I also owned more herds and flocks than anyone in Jerusalem before me. I amassed silver and gold for myself, and the treasure of kings and provinces. I acquired men and women singers, and a harem as well—the delights of the heart of man. I became greater by far than anyone in Jerusalem before me. In all this my wisdom stayed with me.
>
> I denied myself nothing my eyes desired;
>   I refused my heart no pleasure.
> My heart took delight in all my work,
>   and this was the reward for all my labor.
> Yet when I surveyed all that my hands had done
>   and what I had toiled to achieve,
> everything was meaningless, a chasing after the wind;
>   nothing was gained under the sun (Eccl 2:4–11).

What Solomon discovered, albeit via a long detour, was that we are created by God and for God.[82] That is an exclusive relationship that allows everything else to fall into its proper place and come together in a splendid harmony and beauty of its own. Because we are created

---

80. Marcia Flak, quoted by Fox, *Love Songs*, 175.
81. See day 1.
82. Ecclesiastes 12:1, 13–14.

by God and in his image, the same is true of the love between a man and a woman. We can know the joy and passion of belonging to each other alone, or else we will discover the indignity of being regarded as property and conquest.

The Shulammite has proved it. For the first time in her life, she radiates with joy and confidence. These are the fruits of love.

MEDITATION

*In Faithfulness to God, and in Union with Christ,
We Are Given Freedom*

See, I set before you today life and prosperity, death and destruction. For I command you today to love the LORD your God, to walk in his ways, and to keep his commands, decrees and laws; then you will live and increase, and the LORD your God will bless you in the land you are entering to possess (Deut 30:15-16).

I will sing for the one I love
  a song about his vineyard:
My loved one had a vineyard
  on a fertile hillside. . . .

The vineyard of the LORD Almighty
  is the house of Israel,
and the men of Judah
  are the garden of his delight (Isa 5:1, 7).

"I am the true vine, and my Father is the gardener. He cuts off every branch in me that bears no fruit, while every branch that does bear fruit he prunes so that it will be even more fruitful. . .

"I am the vine; you are the branches. If a man remains in me and I in him, he will bear much fruit; apart from me you can do nothing" (John 15:1-2, 5).

He is the image of the invisible God, the firstborn over all creation. For by him all things were created: things in heaven and on earth, visible and invisible, whether thrones or powers or rulers or authorities; all things were created by him and for him. He is before all things, and in him all things hold together. And he is the head of the body, the church; he is the beginning and the firstborn from among the dead, so that in everything he might have the supremacy (Col 1:15–18).

PRAYER

Lord, I praise you for the joy and the freedom you have given us by treating us as your bride. Thank you for the love and dignity that is ours in Christ.

Forgive us, Lord, for all the times we have been unfaithful and found ourselves enslaved again as if we were not your sons and daughters!

Teach me this day to live in freedom and dignity so that I might have the strength to oppose the wrong, the grace to avoid the traps of the evil one, and most of all, the joy of living my life in praise of you. Amen.

Day 48

Poem 23 (8:13–14)

Happily Ever After?: "Let me hear your voice"

Man
You who dwell in the gardens
  with friends in attendance,
  let me hear your voice!

Friends
Come away, my lover,
  and be like a gazelle
or like a young stag
  on the spice-laden mountains.

NOT YET

Here we are at the end of the Song of Songs waiting for its happy ending. We want the shepherd and Shulammite to be strong, healthy, and well put together, prospering in love and in their relationships. If it is not "happily ever after" for this couple, then what hope is there for any of us that it can be?

We have to admit that here in the closing lines of our Song there is a certain tension in the air. "An indefinite sense of longing governs the scene."[83] The poem expresses a yearning for union.[84] "Let me hear your voice" is an imperative,[85] a command. Our English text flows a little too

---

83. Keel, *Song*, 285.
84. Longman, *Song*, 220.
85. Keel, *Song*, 285.

smoothly. There is a terseness in the Hebrew. We would have a better sense of this if it read,

> Man
> You who dwell in the gardens,
>   companions are listening,
>   let me hear your voice.[86]

"The sense of the verse is that the woman is in the garden but estranged from the man. He yearns to be in her close proximity; thus he asks that he might hear her voice."[87] Her companions appear to be getting in the way, almost as rivals. These companions are probably to be understood not merely as "the daughters of Jerusalem" who have been in attendance throughout the Song, but also as the wider circle of friends who had been at the wedding.[88] Even they can get in the way! The man apparently feels crowded out and even neglected, if not abandoned. "There seems to be some rupture in the relationship, or at least a misunderstanding on his part."[89]

There is static on the line. Some suggest that the foxes have come back. The man appears to be indicating that there is too much competition around and that maybe she is paying him insufficient attention. Perhaps he is even suggesting that there is a rupture in their relationship and he can't seem to find her, at least metaphorically.[90] Like God in the garden with Adam and Eve, someone still seems to be hiding, and once again, there are problems with hearing the voice of the other.

The Song appears to be coming to an end with the lovers still caught in "the endless cycle of love, its restless ebb and flow and fluctuating moods."[91] There is tension here between freedom and dependence, of not being able to live with each other and not being able to live without each other. Are we to be left thinking that love is a storm in which they are left swirling around each other, able to be lifted to heights of ecstasy or plunged into depths of despondency? If so, it is emotionally and ner-

---

86. Longman, *Song*, 221.
87. Ibid.
88. Carr, *Song*, 175.
89. Gledhill, *Song*, 243.
90. See the comments in ibid.
91. Ibid., 244.

vously exhausting[92] and would make for a peculiar ending.[93] Can it be that we are going to end the book with our lovers still caught in a storm of communication problems?

A more positive reading would emphasize that all lovers "spiral around each other, sometimes drawing closer in deepening intimacies of intercourse, physical, emotional, psychological, intellectual and spiritual; sometime withdrawing, letting each other find our own separate pathways, yet always secure in the knowledge of our ultimate mutual acceptance and attraction." In that case we understand that, "Each cycle of movement towards and away from each other must bring a deeper sense of that underlying commitment which is the true bond of freedom."[94]

Nevertheless, all of this suggests that love is never satisfied, and it is always longing for more.[95] It ends with an anticipation of love not yet fulfilled. In the end, they have not yet arrived.[96]

"ALREADY"

At the same time, while not denying this realization, we have to say that something is already and still happening that is good, wonderful, and to be celebrated. Her invitation, "Come my lover . . . and be like a gazelle" seems to be asking him to assert his independence,[97] extricate himself from this awkward situation, and have them "sneak away from anything and anyone that separates them from each other and come to her."[98] There is a gentleness and understanding in her response that is to be admired.

It is an acknowledgment that they find that their love must be characterized by the deepest mutual understanding and sufficiency in one another. They recognize that, when necessary, they must be able to shut out the world in this way and learn to live even in the midst of "the attentive eavesdropping" of their friends.[99]

---

92. See the discussion in ibid., 244–45.
93. Fox, *Love Songs*, 177.
94. Gledhill, *Song*, 245.
95. Longman, *Song*, 222.
96. Gledhill, *Song*, 245.
97. Ibid., 244.
98. Longman, *Song*, 222.
99. Keel, *Song*, 285.

The invitation is, of course, also highly erotic.[100] She wants him to be like a gazelle or young stag on the spice-laden mountains. He is to "come away" with her, which at the very least lets him know that she can hardly wait for them to be alone and enjoying each other.[101] Here at the very end of the Song the joys of physical union and mutual enjoyment are once again stamped with God's approval.[102] This is hardly a negative ending or a pessimistic conclusion.

Something else is also going on here. The last time he asked to hear her voice, she replied with the enigmatic lines about catching the little foxes that ruin the vineyard. That, however, was also followed by an invitation to "turn my lover, and be like a gazelle," resulting in her seeking and finding him.[103] Now her answer is even more cogent; she invites him to join her.[104]

The real point, however, is that her invitation leads us back into the Song,[105] and her final outburst returns us to the very beginning with its passionate optimism.

> Let him kiss me with the kisses of his mouth—
> for your love is more delightful than wine.

Far from being anticlimactic, this is an inspired ending. Instead of bringing our Song to a closure followed by "The End," we are being assured that the Song will never end, and that love's game of seeking and finding always goes on.[106] It is not that they have come full circle and we are disappointed to find them, or ourselves, back where we began. It is that love never arrives or comes to its conclusion. It is an open-ended movement, always renewing and being renewed. Nothing can stop this love with all of its passion of finding and having been found.

---

100. Carr suggests that the words "come away" indicate, "Some erotic imagery may also be present, for the idea of piercing or penetration occurs in Exod 36:33 of bolts (Heb. *beriah*), and in Isa 27:1 of the piercing serpent. This latter is a very common sexual symbol." *Song*, 175.
101. Longman, *Song*, 222.
102. Carr, *Song*, 245.
103. Song of Songs 2:14–17, 3:1–4. Exum, *Song*, 263.
104. Murphy, *Song*, 200.
105. Exum, *Song*, 261.
106. Ibid., 261, 263.

REFLECTION

This final poem is a short interchange between the man and the woman that expresses a continued yearning for a perfect union. We might wish that it would end with our lovers having come to a complete, unbounded, and unbreakable intimacy, but our Song is wiser than that. It better expresses a true love in the real world.

Love is always a work in progress. God is not finished with us yet. It is not that we give up and wait for a better day. It is that in the end, no matter how splendid the heights we might achieve in love, sex, marriage and relationships, these are not all there is. Having tasted of love, we know there is more to come, and until then, we live lives of patience, passion, perseverance, and joy. We do this because love has poured grace into our lives. We understand that we yearn and hope for and occasionally get more than glimpses of a deep and satisfying relationship, but complete union is reserved not for this world but for what is yet to come. "Earth is a foretaste, or a foreplay."[107] This being the case, "we might use the term 'consummation' in more than one sense to describe the world to come."[108]

Love is a taste of grace. It has already found joy but having tasted it, realizes that there is more to come. The best-known passage on love in the Bible says the same thing. While celebrating what we have been given and rejoicing in the renewal that it brings, it still ends up looking forward for more to come.

> Now we see but a poor reflection as in a mirror; then we shall see face to face. Now I know in part; then I shall know fully, even as I am fully known.
>
> And now these three remain: faith, hope and love. But the greatest of these is love (1 Cor 13:12–13).

MEDITATION

There Is More to Come. We Can't Wait!

> I will listen to what God the LORD will say;
> he promises peace to his people, his saints . . .

---

107. Kreeft, *Three Philosophies*, 101.
108. Longman, *Song*, 220.

> Faithfulness springs forth from the earth,
>   and righteousness looks down from heaven.
> The LORD will indeed give what is good,
>   and our land will yield its harvest.
> Righteousness goes before him
>   and prepares the way for his steps (Ps 85:8, 11–13).

> The Sovereign LORD is my strength;
>   he makes my feet like the feet of a deer,
>   he enables me to go on the heights (Hab 3:19).

Then I saw a new heaven and a new earth, for the first heaven and the first earth had passed away, and there was no longer any sea. I saw the Holy City, the new Jerusalem, coming down out of heaven from God, prepared as a bride beautifully dressed for her husband. And I heard a loud voice from the throne saying, "Now the dwelling of God is with men, and he will live with them. They will be his people, and God himself will be with them and be their God . . .

He who was seated on the throne said, "I am making everything new!" Then he said, "Write this down, for these words are trustworthy and true" (Rev 21:1–7).

PRAYER

Father, thank you for the new life that you give to us in Jesus Christ, and that you will complete what you have begun. Thank you for your love, which is always seeking and finding.

Forgive me when I have been impatient and doubted that there is more to come.

Teach me to live all my life longing for the day when you will come and complete your new creation. Cause the vision of what you will do to make me live in such a way as to be dissatisfied with the wrong and filled with joy in the presence of the right. Amen.

Appendices

Day 49

Appendix 1

God: The Garden and the Song

WHAT'S GOD GOT TO DO WITH IT?

Here we are at the end of the Song of Songs, and perhaps we have failed to notice that the name of God has not even been mentioned once in the text![1] There have been a couple of places where we have said that God's name is strongly inferred,[2] but that is about as far as we can go.

For some readers, this may be no more than an incidental curiosity, but we must ask the question, "How can the Song be collected as a part of that official 'library of books' held in awe in the Judeo-Christian tradition, described as 'the Scriptures' or holy writings, and not mention the name of God even once?" It is no small accomplishment to be recognized as a part of God's word and have the divine name missing from the action!

Rabbis, priests, and pastors have rarely been bothered by this.[3] One ancient rabbi went as far as to say, "For all the ages are not worth the day on which the Song of Songs was given to Israel; for all the Writings are holy, but the Song of Songs is the Holy of Holies."[4]

In part this is because the Song has often been read as an allegory. Rather than being taken as a book about the love between a man and a

---

1. Jones, *The Jerusalem Bible* does use God's name "Yahweh" in 8:6.

2. In our comments on 8:6, we mentioned that the reading "burns like blazing fire" implies a bolt of lightning and that buried within the Hebrew is the possibility of a "God fire." In 2:7, we referenced the fact that in the original text the oath "by the gazelles and by the does of the field" sounds very much like an "imitation of an invocation of God."

3. Theodore of Mopsuestia (AD 350–428) is an exception. See also John Calvin's refutation of Sebastian Castellio discussed in Longman, *Song*, 38–39.

4. Rabbi Aqiba (c. AD 100), quoted in Murphy, *Song*, 6.

woman, it was understood as a description of God's love for his bride, Israel, the church. As one can imagine, the project flounders on the sexually explicit passages, but it falls when one begins to say which details mean what. Rarely do any two interpreters agree; but worse yet, it ends up with the reader determining what the text means. That is a fatal mistake, because the word of God interprets truth for the reader and not the other way around.

We do better to let the Song literally say what it says, taking into account, of course, its images, metaphors, and poetry. It is about the love between a man and a woman. It is all about relationship.

THE MORAL OF THE STORY

It would be a mistake, however, to take this to mean that God has given us this book so that we can have a manual on relationships. "When all else fails, read the directions." When we do that, the leaping and loving are soon lost, the song and the dance disappear, and the beauty of the poetry evaporates. The Song is about love, not following the instructions. Worse yet, "Do what it says," soon gives way to an insipid moralism that sucks the life and joy out of us.

Moralism is the spiritual version of the slogan, "Just do it." We set out to obey the Lord so that we can have his help and blessing. When we run out of energy, we remember to "rely on him" or to be "filled with the Spirit." So we head off to the spiritual gas station to fill up on some spiritual high-octane fuel to keep us going at least until we find ourselves running on "empty" again.

The problem with moralism is that is exhausting and debilitating and leaves us discouraged and depressed. Or else, depending on our personality, it leaves us filled with pride, relying on our own righteousness, and chasing everyone away from us because we are constantly recounting what it is that proves, to our own satisfaction at least, that we are "pleasing God" and are "good Christians."

Grace sings and dances because it is infatuated with what God has done for us. It is quite convinced that there is "no way" we should have been loved like this and derives its energy from the fact that despite everything that should be to the contrary, we have been loved and wonder of wonders, are still being loved. We are blessed, but it is has nothing to do with us and everything to do with the grace of God and the love of our Lord Jesus Christ. That being the case, we find ourselves "in love," singing and dancing in the Spirit. Faith is all about a relationship that grows out of grace.[5] It is not an act of the will that rewards us with salvation and returns us to salvation by our own works.

Even the Ten Commandments are prefaced with the line, "I am the Lord your God who brought you out of Egypt and out of slavery" (Exod 20:2). Who God is and what he has done for us—his grace poured out upon us—fills us with gratitude and makes walking with him a joy, not a burden. More often than not, the Israelites didn't quite get this and the Lord had to promise that he would give them a new heart.[6]

When Jesus was asked the question, "Which is the greatest of the commandments?" he turned the question and the questioner upside down by changing the terms of reference. He replied, "'Love the Lord your God with all your heart and with all your soul and with all your mind. This is the first and greatest commandment. And the second is like it: 'Love your neighbor as yourself'" (Matt 22:36–38).

Our Song is about love. "And the point of the real story of life is love. The whole Bible is a love story, because God, the author, is love."[7] That is what provides the clue for understanding why it has found such a secure place in the Scriptures. "God is love" (1 John 4:16).

THE GARDEN

More than that, the Song is filled with the vocabulary of love and of the Scriptures. The "garden," for example, is repeatedly referenced,[8] and even when not explicitly referred to, the lovers are seeking it, finding it, entering it, and enjoying it. It is strewing its flowers and spreading its fragrance everywhere in the book.

On one occasion, our infant son was quite ill on a Sunday afternoon, and our family doctor invited us to bring our child over to his home. While the doctor was busily examining him, I remarked on the beauty of their garden to his wife. She stopped for a moment and looked

---

5. For example, see Ephesians 2:4–5, 8–9: "But because of his great love for us, God, who is rich in mercy, made us alive with Christ even when we were dead in transgressions—it is by grace you have been saved. . . . For it is by grace you have been saved, through faith—and this not from yourselves, it is the gift of God—not by works, so that no one can boast."

6. Jeremiah 24:27; Ezekiel 36:25–28; 31:31–34. Cf. Hebrews 10:15–18.

7. Kreeft, *Three Philosophies*, 99.

8. Song of Songs 4:12, 15, 16; 5:1; 6:2; 8:13.

out over the flowers, into the fields, and then beyond them to the mountains, and quite spontaneously remarked, "I don't know how anyone can say that God does not exist."

Beauty, not science, was her answer. God's name may have as well have been written on the garden because she recognized him as everywhere present in it. What many generations have recognized is that God is everywhere present in the Song of Songs, and he speaks to us there.

If we dare to enter this book and explore the fact that we are designed for love, and if we begin to celebrate not only the beauty of love, but also to meditate on the nature of relationships, we are going to find ourselves walking in God's garden.

This book is precisely what we want and what we need because we have seen that love has a certain transcendent quality to it that causes us not to be able to find it under the microscope. And yet at the same time, we understand that love and relationships have to be lived out in the real flesh and the blood of the garden.

Love is vertical and horizontal, divine and human,[9] but it is not that God is everywhere present in the book symbolically, as if the man stands for God and the bride represents the soul, Israel, the church.[10] It is better said, "In God's story human beauty, intimacy and sexuality are not ends in themselves. They are transcendental longings, whispers of immortality. Like all of creation they point beyond themselves to their divine author, who in this *Song* is nowhere mentioned but everywhere assumed."[11]

THE LIBRARY

In fact, the moment we take down Genesis, the first volume that is housed in that library that we call "the Scriptures," we find ourselves not only entering the garden, but also in the presence of God. We immediately discover the first man and the first woman living there and later realize that they get thrown out of the garden, and that this is paradise lost. When we put the first volume back in place and take down the Song of Songs, we once again encounter a man and a woman, lovers trying to discover, sometimes against great odds, the joy of the garden and the

---

9. Kreeft, *Three Philosophies*, 100.
10. Ibid., 99. Kreeft's position remains closer to allegory than analogy.
11. Gledhill, *Song*, back cover.

fruits of living in it. By the time we get to the final chapter of the last volume in our library, the Revelation, we find ourselves once again in the garden, this time in paradise regained.[12]

It is not that we cannot help but make these associations; it is that we are meant to make these connections. They are all part of "the greatest story ever told," and it is being told to us by its author, God. Put another way, it is precisely for that reason that we find all these books, including the Song of Songs, bound together in that one great volume, the bestseller of all time, in that book that we call the Bible.

THE READER

By now you have discovered the joys and prejudices that we bring to the reading of the Song. If we were antiquarian scholars of Ancient Near Eastern poetry, we might be able to take the Song and allow it to stand all by itself. But we are not. We are Christians, seekers after the truth, people who have been found by grace, and lovers of life and of God. We find the Song bound into our Bibles, and when we read about the true nature of love when best exemplified between the man and the woman, we cannot help but say, "That is just how God loves me!"

We are right in doing this because we are made in the image of God, and how he loves us is how we are to love one another. For us this is not an academic idea. It is about life, loving, and living. It is about splashing around in God's creation, finding ourselves marveling at the love of God, delighting in his garden, and breathing his air, which of course is love.

MEDITATION

God Is Everywhere Present, and in His Presence We Find Life, Love, and Joy

> Now the LORD God had planted a garden in the east, in Eden; and there he put the man he had formed. And the LORD God made all kinds of trees grow out of the ground—trees that were pleasing to the eye and good for food. In the middle of the garden were the tree of life and the tree of the knowledge of good and evil. . . . Then the man and his wife heard the sound of the LORD

---

12. Revelation 22:1–3.

God as he was walking in the garden in the cool of the day . . . (Gen 2:8–9, 3:8).

The heavens declare the glory of God;
   the skies proclaim the work of his hands.
Day after day they pour forth speech;
   night after night they display knowledge. . . .
Their voice goes out into all the earth,
   their words to the ends of the world.
In the heavens he has pitched a tent for the sun,
   which is like a bridegroom coming forth from his pavilion,
   like a champion rejoicing to run his course (Ps 19:1–2, 4–5).

From the fullness of his grace we have all received one blessing after another. For the law was given through Moses; grace and truth came through Jesus Christ. No one has ever seen God, but God the One and Only, who is at the Father's side, has made him known (John 1:16–18).

Dear friends, let us love one another, for love comes from God. Everyone who loves has been born of God and knows God. Whoever does not love does not know God, because God is love (1 John 4:7–8).

PRAYER

Father, thank you for your love and for your presence in your world and in our lives. Thank you for the new creation that has begun in your Son, Jesus Christ, and for already beginning to bring us back into your garden.

Forgive me for the times that I have lived as one outside of your garden.

Teach me to delight in your presence and to allow your love to transform all of my relationships, both with you and with others. Amen

Day 50

Appendix 2

Redemption: The Son and the Song

WHERE IS THE CHRIST?

If we have been surprised to discover that the name of God is not anywhere present in the Song of Songs, we will not be shocked to realize that neither is there any reference to the Christ, the promised Son of David.

We may, however, be taken aback to hear it said that the absence of any reference to the Christ creates a larger quandary for the Christian interpreter than the absence of God's name. God, we have seen, can appear to be absent and yet be everywhere present and at work. But if Christ is absent, then redemption is not present, and all that we have left is a self-help book, which, although interesting, lacks the compelling nature of Scripture, which this is claimed to be.

The only other book in the Bible that does not mention the name of the Lord is the book of Esther. There we find a young woman who is living in exile, along with the people of God, under the Persians. Through a number of remarkable circumstances, she comes to the attention of the king, who marries her at the very time that the enemies of the people of God are plotting to wipe them out. She places her life on the line and become the deliverer of her people, Israel.

God's name is not mentioned in Esther, but he is everywhere "present" in the book in the salvation of his people, who are the bearers of the promise of the Christ. In this moment, God shows us not just his care for his people, but also his intention to redeem them and to do what it takes to bring his covenant promise to fulfillment in the Christ.[13] In his

---

13. Genesis 15:4–6.

so doing, we learn how to be a part of his purposes in the circumstances of our lives.

Of great importance to us are the words of Jesus himself. After his crucifixion, two of his dejected followers were walking on the road to Emmaus, where they failed to recognize that it was the risen Christ who had joined them. When Jesus asked what it was that was disturbing them so much, they retorted, "Are you only a visitor to Jerusalem and do not know the things that have happened there in these days?" After explaining to Jesus what had transpired, including the crucifixion and now the reports of the resurrection, Jesus replied to them, "'How foolish you are, and how slow of heart to believe all that the prophets have spoken! Did not the Christ have to suffer these things and then enter his glory?' And beginning with Moses and all the Prophets, he explained to them what was said in all the Scriptures concerning himself."[14]

If all of the Scriptures are all about the Christ, and if they take their character as the word of God from the one who is the word,[15] then how do we make sense of the Song of Songs?

THE REDEMPTIVE THREAD

There at least three or four ways that Christ presents himself to us in the Old Testament.[16] Very often there are explicit promises of the great kingdom that is to come and to the Son of David who will bring that redemption. Sometimes, a particular person or institution like David or Melchizedek, or the temple or the Passover, will dramatically enact beforehand what Christ will be like and what he will do for us. Both of these first two principles come together in someone such as Moses, to whom the New Testament makes reference and of whom it is said, "I will raise up for them a prophet like you from among their brothers; I will put my words in his mouth, and he will tell them everything I command him."[17]

By far the most common way in which we see the great thread of redemption running through that tapestry that is the Old Testament is simply by looking at where the text comes on this road to Christ and

---

14. Luke 24:13–25.
15. John 1:1.
16. For an excellent explanation, see Chapell, *Christ-Centered Preaching*, 263–86.
17. Deuteronomy 18:18. See the reference to this in Acts 3:22–24.

what it brings to the overall picture that is being presented. As we locate its place in the history of God's redemption, we see both where it is taking us and the Christ to whom we are being led. There is an organic development that, as it grows, helps us to understand who Christ is and why it is that he came.

In other texts, we simply hear a crying need for the Christ. We understand, for example, that as wonderful as was David's kingdom, it was not enough. It fell apart under his son Solomon, and the hearts of his people would lead them into exile in Babylon. Israel needed new hearts.[18] And then there was David's personal life. His notorious sin with Bathsheba led him to bare his soul in his poetry, confess his need for salvation, and show us the wonders of forgiveness that would be later explained more fully to us in the New Testament.[19] David and his kingdom are looking forward to the Christ!

We expect, therefore, that every part of the word of God is going to show us either the nature of God that provides for the redemption that is in Christ or else that aspect of human nature that is displayed in the text and that is crying out for the making of all things new in Jesus the Savior and Christ.[20]

REDEMPTION SONG

Here is how the Song of Songs fits into all this. Let us imagine the story of God's redemption as a huge painting on the wall of a gallery. On one side of the canvas the setting for the coming redemption would be portrayed, beginning with the wedding in the Garden of Eden. Here, there, and everywhere there would be vignettes of gardens and vineyards, of Israel and God's care for his often reluctant and unfaithful bride. Our eyes would quickly go in search of Jesus, only to find him at his first miracle at the wedding in Cana of Galilee. We would notice him telling his parables of the wedding feast. We would especially make a point to see how the narrative portrayed in the painting ends, and there would be the bride—the New Jerusalem, the people of God—coming down from heaven beautifully dressed for her husband.[21]

18. See Hebrews 8:7–12.
19. Cf. Psalm 51:32 and Romans 4:4–8.
20. Chapell, *Christ-Centered Preaching*, 277.
21. Genesis 2:8–25; John 2:1–11; Matthew 22:1–14; Revelation 21:2.

Now for the Song. Buried somewhere in the heart of this great painting, there would be a stunning love story with the wedding at the heart of it all. This would be the Song of Songs, giving sparkle to the wedding theme but more importantly, providing the color and the setting; that is, the love that is everywhere present in the narrative of the picture.

This history of redemption is, after all, all about love, and nowhere is that explored in all of its magnificent physical, social, emotional, and psychological complexity than in the Song of Songs. What we learn from the Song is that the complex web of relationships that are woven through our lives are all to be about love, and that we have learned this from the God who is love.

Love Song

Love is all about redemption. If there had not been a fall, then men and women, and indeed all creation, would be living in perfect harmony. Those relationships would be immensely enjoyable, but technically, they would not be characterized by love. Each person would be perfectly whole with the other, but no one would need love to pick him or her up, encourage him or her, or bring fulfillment. There would really be no need for love or redemption. Were it not for the fall, we would never have known that "God is love," nor would there have been any need for the verse, "God so loved the world that he gave his one and only Son . . ." (John 3:16).

Love implies meeting a need. If there is no need, there is no need for love. If we were not fallen and God had not sent his Son to die for our sins and clothe us in his righteousness and make us a part of his new creation, we would not have known what it is to be loved by God. Or, as someone has said, "It is good that there be fear so that love can cast it out. If there is no fear for love to cast out, love falls on unprepared soil."[22]

What we understand is that we have tried to keep the "laws," and we have failed to find the relationship. We have come to recognize that by its very nature love is to be celebrated, not manufactured. In fact, it is so elusive that almost intuitively we realize that it belongs more to the realm of worship and the spirit than to law and the efforts of the self. Indeed, we might even say that love is about being found by this thing

---

22. Kreeft, *Three Philosophies*, 127.

called *grace*. When someone walks into our life and turns everything upside down, we know that grace is a gift more often than not quite unplanned and unexpected. It is a grace that finds us even more than it is a love that we have searched for and found.

When it comes to laws for relationships, we have "been there and done that." If our relationships could be manufactured and if they were running according to plan, we wouldn't be reading this. And if we are reading this, it is because we realize that we need a redeeming presence in our lives and in our relationships, and that thing that we need is called *love*.

What we discover is that the language of this Song, with its lovers found in the garden, will be suffused into the rest of God's word. In the Song of the Songs, we enter not only the real world of love and broken relationships, but also of redemption and reconciliation. We come to understand the nature of love and the need for redemption, and we find ourselves grasping, perhaps for the first time, the love of God that is in Christ.

At some level or another, we end up saying that this great book, the Song of Songs, "describes the ultimate purpose of life. . . . This is the highest and holiest and happiest hope of the human heart, the thing we are all born hungering for, hunting for, longing for. This is the last chapter of life's story, the point and purpose of it all. . . . And the point of the real story of life is love."[23]

Love is the language of God. God is love and has shown us that love in Christ, his Son, through whom we have been, or can be, brought back to be his bride. "Life is a quest for love and a quest for God."[24] In the Song love is found, and all of life becomes a love song. In this great book, we hear the music as nowhere else, but it always ends in the Christ who is our song.

MEDITATION

Christ Is Our Song

> I will sing of the LORD's great love forever;
> with my mouth I will make your faithfulness known through all generations.

23. Ibid., 99.
24. Ibid., 110.

> I will declare that your love stands firm forever,
>> that you established your faithfulness in heaven itself.
>
> You said, "I have made a covenant with my chosen one,
>> I have sworn to David my servant,
> 'I will establish your line forever,
>> and make your throne firm through all generations'" (Ps 89:1–4).

> "Sing, O barren woman,
>> you who never bore a child;
> burst into song, shout for joy,
>> you who were never in labor;
> because more are the children of the desolate woman
>> than of her who has a husband,"
>>>> says the LORD. . . .
>
> For your Maker is your husband—
>> the LORD Almighty is his name—
> the Holy One of Israel is your Redeemer;
>> he is called the God of all the earth. . . .
> Though the mountains be shaken
>> and the hills be removed,
> yet my unfailing love for you will not be shaken
>> nor my covenant of peace be removed,"
> says the LORD, who has compassion on you (Isa 54:1, 5, 10).

Then Jesus told them this parable: "Suppose one of you has a hundred sheep and loses one of them. Does he not leave the ninety-nine in the open country and go after the lost sheep until he finds it? And when he finds it, he joyfully puts it on his shoulders and goes home. Then he calls his friends and neighbors together and says, 'Rejoice with me; I have found my lost sheep.' I tell you that in the same way there will be more rejoicing in heaven over one sinner who repents than over ninety-nine righteous persons who do not need to repent" (Luke 15:3–7).

This is how God showed his love among us: He sent his one and only Son into the world that we might live through him. This is love: not that we loved God, but that he loved us and sent his Son as an atoning sacrifice for our sins. Dear friends, since God so loved us, we also ought to love one another. No one has ever seen God; but if we love one another, God lives in us and his love is made complete in us (1 John 4:9–12).

PRAYER

Father, thank you for your extraordinary love that found us and brought us back into your presence. Thank you for your Son, Jesus Christ, who, at the cost of his own life, has given us new life.

Lord, I have not loved you as you have loved me.

By the grace of your Holy Spirit, fill me with your love, so that in all of my relationships, the joy of your love may overflow in gratitude and service. May your love take root in our hearts so that we may know the joy of your salvation and become a part of what you are doing in the world. Amen

Bibliography

Babcock, Maltbie D. "This Is My Father's World." In *The Worshipbook: Services and Hymns*, 602. Philadelphia: Westminster, 1972.
Balchin, John. "The Song of Songs." In *New Bible Commentary*, edited by G. J. Wenham, et al., 619–28. Downers Grove, IL: Inter-Varsity, 1997.
Barth, Karl. *The Word of God and the Word of Man*. Gloucester, MA: Peter Smith, 1978.
Bloch, Chana, and Ariel Bloch. *The Song of Songs: The World's First Great Love Poem*. New York: The Modern Library, 1995
Calvin, John. *Institutes of the Christian Religion*. Edited by John T. McNeill. Philadelphia: Westminster, 1960.
Carr, G. Lloyd. *The Song of Solomon*. Downers Grove, IL: Inter-Varsity, 1984.
Chapell, Bryan. *Christ-Centered Preaching*. Grand Rapids: Baker, 1994.
Curtis, Edward M. *Song of Songs*. Grand Rapids: Zondervan, 1988.
Exum, J. Cheryl. *Song of Songs*. Louisville: Westminster John Knox, 2005.
Falk, Marcia. *The Song of Songs: Love Lyrics from the Bible*. Translated by Marcia Falk. Waltham, MA: Brandeis University Press, 2004.
Fee, Gordon D. *The First Epistle to the Corinthians*. Grand Rapids: Eerdmans, 1987.
Fox, Michael V. *The Song of Songs and the Ancient Egyptian Love Songs*. Madison: University of Wisconsin Press, 1985.
Gledhill, Tom. *The Message of the Song of Songs*. Downers Grove, IL: Inter-Varsity, 1994.
Glickman, S. Craig. *A Song for Lovers*. Downers Grove, IL: Inter-Varsity, 1976.
Hall, Daniel E. "Religious Attendance: More Cost-Effective Than Lipitor?" *The Journal of the American Board of Family Medicine* 19 (2006) 103–9.
Jobes, Karen H. *1 Peter*. Grand Rapids: Baker Academic, 2005.
Jones, Alexander. *The Jerusalem Bible*. New York: Doubleday, 1974.
Keel, Othmar. *The Song of Songs*. Minneapolis: Fortress, 1994.
Kreeft, Peter. *Three Philosophies of Life, Ecclesiastes: Life as Vanity, Job: Life as Suffering, Song of Songs: Life as Love*. San Francisco: Ignatius, 1989.
The Larger Catechism. In *The Westminster Standards: The Confession of Faith, The Larger Catechism, The Shorter Catechism*. Suwanee, GA: Great Commission, 2003.
Longman III, Tremper. *Song of Songs*. Grand Rapids: Eerdmans, 43.
Luther, Martin. "The Freedom of a Christian." In *Martin Luther's Basic Theological Writings*, edited by Timothy F. Lull. Minneapolis: Fortress, 1989.
Morris, Leon. *1 Corinthians*. Carol Stream, IL: Tyndale, 1969.
Murphy, Roland E. *The Song of Songs*. Minneapolis: Fortress, 1990.
Pope, Marvin H. *Song of Songs*. Garden City, NY: Doubleday, 1977.
Taylor, James Hudson. *Union and Communion, or Thoughts on the Song of Solomon*. New York: Cosimo Classics, 2007.
Thomas, Derek and Rosemary. *A Biblical Guide to Love, Sex and Marriage*. Webster, NY: Evangelical, 2007.
"The War on Baby Girls: Gendercide." *The Economist*. 394: 8672 (March 6, 2010) 13, 77–80, 104.